Money in the House

TRANSFORMING AMERICAN POLITICS

Lawrence C. Dodd, Series Editor

Dramatic changes in political institutions and behavior over the past three decades have underscored the dynamic nature of American politics, confronting political scientists with a new and pressing intellectual agenda. The pioneering work of early postwar scholars, while laying a firm empirical foundation for contemporary scholarship, failed to consider how American politics might change or to recognize the forces that would make fundamental change inevitable. In reassessing the static interpretations fostered by these classic studies, political scientists are now examining the underlying dynamics that generate transformational change.

Transforming American Politics brings together texts and monographs that address four closely related aspects of change. A first concern is documenting and explaining recent changes in American politics—in institutions, processes, behavior, and policymaking. A second is reinterpreting classic studies and theories to provide a more accurate perspective on postwar politics. The series looks at historical change to identify recurring patterns of political transformation within and across the distinctive eras of American politics. Last and perhaps most important, the series presents new theories and interpretations that explain the dynamic processes at work and thus clarify the direction of contemporary politics. All of the books focus on the central theme of transformation—transformation both in the conduct of American politics and in the way we study and understand its many aspects.

BOOKS IN THIS SERIES

Money in the House

CAMPAIGN FUNDS AND CONGRESSIONAL PARTY POLITICS

Marian Currinder

The Government Affairs Institute at
Georgetown University

A Member of the Perseus Books Group

Find us on the World Wide Web at www.westviewpress.com.

Westview Press books are available at special discounts for bulk
purchases in the United States by corporations, institutions, and
other organizations. For more information, please contact the
Special Markets Department at the Perseus Books Group, 2300
Chestnut Street, Suite 200, Philadelphia, PA 19103, or call (800) 810-4145,
extension 5000, or e-mail special.markets@perseusbooks.com.

Set in 10.25 point Minion by the Perseus Books Group

Library of Congress Cataloging-in-Publication Data

Currinder, Marian.
    Money in the House : campaign funds and congressional party politics
/ Marian Currinder. — 1st ed.
        p.   cm. — (Transforming American politics)
    Includes bibliographical references and index.
    ISBN 978-0-8133-4379-2 (pbk. : alk. paper) 1. United States. Congress.
House. 2. United States. Congress. House—Elections. 3. Campaign
funds—United States. 4. United States—Politics and government—
1945–1989. 5. United States—Politics and government—1989– I. Title.
JK1319.C88 2008
324.7'80973—dc22   2008013147

10 9 8 7 6 5 4 3 2 1

Contents

Introduction

In the November 2006 midterm elections, forty-two Democrats challenging for seats in the U.S. House of Representatives won election and propelled their party into the majority for the first time in twelve years. Known as the majority makers, these newly elected Democrats had campaigned as agents of change and had promoted ethics reform, fiscal responsibility, and an end to the war in Iraq. Many of them had also emphasized conservative social values. As a result of their election, the new Democratic majority looks quite different from the last one in 1994. The party's liberal majority has been tempered by an influx of new members who must walk a fine line between supporting traditional Democratic policies and representing conservative constituencies. Perhaps no one is more attuned to this intraparty dynamic than House Speaker Nancy Pelosi (CA). As Speaker of the House, Pelosi is responsible for setting the House's legislative agenda—a task that requires her to negotiate compromises among her party's diverse factions. On any given policy, differences may surface between members of the Congressional Black Caucus, the Congressional Hispanic Caucus, the Progressive Caucus, the conservative Blue Dog Coalition, the New Democrat Coalition, and the freshman Democrats, who, because of their large numbers, sometimes act as an informal caucus. The challenge for Speaker Pelosi is to produce a record of Democratic policy accomplishments on which all Democratic incumbents can successfully run in 2008.

Building majority coalitions within a diverse caucus is not so much a remarkable leadership strategy as it is a necessary one. More remarkable

1

is Speaker Pelosi's financial strategy for retaining majority status: She has committed to contributing $800,000 to the Democratic Congressional Campaign Committee (DCCC) and to raising an additional $25 million for the committee during the 2008 election cycle. The DCCC is the campaign committee for House Democrats and works to help the party gain or retain majority status. The committee's strategies depend on a number of factors, but today they center primarily on fundraising to help Democratic incumbents in close races and promising Democratic challengers and candidates for open seats.[1] The National Republican Congressional Committee (NRCC) is the campaign committee for House Republicans and, like the DCCC, focuses on gaining or retaining majority status, primarily through fundraising.

Speaker Pelosi's commitment to raising over $25 million for the DCCC is stunning. No House leader has even come close to raising that much money for a party campaign committee during a single election cycle. In fact, the combined fundraising commitments of the other eight current House Democratic leaders total less than Speaker Pelosi has pledged to raise on her own (Davis and Newmyer 2007). Fundraising is as central to her strategy for retaining majority control as producing policy results; winning elections requires both.

As part of her plan to protect the freshman majority makers, Speaker Pelosi directed the DCCC to help them build up their campaign war chests. A hefty campaign account signals strong financial support that can scare away potential challengers. As soon as the newly elected freshmen arrived in Washington, the committee began working with them to raise funds. Those facing the toughest races in 2008 qualified for the DCCC's Frontline program, which helps vulnerable members raise money early and provides them with logistical support. During the first half of 2007, the forty-two freshman Democrats outdid their thirteen Republican counterparts in fundraising $21.8 million to $4.3 million, for an average of $520,000 per Democrat to $330,000 per Republican (Sabato 2007). At the end of 2007, seven freshmen had more than $1 million in their campaign accounts, and more than half were safely positioned to win reelection. In addition, the DCCC ended 2007 with a more than eleven-to-one cash advantage over the NRCC. This advan-

tage translated into even more potential support for endangered freshmen (Kane 2007a).

The freshman members also get special treatment from their leaders
and meet once weekly with Speaker Pelosi and Majority Leader Steny
Hoyer (MD). In addition, Democratic Caucus Chair Rahm Emanuel
(IL) and DCCC Chair Chris Van Hollen (MD) meet frequently with the
freshmen to advise them on how to vote. Despite the intensity of leadership support, the freshman Democrats still regularly vote with the Republicans. And they do so with the full support of their leaders. Many of
the freshmen represent conservative or moderate constituencies; while
they generally support the leadership's agenda, they need to distance
themselves from the party's liberal leaders as they prepare for their first
reelection campaign. As part of their strategy to defeat vulnerable Democrats in 2008, House Republicans launched a Web site that tracks the
percentage of votes that Democratic freshmen cast with the Speaker.
Pelosi, a liberal Democrat from San Francisco, is a polarizing figure in
many conservative districts, and some of the most vulnerable freshmen
have responded to the Republican tactic by voting with the Republicans
on procedural matters that have no bearing on the Democratic leadership's agenda. For example, the chamber votes each day on approving
the House Journal (essentially, the minutes from the previous day). The
majority party routinely votes in favor, and the minority party votes in
opposition. By voting with the Republicans, the freshman Democrats
can up their "Pelosi opposition" scores without adversely affecting their
party's agenda. "We've given them very simple advice: Make sure you
vote your district," said DCCC Chair Chris Van Hollen (Kane 2007). For
many of the Democratic freshmen, voting their districts means opposing the liberal leadership on occasion. And leaders figured out a way for
them to do just that, without actually hurting the party.

Ideological differences aside, Speaker Pelosi and the freshman Democrats share the goals of wanting to win elections and retain majority
status—aspirations that explain their willingness to engage in financial
and procedural protectionist strategies. Speaker Pelosi's extraordinary
financial commitment to her party, and especially to her party's vulnerable members, illustrates the overriding emphasis that congressional

political parties and members place on money. And her encouragement
of selective "opposition votes" demonstrates the complexity of governing in a highly partisan and highly competitive political environment.

Beginning in the early 1990s, two factors—campaign money and
close partisan margins—started to dominate congressional party politics. As competition between the parties increased, electoral strategy
became as important as legislative strategy in securing majority control. Campaign money has figured prominently in electoral party politics for decades, but it became central during the 1990s and remains so
today. As the margins between the parties in the House shrank and
electoral competition increased, party leaders sought out new sources
of money for the congressional campaign committees (CCCs). In addition to requesting money from individual contributors and political
action committees (PACs), the CCCs began asking incumbent members to contribute their excess campaign funds. They reasoned that
retaining or gaining majority status was a group goal, and that all
members who could afford to give should do so for the good of the
whole. They also believed that incumbent giving would inspire potential outside contributors to support the party.

As more and more members began to participate in the CCCs'
fundraising efforts, party leaders began to view member fundraising as
a sign of party loyalty. The presence of real competition in the House
meant that House leaders had to enforce strict party discipline to pass
(or block) policy. By rewarding loyalty, leaders could maintain some
degree of control over members who were anxious to promote their
own political and policy agendas rather than the party's. Eventually,
members understood that their ability to successfully pursue their own
ambitions depended on their willingness to vote with their leaders and
raise money for their parties.

Members can contribute to the CCCs using funds from their personal campaign committees and from their leadership PACs. Members
typically use their personal campaign committees to raise money for
their own election and reelection campaigns. Leadership PACs are
generally created to promote the politicians who establish them. Like
other PACs, leadership PACs solicit donations and make contributions

to candidates and party committees. Members also use their leadership PAC funds to pay for travel, and for a broad range of campaign-related expenses. Members can make unlimited transfers from their personal campaign committees to party committees, but they can contribute a total of only $15,000 per election cycle from their leadership PACs to the national party committees.

Member contributions to the CCCs have increased dramatically since 1990. House Democrats contributed $0.3 million to the DCCC during the 1990 election cycle, then upped that amount to $7.8 million during the 2000 cycle. In 2006, House Democrats contributed $33.7 million to the DCCC. House Republicans gave $0.001 million to the NRCC during the 1990 cycle and $14.7 million during the 2000 cycle. In 2006, they gave $31.6 million to the NRCC (Bedlington and Malbin 2003, 134; Campaign Finance Institute). Flash forward to the 2008 election cycle: The DCCC has requested that House Democrats raise a total of $155 million, and the NRCC has established unprecedented fundraising targets for all House Republicans. These figures reflect the escalating cost of running competitive campaigns; they also reflect significant changes in how congressional parties compete for majority status.

House members have also increased their efforts to raise money for each other and for same-party candidates. Members can give $2,300 per candidate, per election, out of their personal campaign committees and $5,000 per candidate, per election, out of their leadership PACs. In 1990, House Democrats contributed a total of $1.8 million to incumbents, challengers, and open-seat candidates; ten years later, they contributed $7.8 million. In 2006, House Democrats gave candidates for the House $14 million. House Republicans contributed $0.9 million to incumbents, challengers, and open-seat candidates in the 1990 elections and $9.6 million in the 2000 elections. In 2006, House Republicans gave $24.6 million to Republican House candidates (Bedlington and Malbin 2003, 134; Campaign Finance Institute). These figures have continued to rise as members have become more attuned to the collective and individual returns such contributions provide.

The increasing amount of money that House members contribute to the CCCs and to other members and candidates is one of the most significant developments in congressional party politics since the late 1990s. As the CCCs' fundraising activities have become more important, congressional party leaders have moved from encouraging members to contribute money to the committees to requiring them to do so through dues systems and commitment contracts. While these party-orchestrated fundraising programs promote the collective goal of majority status, redistributing money can also help members promote themselves—a strategy that became more important in the postreform Congress.

This book is about how and why a system evolved that places a premium on members' ability and willingness to raise and redistribute money. It is also about the consequences of such a system. The career trajectory of ambitious members changed significantly following the 1970s House reforms. Under the seniority system, House members moved up the chamber's power ladder through extended service. Committee chairs were the majority party members who served on the committees the longest, and party leaders earned their posts by slowly progressing up through the ranks. The contemporary House operates under a dramatically different set of rules. Both parties permit all members to compete for leadership posts, chairmanships, and even committee seats. When the margins between parties are narrow and the political atmosphere is fiercely partisan, party loyalists are favored for higher positions in the chamber. Ambitious members can demonstrate their loyalty through party-line voting, but they can no longer distinguish themselves this way because congressional leaders push all members to vote with their parties. Members can, however, distinguish themselves by raising money for the party and its candidates. Those who raise money for the good of the whole demonstrate that they are loyal, and that they are team players—qualities that members want to see in their leaders.

Party leaders in the House are now expected to raise tremendous amounts of money for the CCCs and for party candidates. Because narrow margins mean that control of the House is at stake every two years, fundraising has become enormously important. Just before the 2006 elections, Nancy Pelosi's staff estimated that her constant travel and phone calls on behalf of the DCCC, individual candidates, and her leadership PAC generated about $50 million that election cycle. This money encouraged grateful House Democrats to support her bid to become Speaker (Epstein 2006). Leaders must be well connected to the outside interests that can provide campaign funds, and they must also be willing to build new financial connections. Because more money is raised at the ideological extremes, House members at the far ends of the liberal and conservative spectrum tend to attract more money than centrists. And the ability to raise large amounts of money propels these members to leadership posts that they otherwise might not have won (Heberlig, Hetherington, and Larson 2006). Selecting leaders who do not represent the median party member may advance policy agendas that are more extreme than many party members prefer. Leaders who raise large sums of money may also feel compelled to advance agendas that reflect the preferences of those who funded their leadership campaigns.

As money has become central to securing majority control, the CCCs have expanded their fundraising requirements to include all incumbent members. Unless they are facing close reelection campaigns, incumbents are assessed "fundraising goals" according to their clout in the chamber. Some members, however, find meeting the fundraising requirements more difficult than others. Representative Alcee Hastings (D-FL), for example, claimed he did not have the spare funds to pay his 2007 dues to the DCCC. "I only have $13,000 in my campaign account," he said, adding that he has two challengers in 2008. "My overall feeling is when I get to the point where I raise the money, I'll pay the dues" (Hearn 2007a). Members who represent poor constituencies or constituencies with expensive media markets may also find it difficult to raise money beyond what they need for their own campaigns. Other members lack wealthy connections, or simply find fundraising distasteful. But members' ability to raise money determines in part their ability to successfully compete for leadership posts, committee chairs, or committee seats. It may also determine their ability to get their bills heard in committee or scheduled for action on the House floor. The DCCC and the NRCC have become increasingly aggressive in the tactics they use to compel members to meet their fundraising requirements. In 2006, then–DCCC Chair Rahm Emanuel prevented delinquent members from using the DCCC offices to make their own fundraising calls until they had paid their committee dues.[2] House leaders have even adjusted the chamber's floor schedule to make more time for members to raise money.

All of this adds up to an almost constant focus on fundraising. House members must devote tremendous amounts of time to raising money for their own campaigns and for their party campaign committees. They must also devote time and energy to cultivating relationships with potential donors. As a result, members have less time to spend on policy. Most committee hearings are poorly attended and floor debates often feature just a handful of members. The link between members' ability and willingness to raise money for the party and their ability to obtain more power in the chamber also raises important questions about the criteria by which potential leaders are judged. If fundraising skills are deemed as important as policy expertise and institutional experience, what are the benefits in developing an expertise or in long-term service? Whose interests are prioritized in a system that requires policymakers to focus constantly on fundraising and that rewards those who raise the most? Assessing the institutional consequences of a system so focused on campaign money requires first understanding how and why this system evolved. In the next chapter, I present a broad, historical overview of member-to-member and member-to-party giving in the House. The themes in this chapter are further developed in the book's remaining chapters.

Chapter 2 presents a theory of the relationship between House members and the congressional party organizations. Congressional parties are hindered by being made up of self-interested actors who are interested in maximizing their own electoral security, and who pursue politics and policies that are consistent with this goal. The challenge for party leaders is to convince members that promoting the party agenda is just as important as promoting their own personal agendas. The ongoing tension between self-interested members and team-oriented parties affects how money is redistributed in the chamber. When partisan margins are small and power is centralized in the leadership, party leaders are better able to direct member contributions so as to satisfy party goals. But when the margins between parties are sizable and the party leaders are less assertive, members can redistribute money so as to satisfy their personal goals. As the political environment shifts, and as the structure of opportunities available to members changes, so do member contribution strategies.

Chapter 3 examines how the 1970s House reforms helped to create a political environment that fostered the growth of member-to-member giving. The reforms sought to democratize the chamber by redistributing power throughout the majority party membership. Before the 1970s, committee chairs—many of whom were southern conservatives— exercised almost total control over the House's legislative agenda. As the Democratic Party's progressive wing expanded, members began to push for changes that would remove some of the excessive power held by the committee chairs. The seniority rule was replaced with new rules that required secret ballot elections of chairs and leaders. These reforms, in addition to a number of others that were designed to open the legislative system and enhance member participation, created a more active and competitive political environment. Broader contextual changes in the sociopolitical environment also affected congressional and electoral politics. All of these changes encouraged ambitious members to find new ways to impress their colleagues, and by the late 1970s, members seeking higher posts within the chamber began to redistribute money as part of their leadership campaigns.

Chapter 4 focuses on the postreform House. The decade following the 1970s reform movement saw major changes in how parties compete for majority control. As the congressional parties became more ideologically polarized, party leadership was strengthened. The ascension of Representative Jim Wright (D-TX) to the Speakership marked the beginning of a new era of aggressive partisan politics, and the parties were further divided by the rise of Representative Newt Gingrich (R-GA) during the 1980s. As they helped their parties compete for majority control, the CCCs also became more aggressive; they greatly expanded their candidate-oriented services and focused increased attention on their fundraising operations. Seniority was no longer the sole criterion in determining leadership and committee chair posts, so these races became more competitive. In competing for higher positions, members highlighted their fundraising abilities, among other factors, and handed out large amounts of campaign money to their colleagues. Rank-and-file members also became more actively involved in redistributing money, though most of their contributions were small and directed to candidates in competitive races or to regional and personal acquaintances. As more and more members gave to each other for a range of reasons, redistributing money became an institutionalized practice during the 1980s.

In chapters 5 and 6, I examine the House Republicans' rise to power in the early 1990s and the party's twelve years in the majority. After winning majority control in the 1994 midterm elections, the Republicans elected Representative Newt Gingrich as Speaker and centralized power in the leadership. The Republicans passed the most far-reaching House reforms since the 1970s, including new rules that limited party leaders and committee and subcommittee chairs to six-year terms. Small partisan margins, combined with increased intraparty preference agreement and interparty preference conflict, set the stage for conditional party government (CPG) throughout the 1990s. Under the CPG model, members are willing to grant their leaders additional powers because they believe doing so will benefit them electorally (Aldrich and Rohde 2001, 275–276). During the 1990s, the redistribution of campaign money to members, outside candidates, and the CCCs increased exponentially. Republican and Democratic leaders began to require their members to donate to the CCCs, and contributions from members' personal campaign committees to the CCCs grew rapidly as leaders began to link intrainstitutional advancement to fundraising abilities. Leadership and committee chairmanship competitions were likened to financial arms races because many of the candidates for these posts competed by redistributing large amounts of campaign money. Together with the highly partisan political environment, the Republican reforms institutionalized competition in the chamber. And because most members competed by raising money for the party and its candidates, the party benefited from its members' intrainstitutional pursuits.

Chapter 7 looks at the new Democratic majority and examines the party's attempts to advance the redistribution of campaign money. Partisan margins have remained narrow. As a result, party leaders have continued to enforce strict party discipline. Party loyalty, as expressed through fundraising and support for the leadership, continues to be the pathway to power in the House. The chapter concludes by considering the consequences of this system.

Notes

1. See the preface of Robin Kolodny's *Pursuing Majorities* (1998) for a discussion of how different variables affect the strategies the congressional campaign committees use to pursue majority status.

2. Federal law prevents members from making fundraising phone calls from their congressional offices, so most members use the party offices to make their phone calls. Both parties have offices close to the Capitol Building so that members can make phone calls between hearings, floor votes, and meetings.

1

Campaign Funds and Congressional Party Politics

An Overview

In *Federalist No. 51*, James Madison argued that the interests of men who serve in federal government must be connected to the institutions in which they serve. The U.S. Constitution endows each branch of government with rights that both empower and protect those who serve. Madison assumed that human nature would drive federal officeholders to seek power beyond that granted by the Constitution. However, one branch's attempt to encroach on another branch's power would be blocked by the natural tendency of men to guard their own interests. "Ambition," according to Madison, "must be made to counteract ambition." Federal politicians who understood the constitutional powers of the institutions in which they served could use those powers both to build influence and to protect themselves. In linking the ambitions of federal politicians to their institutions, Madison sought to further strengthen the principle of separation of powers. He also recognized the interplay between personal ambition and collective, institutional ambition. By expanding their institution's powers, federal politicians could claim more personal power for themselves. While Madison seemed to suspect that the relationship between individuals and their institutions would be a defining feature of federal government, he could not have predicted how this relationship would transform and expand over time. At every stage in our political history, the interaction between personal and collective ambitions has shaped congressional politics.

Less than a decade after the Constitution was ratified, the first ad hoc parties formed, and Madison's arguments about individual and collective ambitions took new shape. Members of Congress began to organize themselves according to their collective goals, voting as blocs on matters having to do with support for the administration and foreign affairs.[1] However, there was little consistency in congressional organization, and a formal party structure still did not exist. By 1828, the contours of a two-party system were beginning to form. Supporters of President Andrew Jackson labeled themselves the Democratic-Republicans and opponents of the Jackson administration called themselves the Whigs. The foundations of mass political parties took root as both the Democratic-Republicans and the Whigs developed extensive grassroots networks, held nominating conventions, and developed policy platforms.

In the 1840s, party loyalties were well established, and voter turnout rates reached record highs. Stable party preferences in the electorate and high voter turnout rates stayed consistent into the early 1850s, as did partisan voting in Congress. While Madison had envisioned a system in which individual members would be connected to Congress, the system that developed emphasized members' connection to their parties. In order to gain power in the chamber, members advanced the collective goals of their parties rather than the collective goals of the institution. By the mid-1850s, the Whig Party had collapsed, primarily over the issue of slavery. The Republican Party emerged in the vacuum left by the demise of the Whigs, to become the chief rival to the Democrats (formerly the Democratic-Republicans). Republicans won the presidency in 1860, and after the Civil War, the Democrats emerged as the defenders of the white South. While the Republicans stood for economic and moral progress, the Democrats emphasized states' rights, individual liberty, and laissez-faire governance. For the next thirty years, Democrats remained largely in control of the House, but Republicans generally held the White House—a pattern that led to political stalemate. Voter turnout was quite high during this era, and the parties dominated in both the electoral and congressional arenas.

An influx of third-party activity during the late nineteenth century ushered in the Progressive Era. The Populist Party, which posed a serious threat to the Democrats' long-standing control of the South, and several other single-issue parties disrupted the dominant two-party equilibrium. The outcome was an extended period of Republican Party dominance; between 1896 and 1932, Republicans lost the presidency only twice. The election of 1896 marked the first time a presidential candidate used money to significantly undercut his competition. Republican presidential candidate William McKinley beat Democrat William Jennings Bryan by organizing his wealthy supporters to challenge the grassroots support Bryan received from farmers and laborers. McKinley's campaign manager, Mark Hanna, devised a fundraising strategy that assessed corporations a percentage of what he determined was their "stake in the general prosperity." The yield for McKinley was $6 million—almost ten times more than Bryan raised and spent (Thayer 1973, 49–50). The Progressives focused on reforming government, primarily by diminishing the influence of the political parties. As a result, voter turnout declined, as did partisanship in Congress. Changes in the House rules weakened the power of the Speaker and basically disconnected the committees from the party leadership.

The midterm elections of 1930 began an era of Democratic Party control in the House that would last for just over sixty years. With the election of Franklin D. Roosevelt in 1932, the Democrats surged to dominance by reinventing themselves as the party of strong executive leadership, the welfare state, and internationalism. Voter turnout rates in the 1930s and 1940s returned to the record levels reached in the mid-nineteenth century. While Democrats lost the presidency twice in the 1950s, they generally continued to dominate in Congress and in the electorate, where a majority of voters tended to vote a straight Democratic ticket. While parties still organized the House, the power to set the legislative agenda rested with the powerful committee chairs. House Democrats held large majorities but did not promote and advance a collective agenda as their counterparts in the mid- to late nineteenth century had.

The Progressive Era reforms that weakened party leaders in the House led to the rise of the seniority system. Committee chairs, who dominated House politics for the first half of the twentieth century, were selected according to their time in office. These chairs maintained their positions until they decided to retire, run for higher office, or step down for some other reason, so members who aspired to committee chairs could do little more than patiently build up seniority and wait their turn. The seniority rule thus led to longer terms of service in the House: Throughout the nineteenth century, House members rarely served more than two terms in office; by the 1950s, members were averaging over five terms in office (Polsby 1968, 146). Pursuing policy goals was an option only for members ideologically aligned with the committee chairs, most of whom were conservative and who controlled which bills were heard in committee and sent to the House floor. And because the party leaders were weak, they lacked the ability to organize any sort of collective challenge to the committee chairs. In this environment, ambitious members who lacked seniority found it difficult to build power in the chamber. However, one enterprising junior member from Texas figured out a way to accomplish that feat.

Spreading Wealth the Old-Fashioned Way

In 1940, Lyndon B. Johnson (D-TX) organized a massive fundraising campaign on behalf of his House colleagues. Democrats were short on funds and at risk of losing majority control of the House, so Johnson called on his Texas oil industry allies for help. Oil money flowed into the campaign coffers of House Democrats, and the party managed not only to maintain control of the House, but to pick up an additional eight seats. The money that Johnson redistributed did not come from his own campaign funds; rather, he acted as a conduit for contributions and always made sure that the recipients understood the role he had played. As a result of his efforts, Johnson quickly gained prestige in the chamber; in fact, his reputation as an influential and powerful politician was largely built on his ability to raise and distribute impressive sums of campaign money (Baker 1989; Caro 1990).

Johnson's fundraising activities in the 1940s were technically associated with the Democratic Congressional Campaign Committee, but his relationship with the committee consisted of little more than his handing over money he had raised. He worked out of his own office and with his own staff. The concept of financing congressional races across the country from a single source was not new, but the Democrats had never implemented such a plan. "No one before had ever worked at it," said James Rowe, a Roosevelt White House insider. "Johnson worked at it like hell. People running for Congress in those days never had much money; it had been that way for years, but Lyndon decided to do something about it; he got in it with both feet, the way he did everything, and he raised a hell of a lot of money." In effect, according to reporter Robert S. Allen, he was "a one-man national committee for congressmen" (Caro 1990, 662).

Johnson's approach to redistributing money to his colleagues was a precursor to contemporary leadership PACs. He was indifferent to the political characteristics of those he helped and was willing "to march with any ally who would help his personal advancement" (Caro 1990, 663). Most of the members who received campaign money through Johnson's efforts in the 1940s were northern liberals competing in swing districts. Thus the money Johnson distributed came from contributors who abhorred the politics of those who received their financial support. "He was helping New Dealers with the money of men who hated the New Deal" (Baker 1989, 19). Nonetheless, these contributors trusted Johnson to distribute their money as he saw fit; in return, they expected Johnson to broker policies from which they would benefit.

Though Johnson's fundraising activities were on a scale never before seen, southern members with excess personal campaign funds had made cash-on-hand contributions to their more vulnerable colleagues for decades. Former Majority Whip Hale Boggs (D-LA) is credited with formalizing this practice (Drew 1983). Such contributions were generally viewed as friendly gestures with no strings attached because they were given by members who simply had more campaign cash on hand than they needed for their own reelection. "It was an effort to help people who needed a little help," according to former congressman Richardson Preyer of North Carolina. "If you raised more money than you needed to spend in your campaign, you'd give some to a couple of other members of your delegation who were hard up for funds. This early form of giving was not directed to any particular purpose such as gaining control of a committee or anything of that sort. It was generally sort of good-will giving and in fairly small amounts" (Baker 1989, 17–18). But as member demand for campaign contributions grew, politically ambitious officeholders who faced little or no competition in their own districts began to recognize the strategic value in raising excess campaign money. By virtue of simply having surplus campaign funds, members could prove they had the clout to attract donors. By sharing their campaign wealth with other members, they could prove they were team players.

Before the passage of the campaign finance reforms in the early 1970s, no law required the reporting of these transactions. According to former Representative Richard Bolling (D-MO), "A good deal of money moved around but it was not illegal to have long green. Nobody ever talked about it. Even later on in my career when I was more 'in,' I heard very few specific details. The reason it was legal was because there weren't any laws and a lot of it moved around in cash" (Baker 1989, 23). Whether member-to-member giving during this era played a role in leadership races, committee assignments, or other House proceedings is unknown because such contributions were not documented. However, because the House leadership structure at that time was largely determined by seniority, members who aspired to leadership positions generally had to wait their turn, regardless of their largesse.

The Reform Era

Voter turnout rates began to decline in the 1960s as the Vietnam War, the civil rights movement, and counterculture politics took center stage. Watergate and a poorly performing economy further eroded the public's attitude toward government during the 1970s, and increasing numbers of Americans began to disassociate themselves from the political parties, identifying themselves as independents. Party-line voting in the electorate waned as voters began aligning themselves with particular candidates or issues rather than parties.

These changes led many political scientists to claim that the parties were in a state of decline from which they might never recover (see Broder 1971; Crotty 1984). Historically, parties focused on election activities like recruiting and nominating candidates, fundraising, and registering and mobilizing voters. The introduction of direct primaries meant that the parties no longer controlled the candidate selection process; organized interests replaced the parties as the primary source of candidate campaign funds; and party identification in the electorate declined, as did partisan voting in Congress. The new politics of the 1970s clearly emphasized member and voter independence.

The public had also become disillusioned by the access that many organized interests enjoyed in Washington. President Lyndon Johnson's Great Society programs expanded the role of federal government, as did the emergence of new policy and regulatory issues. As the government became more involved in public life, organized interests increasingly sought to influence federal policy. With profits and benefits at stake, interest groups and their lobbyists worked to build relationships with members of Congress who could help them accomplish their policy goals. As the federal government's agenda grew and as more members became involved in policy formulation and oversight, the number of lobbyists seeking access multiplied. The growing number of "sweetheart relationships" between organized interests and members of Congress eventually led to widespread allegations of political corruption. A series of scandals involving members of Congress and lobbyists during the 1970s confirmed the public's suspicions that the federal government favored those who could afford access (Dodd and Schott 1979, 183–210). In the face of intense criticism, Congress moved to reform its campaign-finance and lobbying laws, and to impose stringent new ethics standards on its members.

The passage of the Federal Elections Campaign Act (FECA) in 1971 strengthened the reporting requirements for campaign contributions and restricted campaign spending. In explicitly requiring PACs to file quarterly reports of receipts and expenditures, the act acknowledged that such committees played a role in campaigns and, in effect, authorized their establishment. Before passage of the FECA, groups made campaign contributions through political committees, but there was no formal means of tracking these contributions.

Public outrage over the Watergate scandal and campaign abuses in the 1972 elections convinced Congress that more regulation was necessary. The FECA amendments of 1974 largely replaced the 1971 act. The amendments significantly strengthened disclosure requirements, set limits on contributions and expenditures in federal elections, created the Federal Elections Commission (FEC), and established a system of public financing for presidential candidates. The amendments also set PAC contribution limits of $5,000 per candidate, per election. In 1975, the Sun Oil Company asked the FEC for an advisory opinion on the legality of establishing a PAC in light of the 1974 FECA amendments. The FEC's opinion provided the most definitive account of the "rights and responsibilities" of PACs and paved the way for more corporations, unions, and other groups to participate in federal elections by establishing PACs (Corrado et al. 1997, 130). As a result, the number of registered PACs grew from 89 in 1968 to 1,653 in 1978. PAC contributions to congressional candidates exploded as well. In 1968, PAC giving to congressional candidates totaled $3.1 million; by 1978, this amount had climbed to $34 million. PACs continued to grow in both numbers and spending power throughout the 1980s but began to level off in the 1990s (see Table 1.1).

Two months after the 1974 amendments were passed, the constitutionality of contribution and expenditure ceilings was challenged in federal court. In *Buckley v. Valeo,* the U.S. Supreme Court declared that the government cannot restrict the speech of the wealthy in order to enhance the relative voice of the poor, and it invalidated all restrictions on campaign expenditures. Yet limits on campaign contributions were left intact. The Court reasoned that contribution limits were justified to prevent the appearance (and possibly the reality) of corruption.

In 1976, Congress attempted to pass legislation revising lobbying laws. The proposed revisions sought to provide a clear definition of lobbying, and to require lobby organizations to register annually and file

Table 1.1 Spending, by Type of PAC, 1977–2004 (in millions of dollars)

Election Cycle	Corporate	Labor	Trade/ Membership/ Health	Non- Connected[a]	Other Connected	Total
1977–78	15.2	18.6	23.8	17.4	2.4	77.4
	(785)	(217)	(453)	(162)	(36)	(1,653)
1979–80	31.4	25.1	32.0	38.6	4.0	131.2
	(1,206)	(297)	(576)	(374)	(98)	(2,551)
1981–82	43.3	34.8	41.9	64.3	5.8	190.2
	(1,469)	(380)	(649)	(723)	(150)	(3,371)
1983–84	59.2	47.5	54.0	97.4	8.7	266.8
	(1,682)	(394)	(698)	(1,053)	(182)	(4,009)
1985–86	79.3	57.9	73.3	118.4	11.1	340.0
	(1,744)	(384)	(745)	(1,077)	(207)	(4,157)
1987–88	89.9	74.1	83.7	104.9	11.7	364.2
	(1,816)	(354)	(786)	(1,115)	(197)	(4,268)
1989–90	101.1	84.6	88.1	71.4	12.5	357.6
	(1,795)	(346)	(774)	(1,062)	(196)	(4,172)
1991–92	112.4	94.6	97.5	76.2	14.1	394.8
	(1,735)	(347)	(770)	(1,145)	(198)	(4,195)
1993–94	116.8	88.4	94.1	75.1	13.7	388.1
	(1,660)	(333)	(792)	(980)	(189)	(3,954)
1995–96	130.6	99.8	105.4	81.3	12.9	429.9
	(1,642)	(332)	(838)	(1,103)	(164)	(4,079)
1997–98	137.6	98.2	114.4	107.8	12.9	470.8
	(1,567)	(321)	(821)	(935)	(154)	(3,798)
1999–00	158.3	128.7	137.2	139.7	15.5	579.4
	(1,548)	(318)	(844)	(972)	(153)	(3,835)
2001–02	178.3	158.0	141.3	165.7	13.3	656.5
	(1,508)	(316)	(891)	(1,019)	(157)	(3,891)
2003–04	221.6	182.9	170.1	255.2	13.1	842.9
	(1,538)	(310)	(884)	(999)	(137)	(3,868)
2005–06	277.8	197.3	208.8	354.5	16.6	1b[b]
	(1,808)	(312)	(1,019)	(1,797)	(155)	(5,091)

Source: Harold W. Stanley and Richard G. Niemi. 2008. Vital Statistics on American Politics, 2007–2008. Washington, DC: CQ Press; Federal Elections Commission, www.fec.gov.

Note: Amounts in current dollars. The number of registered PACs in each category is in parentheses.

[a] This category combines the Federal Elections Commission categories of cooperatives and cooperations without stock.

[b] Total PAC spending for the 2005–2006 election cycle was just over $1 billion.

quarterly reports with the General Accounting Office. The bill, which was opposed by almost every major lobby group in Washington, failed to pass before the congressional session ended. Lawmakers tried repeatedly to reform lobbying laws during the 1970s and 1980s, but no major legislation was passed until 1995, when Congress enacted the Lobby Disclosure Act. Though reform-era attempts to modify the lobby system failed, both the House and the Senate managed to pass fairly stringent ethics codes in 1977. The provisions focused primarily on financial disclosure, outside income, and gifts (Dodd and Schott 1979, 205–210).

House reformers believed that stricter campaign-finance, lobbying, and ethics laws would constrain the influence of outside interests. They also pushed for changes to constrict the powers of entrenched committee chairs, and to empower Congress as an institution. Progressive members of the House Democratic Caucus—many of whom had been elected in the 1960s and 1970s—led these reform efforts. By the mid-1970s, the House had begun to move away from the seniority rule and had changed the procedures whereby committee and subcommittee chairpersons were chosen. Once the power of the House's long-standing committee chairs was dislodged, newer members began to seek their party leaders' help in pursuing their political and policy goals (Price 1992). Junior members thus became more active in their congressional party organizations and moved to strengthen the power of party leaders. Because the reforms required caucus approval by secret ballot vote of committee chairs and party leaders, these positions became more attainable by junior members than they had been under the seniority system, and ambitious members began to pursue them. As a consequence of the reforms, the playing field between junior and senior members became more level and the political environment became more competitive.

While party-line voting remained high on some issues, members were generally less influenced by the party when casting roll call votes. Democratic party leaders were handed more power during the 1970s, but they still lacked the ability to enforce strict party discipline. Members were more likely to listen to their constituents and their own instincts than to the party. Democratic leaders in the postreform House faced a unique challenge: In order to advance the party's policy agenda, they had to promote party cohesion in a political atmosphere that increasingly emphasized individual members over parties (Rohde 1991). The era's new breed of lawmaker was more self-centered and more committed to policy entrepreneurship than to collective action.

Newer members were also enterprising when it came to promoting themselves; anxious to impress their constituents, these members sought the help of professional campaign consultants and strategists. Pollsters, media advisers, policy consultants, and direct mail experts—a group of specialists collectively known as the *elections industry*—were by-products of the 1970s reforms and the new kind of politics they inspired (Mitchell 1989). Television replaced print and radio as the favored medium for campaign advertising because as broadcast markets expanded, candidates found they could reach wider audiences through television. They also could personalize their campaign messages with images of themselves and their families—a tactic that appealed to the era's self-interested politicians. Running for reelection every two years and responding to increasingly active constituencies required incumbent members to travel home more often. Airfare costs significantly strained many incumbents' campaign budgets. As a result of all of these factors, the average cost of running a campaign increased dramatically during the 1970s: Mean campaign expenditures by House candidates in 1974 amounted to $53,384; by 1978, mean expenditures were $109,440; and by 1980, House candidates were spending an average of $153,221 (Malbin 1984, 278). Over the course of six years, campaign expenditures for House candidates had nearly tripled. Gone were the days of all-volunteer, grassroots campaigns. In order to compete, candidates needed to raise a lot of money.

As the community of organized interests rapidly expanded, members actively began to seek out the PAC money many of these groups could provide. Because PACs could contribute $5,000 per candidate, per election, their donations were more attractive than those from individuals, who in the 1980s could contribute only $1,000 per candidate, per election. The campaign finance reforms of the early 1970s authorized PACs in order to better regulate outside contributions to candidate campaigns. While this official authorization was intended to constrain the influence of organized interests, it ultimately advantaged self-interested members who needed to raise campaign money.

Attuned to the increasing value that members placed on campaign contributions, House leaders began helping members raise money with the expectation that these members would repay the favor by supporting the party's agenda. The strategy was mutually beneficial in that it gave the leaders a new way to promote party cohesion and gave the members a new way to raise money. Thus the ongoing quest for campaign funds provided party leaders with a way to balance members' individual goals with the party's collective goals.

Under the seniority system, one member's aggressive networking did not trump another member's rank. While the reforms made it possible for more junior members to pursue committee chairs or leadership posts, to do so successfully required building support in the chamber. Members with leadership aspirations typically pursued a strategy of building support networks in the chamber, but some also engaged in member-to-member giving. Ross Baker describes several cases during the 1970s in which senior members raised money, then distributed it to their colleagues for the purpose of securing support for their own leadership bids. The 1976 Majority Whip race set a new standard in member-to-member contributing in that three of the four challengers gave campaign money to their colleagues for the express purpose of winning their support. One of the challengers, California Democrat Phil Burton, is credited with devising the strategy, which two of his competitors then copied. Texas Democrat Jim Wright won the position by one vote (Baker 1989, 24–26). By the end of the 1970s, House members had begun to redistribute money more strategically.

The Rise of Leadership PACs

In 1978, Representative Paul Rogers (D-FL) retired as chair of the Energy and Commerce Committee's Subcommittee on Health and the Environment, sparking an unprecedented battle. Although the House reforms had made subcommittee chairs elective within committee, the most senior subcommittee member of the majority party was typically still recognized as next in line. But in this case, the most senior subcommittee member was Representative David Satterfield (D-VA), a member who was so far to the ideological right of his Democratic colleagues that the caucus refused to consider him for the chair. Richardson Preyer (D-NC), the next most senior member, announced his candidacy for the position and was expected to win committee approval easily.

Soon after Preyer declared his intentions, Representative Henry Waxman (D-CA), a two-term member who was fourth in seniority on the subcommittee, announced that he, too, would seek the subcommittee chair. Waxman actively lobbied his committee colleagues for the position and called on his allies in the organized-labor community to lobby committee members with large working-class constituencies on his behalf. He also publicly suggested that Preyer's financial ties to pharmaceutical firms and his representation of a tobacco-steeped North Carolina district were jurisdictional conflicts of interest that might affect his ability to be impartial.

Waxman then did something that no member of Congress had ever before done: He established a leadership PAC and contributed $24,000 to his Energy and Commerce Committee colleagues. After a large number of last-minute vote switches, Waxman defeated Preyer by a fifteen-to-twelve vote. "Friends of Henry Waxman," the first leadership PAC established by a member of Congress, was considered instrumental in Waxman's ascension to the subcommittee chair (Baker 1989, 29–32).

While most Democrats, including Preyer, considered Waxman an extremely bright and competent member, many were dismayed by how he had competed for the subcommittee chairmanship. Because member-to-member giving had been practiced only by senior members and party leaders, many members thought Waxman's adoption of the strategy was disrespectful. Other members accused Waxman of simply buying the chair. Rules Committee Chair Richard Bolling (D-MO), one of the House's lead reformers, angrily denounced Waxman's appointment as chair, claiming that "what Waxman did was an institutionalization of something that I think was pernicious when it was hidden. It was clear, however, that it was going to be a precedent" (Baker 1989, 31).

Even though the innovation was not widely imitated at first, Waxman's PAC was an early indicator of what would eventually become a standard strategic tool for enterprising politicians. True to Bolling's prediction, Waxman's leadership PAC set the standard for those who aspired to leadership positions or committee chairs, and for the leaders and chairpersons themselves. In 1988, ten years after Waxman became the first member of Congress to establish a leadership PAC, there were 45 active leadership PACs affiliated with members of Congress (Wilcox 1990). By 1998, 81 members of Congress had established leadership PACs, and by 2000, that number had climbed to 141. The growth in leadership PAC contributions is even more remarkable. In 1978, fewer than 10 leadership PACs gave political candidates a total of $62,485; in 1988, they contributed a total of $3.7 million; and by 1998, leadership PAC contributions totaled $11.1 million (see Table 1.2). The proliferation of leadership PACs in the wake of the reform era suggests that members began to view leadership positions as increasingly attractive (Canon 1989), and that they were seeking new ways to ingratiate themselves with their colleagues.

Leadership PACs were a direct outgrowth of the 1970s House reforms—a reminder that Congress is a political institution, and that any new rule or norm is subject to unexpected adaptations and exploitations. The goal of the reformers was to create a more democratic institution, where every member had a voice as well as the opportunity to pursue his or her own policy and political ambitions. Removing excessive power from the committee chairs was essential to this plan, as was expanding the authority of the party leaders. The message that committee chairs would be held accountable became clear in 1975, when the Democratic Caucus ousted three long-standing chairs who were considered out of touch with the party. Because the structure of opportunities available to members gradually changed, so did member incentives.

When power is centralized in the party leadership, leaders are typically better able to promote party cohesion. Members have an incentive to follow leadership directives when leaders determine committee assignments and control which bills go to the House floor. However, party leaders in the postreform era were not altogether successful in enforcing party discipline. Despite their enhanced powers, leaders rarely punished members for defying the party or for pushing their own agendas rather than the party's. The Democratic leadership's inability or unwillingness to exercise strong control over members may have been a reflection of

Table 1.2 Leadership PAC Growth, 1978–2006

Year	Number of Registered Leadership PACs	Total Leadership PAC Contributions (in dollars)
1978	<10	62,485
1988	45	3.7 million
1998	120	11.1 million
2000	167	16.9 million
2002	201	24.6 million
2004	230	27.9 million
2006	291	41.9 million

Sources: The Center for Responsive Politics, www.crp.org; Ross K. Baker. 1989. *The New Fat Cats.* New York: Priority Press; Clyde Wilcox. 1989. Share the Wealth. *American Politics Quarterly* 17, no. 4:386–408.

Note: Figures include all leadership PACs registered to federal politicians.

the seniority rule's still generally being followed in the selection of committee chairs. Respecting seniority even though it was no longer a formal rule suggested that the seniority system was virtually unbreakable and that the result would be a system in which committee chairs acted independently and power was decentralized (Polsby, Gallagher, and Rundquist 1969). But as Norm Ornstein (1981, 374) argues, the meaning and impact of seniority were altered in the postreform Congress. While seniority still gave members a clear edge in chair races, it by no means guaranteed total insulation from removal thereafter.

The inability of party leaders to exercise strong authority over members was also a sign of the times. Newer members of Congress saw themselves as political and policy entrepreneurs first and party members second. Leadership PACs were part of the broader trend toward greater member autonomy in that they provided ambitious members with a way to promote their own self-interests. Member-to-member giving in the prereform era emphasized party building; politicians like Lyndon Johnson certainly understood that they would benefit personally by helping their colleagues, but the contributions they made were more about securing majority control for the party. Postreform contributors gave to colleagues more to advance their own personal ambitions than to build the party.

While the party organizations focused on the collective goal of getting candidates elected, House members continued to concentrate on their own individual ambitions. In the decade or so after Henry Waxman established Friends of Henry Waxman, most congressional leadership PACs were formed by liberal Democrats who held safe congressional seats (Baker 1989, 35). Democrats had presided over the House since 1940, so it is not surprising that they were the first to form leadership PACs, as they controlled all of the top leadership posts and committee chairs. Most Democrats who formed leadership PACs followed Waxman's example and used them for the purpose of garnering colleague support for their own ambitions.

The 1986 House Majority Whip race pitted California Democrat Tony Coelho against Charles Rangel of New York and W. G. (Bill) Hefner of North Carolina. Coelho was the early favorite, having raised tremendous amounts of money for Democratic House candidates during his tenure as chair of the DCCC. He was also a member of the California Democratic delegation, which was populated by a number of strong fundraisers like Phil Burton and Henry Waxman. Many California Democrats were alumni of the California state legislature, and in that legislature's system, party leaders were traditionally chosen for their ability to raise campaign money for party members (Jacobson 1985–1986, 623). Charles Rangel, one of the leading African-American House members, was Coelho's primary competition. Rangel was a well-respected and well-liked member of the Democratic Caucus who was supported by the Speaker, as well as by the Congressional Black Caucus. However, Coelho had one advantage: a leadership PAC. Following the California precedent, Coelho established the Valley Education Fund PAC once he had decided to run for Majority Whip. Rangel claimed he was personally and politically opposed to leadership PACs and refused to compete with Coelho on those terms. He also suggested that giving members money was akin to buying votes and claimed he did not want to embarrass his colleagues by putting them in an awkward position.

As the Whip's race heated up, Rangel changed his mind and established the Committee for the 100th Congress leadership PAC. In doing so, Rangel set out to compete with Coelho on a field where Coelho was virtually unbeatable. Coelho contributed $570,000 to 245 Democratic House campaigns and Rangel contributed a total of $225,000 to about 100 candidates. Coelho won the Whip's race by a comfortable margin, despite some grumbling about the role fundraising had played in the race's outcome (Baker 1989, 35–36).

Two years later, Pennsylvania Democrat William Gray established a new precedent in member-to-member giving when he ran for chair of the House Democratic Caucus. Running for chair of the House Budget Committee in 1984, Gray had established a leadership PAC and contributed $27,000 to 75 Democratic incumbents and challengers. The caucus selected Gray in a three-way contest for the chair, naming him to a prestigious position from which he could raise even more campaign money for his colleagues. House rules limit Budget Committee chairs to two two-year terms, so Gray announced his intention to seek the caucus chair in 1987, approximately one year before his Budget chair was set to expire. Mary Rose Oakar of Ohio and Mike Synar of Oklahoma also declared themselves candidates in the race and, like Gray, began campaigning for the post one year in advance. In the few months after announcing his candidacy, Gray used excess campaign money that he had raised as Budget chair to give $35,750 in contributions to his colleagues. Oakar contributed to five Democrats (at the request of the leadership), and Synar did not give any campaign money to his colleagues.

As the election drew closer, Gray's self-promotion campaign became even more pronounced. In early 1988, he hosted an extravagant dinner for his colleagues at Occidental, a posh DC restaurant, and used the occasion to promote his candidacy. In addition to enjoying an expensive dinner, members of the Pennsylvania delegation were singled out and given $1,000 campaign checks. Just as they were recovering from their astonishment over the dinner he had hosted, Gray surprised his colleagues again: He established a new leadership PAC called the Committee for Democratic Opportunity and solicited outside contributors to help him in his quest to become caucus chair. This marked the first time a member of Congress had actively sought outsider help in a leadership race. Gray also hosted a breakfast meeting for lobbyists and asked them to contact other Democrats and urge them to support his bid. In the end, Gray's rigorous campaigning paid off, and he was elected caucus chair. His campaign for the position revealed that in addition to establishing leadership PACs, members had numerous options for influencing their colleagues (Baker 1989, 37–40).

William Gray's strategy of incorporating outside interests into leadership races inaugurated a new tactic for leadership aspirants, which House Republicans soon adopted. In 1994, after the Republicans won majority control of the House for the first time in forty years, Republican members were finally in a position to pursue leadership posts and committee chairs. During the 1970s and 1980s, House Republicans did not establish leadership PACs at the same rate as House Democrats, but that equation changed in the 1990s. Republicans who were interested in one day running for a leadership post or a committee chair now understood the value of helping themselves by helping their colleagues.

When Louisiana Republican Bob Livingston decided to run for the House Speakership, he knew that winning the early support of his colleagues was essential. Speaker Newt Gingrich was expected to step down in 1999 to launch a bid for the presidency, and Livingston, as well as House Majority Leader Dick Armey, hoped to succeed him. Livingston was generally well liked by his colleagues, but he sometimes clashed with his party's more conservative members over budgetary matters. And though his chairing of the House Appropriations Committee provided him with impressive credentials, the position was generally not considered a stepping-stone to the Speakership.

Once Livingston had made his Speakership aspirations known, he established a leadership PAC and named it BOB's PAC, an acronym for "Building Our Bases." In its first year of operation (1998), BOB's PAC raked in approximately $1.3 million and doled out $800,000 to Republican House members and candidates. That same year, Livingston also contributed $600,000 from his own personal campaign committee to his party and to Republican candidates. Most of the money raised by Livingston's personal campaign committee and his leadership PAC came courtesy of the businesses he had worked closely with as chair of the House Appropriations Committee, namely, the oil, insurance, and defense industries. James Pruitt, vice president of federal government affairs for Texaco Incorporated and a former Livingston staff member, coordinated the K Street fundraising effort for BOB's PAC.[2] In addition to organizing fundraisers for his former boss, Pruitt worked diligently to convince his skeptical K Street associates that Livingston could actually win the Speakership. A number of business executives ultimately decided to hedge their bets and contributed to Livingston's personal campaign committee and his leadership PAC; less than one year after it was established, BOB's PAC became one of the wealthiest leadership PACs in existence. When Gingrich stepped down following the 1998 elections and Livingston was designated front-runner for the Speakership, BOB's PAC was flooded with even more contributions from corporate PACs eager to signal their support (Babcock and Marcus 1998).[3]

Securing the early financial backing of his friends in the corporate lobbying community was key to Livingston's strategy of establishing himself as an influential player who could assist both his party and his colleagues. "They know Bob helped," Livingston supporter Ron Packard (R-CA) said of members who had received contributions from BOB's PAC. "And when you go and call and ask, it's easier to get their commitment." Explaining the surge of member interest in leadership PACs, Packard concisely observed that "every key member of Congress has had one" (Babcock and Marcus 1998).

The 1990s also saw a rise in the number of junior House members establishing leadership PACs. In 1998, freshman Representative Doug Ose (R-CA) registered his leadership PAC even before he had been sworn into office (Glasser and Eilperin 1999). Other members of Ose's class followed suit and registered leadership PACs during their first term in office. Once limited to a fairly small pool of House leaders and leader aspirants, leadership PACs had moved into the mainstream of congressional politics by the late 1990s.

The Parties Strike Back

During the 1960s and 1970s, some political scientists claimed that the parties were in a state of decline, while others argued they were in a state of transition (Bibby 1981; Conway 1983). As elections became more candidate-centered and as members of Congress became more entrepreneurial, the parties adjusted by providing candidates with a broad range of campaign services. Recognizing that members are primarily concerned with winning reelection, the party organizations began offering media support, polling and survey assistance, campaign training, and targeted fundraising. In other words, the parties figured out ways to remain relevant in a political system that no longer revolved around them. By helping their members secure reelection, the parties could promote the collective goal of majority status.

Unless a party controls the governing apparatus, it cannot reasonably expect that its policies will be adopted, and its members cannot effectively pursue their own political ambitions. Members of the majority party are therefore motivated to maintain control, while members of the minority party are motivated to gain control. Both actions—maintaining and gaining—require that members act as a team. Traditionally, the majority party has had a more difficult time convincing its members to focus on the collective goal of maintaining majority status because these members already enjoy the benefits of majority control. They are typically more interested in using their party's majority status to pursue their own personal policy and political goals (Dodd 1986, 94–96). House Democrats in the 1970s and 1980s rarely worried about losing their majority status, as their party had controlled the chamber since 1954. The Republicans' outlook was quite different; they had been out of power for so long that it was difficult for them to imagine being in the majority. Democrats held comfortable margins over the Republicans throughout the 1970s and 1980s—another factor that contributed to the Republicans' lack of enthusiasm (see Table 1.3). When there is a realistic opportunity to win majority control, the minority party usually pulls together as a team because its members are highly motivated by their desire to take charge of the chamber. Once the majority party begins to fragment as members pursue their own political and policy agendas, a unified and organized minority party can exploit the majority party's weaknesses and promote its alternative agenda.

Competition for House seats increased substantially in the 1990s for a number of reasons. The percentage of incumbents winning with 60 percent or more of the vote dropped from a postwar high of 89 percent in 1988 to 76 percent in 1990, to 66 percent in 1992, then to 65

Table 1.3 Party Margins in the House, 1965–2007

Congress (Years)	# of Democrats	# of Republicans
89th (1965–67)	295	140
90th (1967–69)	247	187
91st (1969–71)	243	192
92nd (1971–73)	255	180
93rd (1973–75)	242	192
94th (1975–77)	291	144
95th (1977–79)	292	143
96th (1979–81)	277	158
97th (1981–83)	242	192
98th (1983–85)	269	166
99th (1985–87)	253	182
100th (1987–89)	258	177
101st (1989–91)	260	175
102nd (1991–93)	267	167
103rd (1993–95)	258	176
104th (1995–97)	204	230
105th (1997–99)	206	228
106th (1999–01)	211	223
107th (2001–03)	212	221
108th (2003–05)	204	229
109th (2005–07)	202	232
110th (2007–09)	233	202

Source: Clerk of the U.S. House of Representatives, www.clerk.house.gov.

Note: Party totals are based on election day results. There are 435 members of the House; a majority is 218 members.

percent in 1994. The competitive balance between Democrats and Republicans also shifted, so that in the 1990s, Republicans began to regularly win more seats than they had between 1946 and 1990. Voting behavior changed as well; the percentage of districts where voters elected a presidential candidate of one party and a House member of another declined considerably after 1984. Reapportionment after the 1990 census also shifted the electoral dynamics in a number of districts, creating more favorable conditions for House Republicans. The postreform southern realignment led to more ideologically homogeneous parties, as many conservative Democrats left their party for the Republican Party. These changes were apparent in the House, where Democrats and Republicans fought their political and policy battles in increasingly partisan terms. Republicans also took advantage of President Bill Clinton's high unfavorable ratings and successfully challenged a number of vulnerable Democrats who had been elected in 1992. In addition, twenty-seven House Democrats decided to retire in 1994 and left open many formerly safe seats. Despite all of the evidence to suggest otherwise, the Democrats still believed they would retain majority status in 1994 (Kolodny and Dwyre 1998, 277–279). Instead, the Republicans finally ended four decades of Democratic control of the House.

The 1994 elections signaled a new era of electoral competitiveness. For the next twelve years, Republicans would remain in the majority, though holding very small margins over the Democrats. Real party competition was a phenomenon House Democrats and Republicans had not experienced for decades. This new dynamic dramatically strengthened the role of the congressional parties in that ambitious members—onetime independent actors—began turning to their party organizations for help in pursuing their personal goals (Schlesinger 1991; Kolodny and Dwyre 1998, 278). Enhanced competitiveness enables party leaders to leverage more control over members because a member's ability to attain power closely depends on the party's ability to maintain majority control. While this is always the case in theory, members are much more likely to abide by leadership directives when the margin between parties is small simply because the parties' majority/minority status hangs in the balance every two years.

The CCCs had made fundraising appeals to incumbent members throughout the 1980s, but most members chose not to contribute for the good of the whole (Jacobson 1985–1986, 616). The presence of real electoral competition throughout the 1990s swayed members to see the value in contributing to and raising money for the congressional party campaign committees, as well as in forming leadership PACs and contributing money to their colleagues. While the collective goal of majority status drove members to contribute, so did the desire to impress their party leaders.

Following their success in 1994, Republican leaders believed that to maintain majority control, the party needed to continue its vigorous fundraising efforts. In 1993, the NRCC broke new ground by convincing members that the party could gain majority status in 1994 if they would contribute money to the committee and to other candidates. NRCC directors Bill Paxon and Newt Gingrich reasoned "that the collective goal of majority status was more valuable to these incumbents than the few extra thousand dollars" they asked them to contribute (Kolodny and Dwyre 1998, 289). Gingrich established a formula for "voluntary contributions" by each incumbent; unless they were in financial trouble themselves, members were expected to contribute (Gimpel 1996, 10). The strategy was hugely successful: Republican House members donated just under $13 million to Republican candidates and to the NRCC, and the money was targeted to outside challengers running against vulnerable Democratic incumbents and to open-seat candidates (Kolodny and Dwyre 1998, 289). As Gimpel notes, the "1994 campaign signaled the coming of a Republican revolution both in terms of message and money" (1996, 11).

Following the 1994 elections, Republican leaders confronted the Madisonian dilemma of how to channel individual ambition for the good of the whole by enforcing party discipline and rewarding members who supported the leadership's agenda. Newt Gingrich believed that fragmentation was at the root of the Democrats' defeat and that strong, centralized leadership was necessary to keep members in line. By rewarding party loyalty more than longtime service, the leaders discovered that ambitious members would serve the party organization as they pursued their own political and policy goals. Though members can demonstrate party loyalty in a number of ways, fundraising and party-line voting rank high on the list.

The emphasis on party-based fundraising efforts in the House suggests that congressional party organizations again have transformed in response to changes in the political environment. Robin Kolodny and

Diane Dwyre contend that because the electoral environment has become so competitive, the parties now act as "orchestrators of electoral activities." In this new environment, the CCCs serve as the "pivotal party organizational actors" because they coordinate the party-orchestrated fundraising for congressional races (1998, 278). How ambitious members pursue their political and policy goals has also been transformed in response to changes in the electoral environment. Because the individual goal of power in the chamber is now inextricably tied to the collective goal of majority status, members understand that if they want to advance in the chamber, they must act in service to the parties. Anne Bedlington and Michael Malbin have documented that House members are now giving a higher proportion of their personal campaign committee money to the CCCs rather than to other candidates. They also document the CCCs' increased reliance on member contributions as a source of campaign funds (2003, 133–136). In the contemporary Congress, members who raise money for the party and toe the party line have considerable opportunities to advance in the House's power structure (Schickler and Pearson 2005, 220).

The Money Pit

Just before the House Democrats voted in the 1986 Majority Whip race between Tony Coelho, Charles Rangel, and W. G. Hefner, Georgia Democrat Ed Jenkins, a Hefner supporter, urged the Democratic Caucus to recognize that the best Whip was not necessarily the best fundraiser (Baker 1989, 37). While money has influenced House leadership races for at least two decades, its current emphasis is unparalleled. Leaders and leadership aspirants, however, are not the only ones expected to contribute for the good of the whole. Under the new rules for the 2008 election cycle, the DCCC asked rank-and-file members to contribute $125,000 in dues and to raise an additional $75,000 for the party. Subcommittee chairpersons must contribute $150,000 in dues and raise an additional $100,000. Members who sit on the most powerful committees (Appropriations, Ways and Means, Energy and Commerce, Financial Services, and Rules) must contribute $200,000 and

raise an additional $250,000. Subcommittee chairs on power commit-
tees and committee chairs of nonpower committees must contribute
$250,000 and raise $250,000. The five chairs of the power committees
must contribute $500,000 and raise an additional $1 million. House
Majority Leader Steny Hoyer, Majority Whip James Clyburn, and
Democratic Caucus Chair Rahm Emanuel must contribute $800,000
and raise $2.5 million. The four Democrats who serve as part of the
extended leadership must contribute $450,000 and raise $500,000, and
the nine Chief Deputy Whips must contribute $300,000 and raise
$500,000. House Speaker Nancy Pelosi must contribute a staggering
$800,000 and raise an additional $25 million (Hearn 2007a).

While the NRCC does not have a formal dues system like the
DCCC's, Republican members are strongly encouraged to contribute
through the use of "commitment contracts" and leadership pressure. In
2000, for example, Speaker Dennis Hastert warned Republican members that the amount of money they raised for the NRCC would help
determine their committee assignments and rankings in the 107th
Congress (Allen 2000). The NRCC assessments for 2007 required that
members of the leadership contribute $375,000. Ranking members on
power committees were expected to contribute $255,000, while those
on nonpower committees were expected to contribute $205,000. Rank-
ing members on Appropriations subcommittees had to contribute
$205,000, while ranking members on other power subcommittees had
to give $180,000. Ranking members on nonpower committees were ex-
pected to contribute $155,000. Rank-and-file members who sat on
power committees were required to contribute $130,000, while those
who sat on nonpower committees were required to give $110,000.
Freshman members were expected to contribute $60,000. The NRCC
also establishes various fundraising programs (such as the Challenger
Fund, which targets money exclusively to challengers and open-seat
candidates) and tasks members with raising money for those various
efforts (Kucinich 2007; Zeller and Teitelbaum 2007).

Given these substantial financial requirements, party leaders and
leadership aspirants must be committed fundraisers. They must also
have the connections necessary to raise enormous sums of money—an
advantage that only some members enjoy. Nancy Pelosi, a protégé of

Phil Burton, is a product of the California system, in which party leaders are chosen in part for their fundraising abilities. Since winning election to Congress in 1987, Pelosi has proven herself a prodigious fundraiser. In 1998, her leadership PAC, PAC to the Future, was second in receipt growth among all PACs. In 2000, she contributed more money to her colleagues than did any other member of the House or Senate. Her ability to raise money helped propel her to the position of Minority Whip in 2001, Minority Leader in 2002, and Speaker of the House in 2006.

Wealthy connections can also jump-start the careers of new members. Like Pelosi, Tom Reynolds (R-NY) arrived in Washington in 1998 with a Rolodex of well-placed connections. During his first term in office, Reynolds impressed party leaders by raising substantial amounts of money for the party. In 2000, during his second term, he was appointed to lead the Republican Party's Battleground 2000 fundraising campaign. Reynolds's affluent contacts thus enabled him to win a coveted appointment very early in his congressional career. When Debbie Wasserman Schultz (D-FL) was elected to the House in 2002, she began her congressional career by immediately contributing $100,000 in leftover campaign funds to the DCCC. She was appointed to the Democratic Whip organization during her first term and, by her third term, had been named a Chief Deputy Whip and anointed an Appropriations "cardinal" (the lofty title given to Appropriations subcommittee chairpersons).

For members who regularly face hotly contested races or lack the connections needed to raise large amounts of campaign money, party-based fundraising requirements present a challenge. And when leaders tie members' ability to move up the chamber's power ladder to their ability and willingness to raise money for the party, members who lack wealthy connections are at a distinct disadvantage. In an environment that emphasizes fundraising, how do the parties evaluate the non-financial contributions that members make to the party? According to Diane Watson (D-CA), the pressure to raise money prevents members from focusing on the issues. "For anything up over $100,000, you've got to focus full-time on fundraising. . . . We're going to have to come to grips with this some way. I understand to win these national races, there's a cost to it. . . . Money should not be the only driving force" (Hearn 2007b).

The connection between members' ability to raise money and their ability to attain a leadership post, a committee chair, or a seat on a power committee also raises questions about the level of influence that outside interests exercise in the choice of leaders and committee appointees. By supporting some members with sizable contributions, and not others, outside interests indirectly signal to the rest of the chamber their own votes of confidence. Members who gain the financial backing of large campaign donors as candidates for leadership posts should be able to secure continued support—for both the party and its members—from these donors once they become leaders. But what, if anything, do these donors expect in return?

Conclusion

During the reform era, progressive House members pushed for changes that would redistribute power and democratize the chamber. The reformers believed that all Democratic Caucus members should have the opportunity to participate in the policy process, and to mount challenges for higher positions in the chamber. However, ambitious lawmakers exploited the reforms for personal advantage and prospered in the postreform Congress. As a result, today's system is quite different from what House reformers in the 1970s envisioned. Although members do have the opportunity to participate in the process and vie for higher positions, the rules of the game have changed. The individual pursuit of power is inextricably linked to the collective pursuit of majority control in ways the reformers did not anticipate, and campaign money has become central to this pursuit. All members are expected to contribute to satisfy the party's fundraising goals, as well as their own intrainstitutional goals. Thus the quest for campaign money has fundamentally altered how parties compete for majority control and how members compete for power. Understanding why this system evolved requires a consideration of the dynamics that affect the interactions between self-oriented members and team-oriented parties.

Notes

1. The following summary of the five party systems is drawn from Shade (1994, 7–22).

2. Washington's K Street is home to many of the city's top lobbying firms.

3. Though he secured the backing of a majority of his Republican colleagues, Livingston ultimately never assumed the House Speakership. After it was disclosed that he had engaged in extramarital affairs, Livingston resigned from office rather than deny or fight the charges. The Republican Conference then elected Dennis Hastert of Illinois as Speaker of the House.

2

Pursuing Ambition in
a Congressional
Parties Framework

To understand why a system that encourages House members to redistribute money to each other and to the party campaign committees evolved requires a consideration of the dynamic relationship between individual members and the congressional party organizations. Members who want to pursue their own political and policy goals must first join together with other like-minded politicians to form goal-oriented teams for the purpose of winning elections. In majoritarian institutions like the House, members cannot expect their policies to be adopted, nor can they successfully pursue their own political goals unless their party controls the governing apparatus (Downs 1957). Therefore all House members share the common goal of wanting to see their party in the majority (Kolodny 1998). As they pursue their own ambitions, members must act within a party framework because their personal success depends largely on their party's ability to either maintain or gain majority status. To this end, party leaders seek to enforce strict party discipline, but their ability to structure the political and policy pursuits of their members depends on factors including how large the partisan margin is, whether power in the chamber is centralized or decentralized, whether government is divided or unified, and the ideological diversity within and between the parties. As the political environment changes and party frameworks shift, House members adjust their goal-seeking behavior. In this chapter, I suggest that the redistribution of campaign money is best explained by member ambitions and the structure of opportunities that shape these ambitions. I also argue that in a competitive political environment, the congressional party organizations can orchestrate the political and policy pursuits of their ambitious members.

Explaining House Member Behavior

Following the 1973 publication of Richard Fenno's *Congressmen in Committees,* generations of congressional scholars adhered to the goal-oriented framework he introduced and explained member behavior via a set of three goals that all members are presumed to share: reelection, good public policy, and power in the chamber.[1] Members emphasize different goals at different points in their career, focusing first on securing reelection, then on sponsoring and passing important policy measures, and finally on obtaining a powerful committee assignment or leadership post. When *Congressmen in Committees* was published, the seniority rule was still in place and members were generally assumed to pursue these three goals in order. Member behavior in the postreform Congress is not nearly as predictable. Some members find it difficult to move beyond the reelection goal because their districts are highly competitive. Some are content to focus on their policy goals, and others begin immediately to pursue power in the chamber. Today, members have access to a structure of opportunities quite different from that available to members in the prereform Congress.

The rational, goal-oriented perspective of member behavior assumes that lawmakers are utility maximizers; when confronted with an array of options, they will choose the one that best serves their objectives (Green and Shapiro 1994, 14). Because reelection is a primary objective of members, it follows that they will make choices that enhance their reelection potential. But whether an abstract goal will influence a member's choices or actions is likely to depend on the issue at hand. As Richard Hall (1996, 77) argues, "The language of members' goals best implies only the central tendencies" that congressional scholars typically ascribe to a random set of choices. Because members set and define their own goals as they make choices about the various issues they confront, Hall suggests an analysis of members' behavior is better focused on the relative importance they place on specific issues. The value that members attach to certain policy issues, for example, does not always reflect reelection goals. A member may support increased funding for cancer research because a close relative or friend died of cancer, not because her or his constituents feel strongly about the issue.

The goal-oriented premise also neglects to consider how the structure of opportunities before members largely determines which policy goals they can reasonably pursue. For example, "a member may be a personally committed environmentalist, but if the issues before her panel involve Social Security cuts or district pork, she is more likely to behave like a constituency-minded delegate—not because of any change of conviction but because the agenda of issues evokes a different kind of calculation" (Hall 1996, 66). Members who take action on a particular policy issue are not necessarily pursuing one agenda at the expense of another; in many cases, pursuing policy is more opportunistic than premeditated.

If member goals are thus understood both as personal and as motivated by the structure of available opportunities, developing a general theory about member behavior becomes all the more complicated. An ideal measurement strategy, according to Richard Hall, "should enable us to tap into members' perceptions rather than simply impute interests to them" and should be "at the level of the member-issue" because members' political and policy interests are issue-specific (1996, 77). Explaining the strategies of members who redistribute money to their colleagues and the party campaign committees requires a similar theoretical approach. Rather than interpret member contribution strategies through a rational, goal-oriented scheme,[2] I focus on how the political environment and the structure of available opportunities shape members' political ambitions and thus their political behavior (Schlesinger 1966). Members define and determine their own ambitions, and they decide which goals to pursue according to the unique personal, political, and institutional circumstances they encounter.

Intrainstitutional Ambition

Built into the U.S. political system is the assumption that certain individuals, driven by their own ambitions, will want to run for elective office. The Founding Fathers were keenly aware of humans' selfish tendencies and sought to create a system of government that would diffuse these inclinations. In his classic study of political careers in the United States, Joseph Schlesinger (1966) argues that because lawmakers respond primarily to their own political ambitions, how and why legislators got to be legislators should not be as great a concern as what they want to be next. By this logic, members act today in terms of the office they hope to win tomorrow. Schlesinger argues that there are discernible patterns of officeholding and that these patterns give direction to members' distinct political ambitions. He identifies three kinds of ambition: discrete, static, and progressive. A politician with discrete ambition wants a particular office for a set period of time; a politician with static ambition wants to make a long-term career of a particular office; and a politician with progressive ambition aspires to an office higher than the one now held (1966, 10). By examining a member's current office position and political behavior, one can reasonably make certain inferences about his or her political ambitions.

Taking their lead from Schlesinger's seminal work, a number of political scientists have examined the role of ambition in politics. While some of this research has borrowed and applied Schlesinger's framework in different political settings, some has sought to build on or supplement Schlesinger's theory of ambition.[3] For the the discussion here, Rebekah Herrick and Michael Moore's examination of intrainstitutional ambition is most instructive. Herrick and Moore (1993, 765) argue that Schlesinger's typology needs to be expanded to account for intrainstitutional ambition. According to Herrick and Moore, lawmakers who have higher ambitions within their present institutions (for example, a House committee chair who wants to be Majority Leader) exhibit different behavior than their colleagues with progressive or static ambition. The behavior of members with intrainstitutional ambition is likely to demonstrate their commitment to the institution and their loyalty to their party, whereas members with progressive ambition tend to engage in more attention-seeking behavior to gain visibility. The behavior of members with static ambition falls somewhere between that associated with intrainstitutional ambition and that associated with progressive ambition. Herrick and Moore found that members with intrainstitutional ambition are more likely to support the party line on roll call votes than are members with progressive or static ambition. They are also more likely to allocate a higher proportion of their staff to their Washington office, whereas members with progressive or static ambition tend to allocate more staff to their district offices.

My assumption is that all House members are ambitious, but not that all members want to hold higher political office.[4] Some House members set their sights on a Senate seat and some decide to pursue a leadership post within the chamber. Others decide that they can be more effective legislators in the House if they are outside the leadership structure. Any approach tying members' ambition to the desire to hold higher office overlooks the personal and complex nature of ambition. Members' ambitions develop and take form as political circumstances change and as various opportunities become available or unavailable (Black 1972). The structure of available opportunities determines which positions can be pursued and which members can reasonably compete for the positions. Some members, then, are able to pursue their ambitions while others are filtered out, at least temporarily. As Gordon Black argues, the system does not directly cause ambition, but it does indirectly determine who among the elected will lead (1972, 158).

Schlesinger's examination of political ambition, as well as many subsequent studies that adhere to the Schlesinger typology, suggests that members' ambitions are shaped by the various offices they may pursue. Several political scientists have tested this hypothesis, assuming, for example, that the logical next step for an ambitious House member is a Senate seat or a governorship (Rohde 1979; Hibbing 1986; Maisel et al. 1997). While this approach helps to explain how particular offices lead members with progressive ambitions to higher office, it neglects some of the finer contextual details at play. John Hibbing argues that "Schlesinger's approach should stress position-seeking, rather than office-seeking. By not doing so, he misses the fact that the numerous committee and party positions in the House make it possible for the entire gamut of position-seeking behavior to be demonstrated by just those people Schlesinger classifies as having static ambition. Progressive behavior can just as easily be displayed by running for party whip as by running for Senate" (quoted in Herrick and Moore 1993, 28). This is an important point for two reasons: First, ambitious politicians who wish to move from one office to a higher office are likely to first engage in intrainstitutional position seeking; and second, some ambitious politicians engage in intrainstitutional position seeking solely to obtain a higher position within the same institution. In addition to inaccurately characterizing members who do not specifically seek higher office as having static ambition, Schlesinger's typology treats a rank-and-file member of the House the same as the Speaker of the House because both hold the same political office—that of U.S. Representative. This characterization neglects the hierarchy of positions within institutions and the personal nature of members' ambitions.

In his book about the rise and fall of former House Speaker Jim Wright (D-TX), John Barry (1989) explains that to Wright, the position of Speaker was in many ways comparable to that of the U.S. president. As the constitutional head of the legislative branch, Wright believed he had the ability to confront a strong president and to dominate a weak one. In other words, he was guided by ambitions that focused on opportunities within the same office rather than a higher one. Herrick and Moore's framework recognizes that opportunities for advancement exist within the House and that members who choose to pursue these opportunities typically do so after evaluating their own personal ambitions, the political context, and the structure of the opportunities before them.

Individual versus Collective Goals

Joseph Schlesinger's claim that politicians act today in terms of the office they hope to win tomorrow also applies to politicians seeking higher positions within the same chamber. Politics at the intrainstitutional level is treated as a "game of advancement" that manifests itself in what Lawrence Dodd (1977) characterizes as a congressional power ladder. Climbing the ladder is an option; as Dodd notes, some members choose to remain on a lower rung. Importantly, members define power in accordance with their own ambitions; thus one member may aim for a particular subcommittee chair while another may not be interested in any position less powerful than the House Speakership (Brown and Peabody 1992). Few members actively pursue top leadership posts during their legislative careers, and those who do are often motivated by reasons other than electoral or legislative advantage. As Lynne Brown and Robert Peabody observe, the factors that lead members to pursue leadership positions are "as varied as the personalities, circumstances, and motives of the individual leaders" (1984, 186). Among these factors, "personal motivations, the desire to be the chosen one among equals, to be at the center of activity, and with fortune, to become 'the elect of the elected'—all figure in the men and women who place themselves in a potential pool of future leaders" (1984, 183–184).

House members who seek to climb the institutional power ladder are often frustrated by the tremendous amount of effort required (Dodd 1977, 1986). But by observing and then emulating the behavior of those who hold leadership posts, members who aspire to higher positions may increase their chances of advancing in the chamber. According to Carl Friedrich (1963), political leaders engage in three primary activities: They initiate by creating a self-image that inspires others to follow; they maintain by building and promoting a favorable impression of the established order for which they are responsible; and they protect by providing their followers with a sense of security. If leaders successfully perform these tasks, members respond by imitating, obeying, and acclaiming. The action-response dynamic between leaders and followers provides the foundation for consensual power relationships in the chamber. Because the ability to exercise influence relies in part on shared value preferences, the ability of a leader to influence colleagues increases as their security (or sense of security) decreases. Friedrich uses the example of a politician who needs campaign funds and claims that the influence of those who can provide such funds will increase. Like leaders, members who aspire to leadership positions must demonstrate their ability to protect their colleagues' interests—particularly their reelection interests.

One way for leaders and would-be leaders to create a favorable image, protect their colleagues, and build influence in the chamber is to redistribute campaign money. Members who establish leadership PACs can use the money they raise to fund their own travel, to host or sponsor various events, and to make campaign contributions. Leaders and leader aspirants can also contribute to candidates and to the party committees using money from their personal campaign committees. Because of changes in the electoral environment, including rising campaign costs, outside-interest participation, and redistricting, almost all House members approach their reelection campaigns with a sense of uncertainty. In most congressional races, the candidate who raises the most money wins. But even if members raise more money than their challengers, they cannot predict or control how much money the opposing party and outside interests will spend trying to defeat them. As electoral security and financial security have become more unpredictable, members have increasingly turned to their leaders for service-oriented assistance like fundraising. According to one House leader, giving money to colleagues does not necessarily get leaders votes, but "it can hurt you if you don't have it. . . . It's not necessarily the amounts. Rather it's a signal that I can help you" (Brown and Peabody 1992, 359). To the extent that leaders and leader aspirants can effectively demonstrate their ability to provide financial assistance, they can exert a certain amount of influence over those members who need help.

Congressional party organizations are limited by the fact that they are made up of self-interested individuals (Cox and McCubbins 1993). Comparing the typical European party system, where party agendas are created before candidates are even selected, to the American party system, where candidates' interests often drive the agenda, Robin Kolodny claims that "it is, at times, remarkable that any party feeling exists at all" in America (1998, 5). Indeed, a "party" in America may represent little more than a general approach to policy issues rather than a precise set of principles. By this measure, both lawmakers and voters decide which party to affiliate with depending on their personal understanding of the party's basic approach (Kolodny 1998, 4). Despite these associational ambiguities, party members in government tend to have distinct goals that vary by institution. Kolodny (1998, 5–7) argues that while traditional political party theory suggests that the goal of party members is total party control of all facets of government, the party interest within each governmental institution emphasizes party control of that particular institution. In other words, House members are interested in maximizing the electoral security of other same-party House members, senators are interested in maximizing the electoral security of their same-party colleagues, and so on. Despite these variations in focus, all members of Congress share the primary goal of wanting to serve in the majority. Whether that goal can be achieved by working with the presidential party or the party in the other chamber is secondary. Self-interested members want to serve in the majority simply because the majority party controls and organizes the chamber; while total party control of the House, the Senate, and the White House is appealing, it is not essential.

This book treats the congressional parties as frameworks within which House members must act as they pursue their own political and policy ambitions. All House members understand that before they can productively pursue their own intrainstitutional goals, their party must achieve majority status. Personal ambitions aside, majority party members have clear political advantages over minority party members simply because they wield more institutional power. It is logical to assume, then, that all members count among their personal ambitions power in the form of majority party control. Some members may be content with majority status alone, while others may perceive majority status as a first step toward attaining a more powerful position in the chamber. Majority status thus serves as a least common denominator where member ambition is concerned.

In order for a party to gain or maintain majority status, its members must coordinate under a specific set of political concerns and legislative goals.[5] The party can then project an image of political unity and purpose as it attempts to win public support for its agenda and its candidates. While centralizing power in the leadership simplifies the often difficult task of coordinating the party's message, self-interested members are typically hesitant to relinquish their autonomy. But because minority party members are essentially prevented from pursuing their political and policy ambitions by virtue of their party status, it is in their immediate interest to focus on winning control of the chamber. They are therefore more willing to follow leadership directives to endorse and promote the party's agenda.

Efforts by majority party leaders to centralize power can create palpable tension because majority party members are generally interested in promoting their own agendas rather than the party's. Having temporarily put their personal ambitions on the back burner to help the party gain majority status, majority party members are anxious to focus on their own pursuits. To reap the more personal benefits of majority status, party members push their leaders to expand the number of power positions members can vie for and to increase institutional resources such as staff and new technologies (Sinclair 1983). They also push for increases in the number of committee and subcommittee seats. Because the committee system provides members with a venue for publicizing constituent concerns, members seek assignments that will enhance their political careers. As a result, committees and subcommittees are typically not microcosms of a diverse chamber, but clusters of constituency-minded members focused on narrowly defined interests (Davidson 1981, 101). Access to additional fringe benefits gives majority party members an edge in their reelection campaigns; the more power and resources they have, the less likely they are to be voted out of office. Over time, however, the advantages of increased institutional power and resources may begin to work against the majority party. The enhanced benefits that majority members enjoy tend to increase member autonomy. And as majority party members gradually shift from the party-oriented focus that helped them win control of the chamber to a self-oriented focus, the party's capacity to act cohesively is undercut. Fragmentation of authority between party leaders, committee chairs, and subcommittee chairs exacerbates these tendencies. The shift in majority-member goal emphasis can gradually damage the party's ability to collectively respond to the public's policy demands and political concerns (Sinclair 1983). However, the party may overlook its declining public approval ratings because its incumbent members typically continue to win reelection.

As the majority party begins to fragment, a well-organized minority party can begin to centralize power and coordinate its message. The minority party can then look for opportunities to attack the majority's performance, highlight its policy failures, and create a sense of crisis. At the same time, the minority party promotes its alternative agenda, recruits and finances strong candidates, and pushes for change. If the majority party refuses to change its structure, to recognize and address public dissatisfaction, and to collectively stand up to minority party attacks, it risks losing its majority status. By virtue of its centralized leadership, strong organization, and unified efforts, the minority party may then gain control of the governing apparatus. Unless the new majority party remains disciplined, it will eventually struggle with the same "self-versus-party" dilemma that its predecessor faced, and the cycle will begin anew.

Promoting the Party by Rewarding Ambition

The strength that the parties exert over individual party members is influenced by various factors in the political environment. Organized interests, institutional reforms, new policy issues, new technologies, and political events shape the environment in which the member and the party interact. When party strength wanes, individual members are encouraged to pursue their own political and policy ambitions. If the party organization is weak, the consequences of neglecting the party are few, while the rewards for doing so are potentially high. During the 1960s and 1970s, political change weakened the party organizations. Independence was rewarded at the voting booth, and candidates reacted by touting their individual qualifications and ambitions, rather than the party's agenda. In the early 1990s, changes in the political environment encouraged the resurgence of strong congressional parties. But in order for the parties to remain strong, member ambitions needed to be redirected in ways that would benefit the party. The interplay between self-interested members and team-oriented parties over the past few decades illustrates how these cycles work.

In the first half of the twentieth century, the parties focused almost exclusively on managing presidential campaigns. At that time, the key to preserving a strong party organization was developing and maintaining strong partisan identification among the voters. Reforms introduced during the second half of the century, including changes in the rules regulating state primaries, voting procedures, and campaign finance, altered party dynamics. The rise of cause-oriented activism in the 1960s and the surge in interest-group formation and activity also affected the party organizations. Because organized interests expanded so rapidly and made specific policy demands, the parties could no longer absorb them as they had in the past (Reichley 1985). Organized interests offered people an alternative to the parties, as well as the opportunity to associate with a group that spoke more directly to their particular issue concerns. The parties seemed unable or unwilling to accommodate the political concerns of newly active groups, including women, minorities, and young people; they were also unable to address the economic, social, and cultural concerns that marked the transition to a postindustrial society (Cigler 1993, 414). In a political environment that downplays the role of the parties, independent-minded candidates thrive.

Beginning in the 1970s, the parties had to adjust to a new kind of House member—one who was more autonomous and less committed to the party. Member independence was encouraged by shifts in voter attitudes toward the political parties. As voters became more educated and more independent, they became less willing to affiliate themselves with a political party. Members of Congress began to run more candidate-centered campaigns as they came to realize that being reelected did not necessarily hinge on supporting the party line. Increasingly, they portrayed themselves as political free agents, willing to put their constituents' concerns first. Rather than turn to their party committees for campaign support, congressional candidates solicited the help of PACs and organized interests. PACs were becoming increasingly important in providing candidates with campaign resources, not only making the parties less important, but also increasing the electoral vulnerability of congressional incumbents, a number of whom were defeated in the 1978 and 1980 elections. By the early 1980s, PACs were spending more than the parties on "direct efforts to influence voter choices among candidates," including voter registration and get-out-the-vote drives (Cigler 1993, 420–421). The more money and organizational support members of Congress could extract from non-party groups, the more independent of the party they could be. The campaign finance reforms of the early 1970s were an attempt to rein in the influence of organized interests in Washington. One unintended consequence of these reforms was a massive increase in the number of registered PACs. The number and variety of sources candidates could tap for campaign money led to further fragmentation, as the candidates attempted to broaden their appeal across PAC issues.

As voters and lawmakers began to shed their partisan loyalties, and as organized interests began to play a more important role in electoral politics, the party committees sought out new ways to remain relevant. Despite dramatic changes in the political environment, one constant was clear: Members of Congress were primarily focused on securing reelection. With this in mind, the parties began transforming into service organizations, focused on electing and reelecting candidates, dispensing technical help including polling, media consulting, advertising, opposition research, and campaign management. By the late 1970s, the congressional party committees had given up their monopoly on candidate control and had begun dedicating the bulk of their resources to service efforts (Aldrich 1995). Allan Cigler argues, "A strong case can be made that party and campaign reform forced both major parties to come to terms with the social as well as technological changes that have characterized the late twentieth century; in the end, these reactions saved the political parties as players in electoral politics, although with diminished roles" (1993, 421). While the service-vendor arrangement that characterizes contemporary party activities evolved out of the shift toward candidate and voter independence, it can also be viewed as a predictable response to a political and electoral system that increasingly emphasizes money. As service vendors, the congressional party committees have adjusted to the "cash economy" of political campaigns and now serve as quasi financial brokers between candidates and contributors (Maisel 1994). The committees coordinate fundraising efforts for incumbents and serious challengers, and they also raise and target campaign money. Despite contributing less money to candidates than do individuals and groups, the parties have proven far more effective in directing contributions to those candidates who are most in need (Cigler 1993, 423).

While congressional party activities have changed significantly in the postreform era, the parties' main goals have not. Congressional parties have continuously sought power in the form of majority control, but the means they have used either to maintain or to gain control have shifted in response to changes in the political environment. In addition to strong leadership and a unified membership, the party that seeks to maintain or gain majority control needs a great deal of campaign money.

By the early 1990s, the political parties were increasingly focused on fundraising as a means of maintaining or gaining majority status in Congress. Changes in the political environment, including shrinking partisan margins in the House and a consequent rise in partisanship, increased the strength of the parties. House Republicans believed they had a realistic chance to win majority control, so beginning in 1992 they willingly unified to challenge the Democrats. Part of the Republican strategy was to fund strong challengers who could beat vulnerable Democratic incumbents. The Democrats increased their fundraising efforts as well but did not aggressively organize until after 1994, when they lost majority control of the House.[6] In addition to canvassing outside donors, the CCCs began asking incumbent members to contribute for the good of the whole. These internal fundraising efforts represented a new strategy initiated primarily by the CCCs. Robin Kolodny and Diane Dwyre note that throughout the 1990s, the CCCs "made unusually proactive efforts to secure House majorities and convince other party-related actors, such as the national committees, PACs, and sitting members of Congress, to assist the CCCs in achieving majorities in the legislature" (1998, 276). Kolodny and Dwyre argue that these party-based efforts are significant enough in effect to warrant a new party role descriptor: party as orchestrator of electoral activities. Political entrepreneurs and other party-based actors served as the catalysts for this reorientation, successfully managing to convince incumbents that helping the party would benefit them personally. By working to promote party goals and convincing their colleagues to do the same, these House members "saw opportunities for their own advancement" (1998, 276).

In order to sustain this kind of system, House members who work on behalf of the party must be recognized at the least and rewarded at the most. Self-oriented members need clear incentives to emphasize the party's goals—particularly when they already enjoy majority status. David Canon observes that "when members' electoral fortunes are only loosely tied to the party, the task of leadership is greatly complicated. Without control over the ultimate sanction, the party is unable to prevent each member from paddling his or her own political canoe in the legislature" (1989, 436). Majority party leaders are well positioned to establish a system that recognizes and rewards supportive members simply because their party controls the chamber. As House members must run for reelection every two years, they tend to greet promises of future rewards with skepticism and expect their efforts to be recognized in the near, rather than the distant, future.

After winning majority control in 1994, House Republicans responded to this collective action challenge by limiting committee and subcommittee chairs to six-year terms. Republican Party leaders were also given six-year term limits. This policy effectively provided ambitious Republicans with a realizable goal. In a system where seniority prevails, junior members have less incentive to serve the party diligently because their efforts will not supplant their ranking. But in a system where turnover is institutionalized and efforts on behalf of the party are rewarded, ambitious members recognize that there are real benefits to be reaped. In 2000 Ken Johnson, then spokesperson for Representative Billy Tauzin (R-LA), claimed that limiting the terms of committee chairs "energized things. . . . You bring in new people with new blood and new ideas. . . . It keeps hope alive that you don't have to make Washington a career in order to get ahead in the conference" (Hirschfield 2000, 2657). The challenge for party leaders, then, is to structure a system in which ambitious members cannot expect to pursue their own political and policy goals successfully without first helping the party reach its collective goals.

Combating the Problem of Fragmentation: Battleground 2000

Battleground 2000, a plan for House Republicans to raise $16 million to support NRCC efforts in the 2000 elections, illustrates how this kind of system works. Republican incumbents who had previously been merely encouraged to contribute to other members and to the party were told in no uncertain terms that their fundraising efforts on behalf of the NRCC would help determine their committee assignments and rankings in the 107th Congress (which convened in January 2001). When he announced the Battleground 2000 plan, House Speaker Dennis Hastert assured his colleagues that the leadership would keep close watch on each member's fundraising progress. Party leaders developed a sliding fundraising scale, based on members' leadership standing, committee membership and rank, and seniority. Individual contribution thermometers were posted outside the party's fundraising offices so that Republican leaders could keep track of House members' efforts and members could compare their totals to those of their colleagues. To make certain that members were staying on target, the leadership created a seventeen-member Whip organization to track member progress and apply pressure if necessary (Allen 2000). Committee chairs were assigned the task of monitoring the progress of their subcommittee chairs. Party leaders, according to a spokesperson for a House power committee chair, made it very clear that "you were at risk of losing your chairmanship if you did not pull your weight" and make sure your subcommittee chairs did the same (interview with author 2001).

Several days before the November 7, 2000, deadline for contributing to the Battleground 2000 effort, Speaker Hastert, accompanied by "a vulnerable House Republican as a form of encouragement," met with groups of members who had not yet contributed. According to one Republican leadership aide, those who did not give would be held accountable in the 107th Congress: "There definitely will be the gave and the gave-nots" (Van Dongen 2000). By November 7, 2000, the Battleground 2000 effort had raised $21 million for the NRCC—an amount that exceeded the party leadership's original goal by $5 million. Some of the effort's most generous contributors were members who were contending for committee chairs in the 107th Congress. Campaign committees and leadership PACs affiliated with twenty-eight potential committee chairs contributed approximately $3.3 million to the NRCC and to other candidates during the 2000 election cycle (Bailey 2001). Money clearly mattered in the selection of new committee chairs for the 107th Congress (see chapter 6).

Just as individual House members found ways to exploit the campaign finance and institutional reforms of the 1970s to serve their own self-interest, the congressional parties have found ways to channel member ambitions in ways that serve the collective interests of the party. Changes in the political environment—namely, small partisan margins and increased electoral competition—have permitted this transformation. Fragmentation is offset by the linking of members' ability to successfully pursue their own ambitions to their ability to help the party pursue the collective goal of majority status.

Explaining Party Power in the House

The strength of congressional parties and party leaders in the House depends on a number of factors. Throughout the 1970s and 1980s, House Democrats enjoyed large majorities over House Republicans. While Democratic leaders encouraged party discipline, it was not strictly enforced as the party could win floor votes even when some members crossed party lines. Democratic leaders were also dealing with a large influx of new members who were not inclined to follow partisan directives. House Republicans, on the other hand, had been in the minority since 1954 and generally viewed majority control as beyond their reach, so, as Roger Davidson (1981, 108) argues, the seniority system was never a "burning issue" for House Republicans. Because of the party's prolonged minority status, senior posts in the Republicans' leadership structure meant less as well. Republican members also tended to retire sooner, so Republican membership turnover was quicker than that of the Democrats. In this environment, individual Democratic members could focus on their own political and policy goals because their party's majority status was not at risk and there were almost no consequences for defying the party. Members who wanted to pursue higher positions in the chamber focused on impressing their colleagues rather than on serving their party. The political environment, which was in part the product of weakened political parties, institutional reforms that dispersed power in the House, the rise of organized interests, and the influx of new Democrats, allowed ambitious members to operate independently in the chamber.

In the late 1980s and the 1990s, the political environment shifted dramatically. House Republicans began to chip away at the Democrats' majority and, in 1994, took control of the chamber for the first time in four decades. Because the Republican majority was quite narrow and remained so for the next twelve years, it was very different from the Democratic majority. The Republican majority was also different in that there was minimal ideological diversity within the party. Congressional Democrats have tended to be a more diverse party, which can make coalition building difficult. Real party competition in the House strengthened the parties as well as the party leaders and contributed to a highly charged partisan atmosphere. Whereas the Democrats treated voting the party line as an option during the 1970s and early 1980s, strict party discipline became essential in the 1990s.

As the dynamics affecting the relationship between House members and the congressional parties shifted, so did theoretical approaches to explaining how members and parties interact. As the margins between House Democrats and Republicans narrowed and electoral competition increased, the parties-in-decline thesis,[7] which was advanced in the 1970s and 1980s, no longer applied to the congressional party organizations. The notion that the parties were in a state of transition[8] rather than in decline seemed more logical by the mid- to late 1980s, as congressional parties became increasingly focused on campaign-related activities. By the early 1990s, the conditional party government thesis effectively captured the new relationship between House members and their parties. In the CPG model, as intraparty preference agreement and interparty preference conflict increase, members become more willing to grant additional power to their leaders (Aldrich and Rohde 2001, 275–276). In other words, as the parties become more ideologically homogeneous, the political and policy divisions between the parties increase. Party members give their leaders the power and resources they need to advance the party's legislative agenda because the members believe that doing so will benefit them electorally (Adler 2002, 172–173). Such was the case in 1994: Republican leaders had recruited a number of strong, like-minded candidates; the Contract with America provided voters with a clear distinction between the Republican and Democratic Party agendas; and interparty conflict was high, due in part to strong Republican opposition to Democratic president Bill Clinton and his legislative agenda. In addition, the Republicans' small majority margin significantly intensified the conflict between the parties. In these circumstances, Republican members willingly supported centralizing power and resources within the party leadership (Aldrich and Rohde 1997; Adler 2002). Because the political environment has remained competitive and partisan, member independence is no longer encouraged. The House's power ladder is firmly planted inside a party framework, and to climb that ladder, ambitious members have to first demonstrate their party loyalty by fundraising and voting the party line. By refusing to participate in this game of give-and-take, members may deny themselves the chance to realize their personal ambitions. While length of service in the chamber still matters, equally important is a member's fundraising proficiency.

Conclusion

The 1970s reforms sought to democratize the House by dispersing power more evenly throughout the chamber. While removing the seniority rule leveled the playing field between junior and senior Democrats, it also increased competition among members hoping to advance in the chamber. Member-to-member giving was an outgrowth of this new, more competitive environment. The reforms also strengthened the party leaders, who began to take full advantage of their new powers during the 1980s. As party leaders accrued more control, the congressional party organizations strengthened. And as the political environment grew more competitive, fundraising became central to party-building efforts. By the 1990s, a new political environment and a new round of institutional reforms had brought self-interested members and strong congressional parties together in unexpected ways. These cycles demonstrate that institutional reforms are subject to adaptation, and even exploitation, over time. They also demonstrate the ongoing tension between self-interested members and team-oriented parties.

Notes

1. During the same time frame in which Richard Fenno published *Congressmen in Committees* (1973) and *Home Style* (1978), several other congressional scholars also introduced important theoretical frameworks for understanding member behavior, for example, David Mayhew (1974), John Kingdon (1973), Morris Fiorina (1977), and Kenneth Shepsle (1978). While these works are by no means inclusive of all the congressional research published during this era, they generally represent the rational, goal-oriented approach to explaining member behavior.

2. For example, see Clyde Wilcox (1989).

3. For example, see Gordon Black (1972), David Rohde (1979), John Hibbing (1986), Linda Fowler and Robert McClure (1989), Thomas Kazee (1994), Richard Hall and Robert VanHouweling (1995), L. Sandy Maisel (1997), Wayne Francis and Lawrence Kenny (2000), Alan Ehrenhalt (1991), John Barry (1989), and Robert Caro (1990).

4. See David Rohde (1979) for an alternative view.

5. The following discussion about the cyclical nature of legislative change is drawn from Lawrence Dodd (1986, 2001).

6. The DCCC began asking incumbent members to contribute to the committee in the 1990 elections, but efforts became much more organized after 1994.

7. For example, see David Broder (1971) and William Crotty (1984).

8. For example, see M. Margaret Conway (1983) and John Bibby (1981).

3

The 1970s Reform Era

The Money Chase Begins

Institutional reform tends to happen in response to changes in the political environment. When House members act to modify chamber rules and procedures, the committee system, and the leadership apparatus, they often have multiple and conflicting goals. As a result, reforms are imperfect compromises. Scott Adler claims that "because members of Congress are elected officials with their own political survival foremost in their strategic calculations, they will oppose any alterations in the policymaking process that disrupt their ability to provide for important constituency needs" (2002, 38). Ambitious reform efforts often fail because there are always members who benefit from the existing arrangements, and they will resist efforts to make changes. Therefore comprehensive institutional reform requires the action of a determined majority.

Like most political compromises, reforms are a constant source of member frustration and institutional tension (Schickler 2001, 3). Given the political nature of Congress, any rule or reform is subject to adaptation. Shifts in the political environment create opportunities for members and parties to exploit institutional arrangements to their own advantage. As a result, reforms often produce unintended consequences. During the 1970s, progressive Democrats pursued broad institutional reforms that would regulate the financing of federal campaigns and redistribute power in the House. These reforms helped foster the growth of member-to-member giving—an unintended consequence with long-term implications for congressional party politics.

While the specific events that mark a particular period of institutional change may be unique, they tend to emerge from a recurring set of political conditions. The principal force that sets and keeps the desire for change in motion is member ambition. But before members can pursue their political and policy ambitions, they must achieve two subsidiary goals: They must master both the organizational politics of Congress and the electoral politics of their constituencies. The pursuit of these two goals generates different levels of organizational and structural tension, which over time compel members to modify the institution's political and policymaking systems (Dodd 1986, 4).

The political landscape of the House was dramatically altered in the 1970s when progressive members pursued institutional reforms that would democratize the chamber in response to the public's demand for greater government accountability. The Vietnam War and Watergate had raised public interest (and distrust) in government and had increased levels of political participation. The interest group community, which grew rapidly during the 1970s, further expanded public participation in the political process and increased the number and complexity of the issues brought before Congress. Together, these forces encouraged the emergence of a new, aggressive breed of federal lawmaker, a growing sense of entitlement among politically active groups, and a surge in policy activism. The events of the 1970s also helped create a political environment that promoted the redistribution of money in the House.

The Rise of the Seniority System

In a 1965 examination of congressional responses to the twentieth century, Samuel P. Huntington argued that government institutions that are incapable of adjusting to social change, as well as to new viewpoints, needs, and political forces, will eventually face an adaptation crisis (1965, 7). According to Huntington, Congress faced such a crisis in the 1960s because it had not effectively adapted to major changes in American society over the course of the twentieth century. Rather than assess transformational shifts and then adjust its responses, Congress sought to maintain a conventional approach to rapid sociopolitical changes. As a result, Congress had evolved into a largely ineffectual institution defined by its insulation from new political forces, its decentralized power structure, and its emphasis on administrative oversight rather than legislative action.

Because Congress remained isolated from the outside forces that were generating social and political change, it was ill prepared to respond to emerging national problems and unable to set legislative priorities. Therefore the institutional power and lawmaking function of Congress declined. Huntington (1965) argues that increasing tenure in office and the rise of the seniority system were particularly instrumental in making Congress ripe for change in the 1970s.

Like congressional-term-limits proponents, Huntington suggests that the longer members serve in Congress, the more isolated they become from the world outside Congress. In 1871, just over 50 percent of all House members were elected to the House more than once. By 1961, 87 percent of all House members had served more than one term. Thus, through the twentieth century, the "biennial infusion of new blood" waned considerably (Huntington 1965, 9). And as more and more members chose to extend their time in office, Congress became more insulated.

As tenures in office increased, the role of seniority became more important. The longer members serve in Congress, the more likely they are to see value in a seniority-based system. And the more important seniority is in helping members attain desirable committee assignments or leadership posts, the more electorally appealing long-serving members become. Though there is some disagreement about when decision making by seniority began in Congress (see Polsby et al. 1969, 791), most accounts point to the 1910 revolt against House Speaker Joe Cannon. At that time, defiant House members pushed for reforms that would curtail the Speaker's powers (particularly his authority to appoint members to and remove them from committees and committee chairs) and disperse power throughout the chamber. The revolt against Speaker Cannon led to a system that emphasized committee independence and weakened party leadership. The rise of the seniority rule was perhaps most apparent in the appointment of committee chairs: In the fifty years following the 1910 revolt, seniority was violated only twice in the selection of committee chairs (Huntington 1965; Polsby et al. 1969). The House's strong committee system, coupled with the use of the seniority rule in naming committee chairs, resulted in the gradual decentralization of power in the chamber.

Though many factors contributed to the push for reform in the 1970s, growing dissatisfaction with the seniority rule was most prominent. The Legislative Reorginization Act of 1946, which consolidated the House committee system into nineteen standing committees and guaranteed committee staff to each of the standing committees, significantly strengthened the seniority system. While the internal structures and processes of the individual committees differed, all committee chairs exercised the power to organize the subcommittees and staff, and to control their committee's agenda (Smith 1989, 20). The act ultimately failed to rectify policymaking inadequacies, but it did further empower committee chairs. Polsby et al. note that after 1946,

> both the discretionary rights of leaders and the rich array of minor committees disappeared with the 'streamlining' of the committee system, and thus from 1946 onward, the rule of seniority is virtually never breached. . . . The House moves after 1947 to a situation where there exists a full-blown seniority system, in which seniority is the single, automatic criterion determining the chairmanships of all committees, and the application of this criterion is not subject to the discretion of any body short of the relatively inactive full party caucuses. (1969, 807)

The Democrats' solid majority in the House and their relatively stable conservative base reinforced both committee power and the seniority system.

While the Legislative Reorganization Act of 1946 was partially responsible for the government-by-committee arrangement that developed in its wake, other factors also contributed to the power and status that committees achieved during this era. The longest-serving members of the majority party were conservative southern Democrats, and they held a disproportionate number of the committee chairs. Because they controlled the legislative process, and because House norms prevented junior members from agitating, conservative Democrats were able to prevent their more liberal colleagues from initiating policy. But by the late 1960s, the apprenticeship norm, which held that new members should observe but not participate, had all but disappeared. The charge to abandon apprenticeship was led by liberal Democrats who were eager to challenge the power and policies (civil rights, for instance) of the conservative majority (Smith 1989, 134–135). As the apprenticeship norm declined, so did deference to the committees. Pressure to respect committee policy recommendations had disappeared by the mid-1970s, as issues became more divisive and as members sought to participate more actively on the House floor (Smith 1989, 139–141).

The Reform Era

Until they are able to advance up the House's power ladder, legislators are typically constrained by the limited resources and opportunities available to them as rank-and-file members. The most logical way for ambitious legislators to acquire the resources they need to pursue their own political and policy goals is to join forces and push for institutional changes that favor the chamber's less senior members (Dodd 1977, 1986). Congress is a body of individuals who either have power or want power; therefore calls for reform are all but constant. However, actually changing the House's rules and procedures requires the action of a critical mass. Gradually, the Democratic Party's liberal wing began to expand, and with this expansion came pressure for change. Progressive and junior Democrats were driven by a shared sense of frustration over their inability to penetrate the House's power hierarchy. As Roger Davidson argues, "One effect of the seniority system was to perpetuate the political triumphs of the previous generation; when the party's factional balance shifted, seniority caused a generation gap between leaders and backbenchers. Such a gap—in region, district type, ideology, and even age—lay at the heart of the Democrats' seniority struggles" (1981, 106).

By the end of the 1960s, the frustration among progressive and junior Democrats who were tired of having their policy efforts blocked by their more senior and conservative colleagues had reached a pinnacle. Southern Democrats comprised less than 30 percent of the Democratic Caucus, yet they held 46 percent of the House's committee chairs. In addition, the average committee chair was sixty-six years old and had almost thirty years of service in the House. The widening gap between the chamber's senior and junior Democrats fueled frustration and resentment because the junior members were virtually powerless (Davidson 1981, 106). The elections of 1958 and 1964 brought more liberal Democrats into the House, and as a result, the conservative wing's long-standing lock on power was threatened. Fueled by their growing ranks, reform-minded members began pushing for changes that would redistribute power within the chamber (Price 1992; Deering and Smith 1997).

A decade or so before the 1970s reforms were drafted, a group of liberal House Democrats formed the Democratic Study Group (DSG). The group organized around a mutual sense of exasperation over their inability to get policy proposals before the House. The DSG worked to provide its members with legislative research and support and tried to coordinate action on its members' policy proposals via a Whip system. Following the election of President Nixon in 1968, the DSG decided to take a more formal approach to pushing its agenda. Though many ideas for accomplishing this task were considered, the group determined that its ultimate goal was to make the Democrats who controlled the chamber—primarily the committee chairpersons—responsible to the party's rank-and-file members. At the time, DSG staff director Richard Conlon claimed, "We are trying to unstack the deck which we feel has been stacked against the majority for the last couple of decades" (quoted in Malbin 1974, 1881). In order to discuss policy issues and to solicit broader support for their reform proposals, DSG leaders began canvassing other rank-and-file Democrats. Before long, they discovered that many Democrats lacked knowledge of the House rules and procedures. The group then decided that unless party members were educated about the House's institutional arrangements, efforts to push reform would be fruitless. Therefore the DSG proposed and secured monthly full caucus meetings. The monthly meetings provided the DSG leaders with the forum they needed to educate their colleagues and promote their own reform proposals.

After distributing to caucus members a DSG-produced report on the history of the House seniority system, the DSG leaders suggested that the caucus create a special committee to study their reform proposals. In March 1970, an eleven-member Committee on Organization, Study, and Review (otherwise known as the Hansen Committee, after the committee's chair, Julia Hansen of Washington) was formed. One year later, the Hansen Committee drafted and put forward for full caucus vote a series of proposals that would provide the framework for the 1970s reforms. While policy goals were the primary motivator of member support for the reforms, they certainly were not the only one. Many members supported the reforms for reasons tied to their own self-interests (Rohde 1991, 17–19).

While Democrats continued to press forward with various caucus-related reform proposals, Congress passed the Legislative Reorganization Act of 1970, which marked the first bipartisan reform effort of the era. Most of the act's provisions were aimed at making the committee system more efficient and open, but they had no direct policy implications. Of note were new rules that required recorded teller votes during the floor amendment process and electronic voting on the House floor. The recorded teller vote provision was the "common carrier for liberal Democrats, Republicans, and junior members of both parties," as it was designed to increase amending activity on the floor and to unravel committee control over the legislative process (Schickler 2001, 216).

Provisions of the Legislative Reorganization Act also opened committee hearings and meetings to the public. Reformers believed that by opening up the bill-amending and -voting processes, rank-and-file members would be less likely to support amendments they opposed but would vote for to satisfy their committee chairs. The reformers also believed that more "sunshine" would increase public trust in government because the public would be able to observe and participate in the process (Sinclair 1983; Rohde 1991; Deering and Smith 1997). But calls for a more open process were not entirely altruistic. Open committee sessions also provided members with a forum for putting themselves on public display for their constituents and for organized interests. Some senior members complained that opening up committee hearings would lead to member grandstanding and hinder the debate necessary to reach compromises. The sunshine reforms also provided organized interests with more opportunities to participate in the legislative process. By some accounts, open meetings did not increase citizen participation, but they did increase the overall influence of organized interests (Schickler 2001, 209–212).

Passing the Legislative Reorganization Act required Democrats and Republicans to find common ground. House liberals recognized that they ultimately lacked the votes necessary to push through the reforms that they wanted the act to include—particularly the recorded teller votes. In an effort to build support, DSG members began meeting with Young Turk Republicans who were also interested in reforms that would increase their influence in the chamber. While senior Republicans often had working relationships with Democratic committee chairs, junior Republicans lacked connections and access. The two groups worked to produce a bipartisan package that appealed to multiple and diverse member interests. Of the ten recommendations, all of which were aimed at weakening committee chairs and dispersing power, nine were adopted by the House (Schickler 2001, 215–216).

The Democratic Caucus adopted the Hansen Committee's first set of recommendations in 1971. These proposals were designed to loosen the committee chairs' excessive hold on power and to distribute power more widely among party members. Specifically, the reforms limited the Democrats to holding one subcommittee chair per member; allowed each subcommittee chair to hire one professional staff person; altered the system for electing committee chairs and committee members so that nominations were presented one committee at a time; and stipulated that a request by ten or more members could initiate debate, a separate vote, and, in the event of a defeat, a new nomination for committee chair by the Committee on Committees (the Committee on Committees was made up of the Democratic members of the Ways and Means Committee). The provision limiting Democrats to one subcommittee chair immediately opened up at least sixteen subcommittee chairs, most of which were then filled by relatively junior liberals (Rohde 1991, 21; Deering and Smith 1997, 36).

The Democratic Caucus continued to chip away at committee chairs' power in 1973, with the adoption of the Hansen Committee's second set of recommendations. Votes on committee chairs were made automatic at the beginning of each Congress and could be made secret if at least 20 percent of caucus members requested a secret ballot. This rule in particular set the stage for potential challenges to long-standing committee chairs. The reforms also expanded the Democratic Committee on Committees to include the Speaker, the Majority Leader, and the caucus chair; created a twenty-three-member Steering and Policy Committee; and adopted procedures to open up floor deliberations.

The Hansen Committee's 1973 recommendations also included a set of reforms known collectively as the Subcommittee Bill of Rights. These reforms removed from committee chairs their power to appoint committee members to subcommittees and to subcommittee chairs; instead, committee members would bid in order of seniority for open slots on subcommittees and for subcommittee chairs. Democrats on the full committee would then vote to approve subcommittee chairs. Subcommittees were also granted fixed jurisdictions, as well as adequate budgets and staff. The reforms also contained a provision requiring that the full committee refer bills to the subcommittees within a fixed period of time. Under the old rules, committee chairs could refer bills to whichever subcommittee they chose, or not refer bills to any subcommittee at all. The Subcommittee Bill of Rights effectively limited the committee chair's ability to determine policy outcomes and to reward or punish committee members for their votes (Sinclair 1983; Rohde 1991, 22; Deering and Smith 1997, 36–37).

The subcommittee reforms were originally devised by liberal Democrats, who lacked a majority within the caucus; to secure adoption, they had to develop reforms that had broad appeal. In canvassing the caucus, liberal members determined that opening up subcommittee chairs appealed to junior caucus members as a whole because the subcommittees had become "more potent power base[s]" (Schickler 2001, 224). Opposition by some senior liberals who stood to lose subcommittee chairs helped convince some conservative Democrats that the reforms were balanced and worth supporting. According to Eric Schickler, "The subcommittee changes passed because liberal Democrats had policy reasons to undercut conservative committee chairmen and found that they could forge a broad coalition for doing so by simultaneously appealing to representatives' power base interests. After all, there were more than 100 subcommittee chairmen and just 20 full committee chairmen" (2001, 226).

The Hansen Committee's efforts in 1973 coincided with a bipartisan effort in the House to review the structure of the committee system. The House Select Committee on Committees, which was chaired by Missouri Democrat Richard Bolling, generated immediate controversy by proposing the elimination of several standing committees and the alteration of long-standing committee jurisdictions. Because of widespread opposition in the chamber, the Democratic Caucus referred the committee's proposals to the Hansen Committee for review. Scott Adler (2002, 145) argues that opponents of the Bolling plan believed that a referral to the Hansen Committee would effectively kill the plan, as a majority of the members who sat on the Hansen Committee publicly opposed the Bolling plan. Caucus members rejected the Bolling package in an effort to protect both their jurisdictional power and their district (and thus reelection) interests (Adler 2002, 169–170). In 1974, the House passed the Hansen Committee's substitute reform package, which contained almost none of the Bolling Committee's original proposals. Committees with more than fifteen members were required to establish at least four subcommittees, the number of committee staff was increased, the minority party was guaranteed at least one-third of the committee's staff, proxy voting in committee was banned, and multiple referrals were authorized.

While the Hansen Committee's substitute reform package was considered fairly weak, the multiple referral rule, which allowed the Speaker to refer the same bill to multiple committees, had considerable implications. Supporters of the rule believed it would enhance the House's ability to deal with policy issues that crossed the jurisdictional lines of several committees. The rule would also support the Democrats' goal of enhancing the Speaker's powers. And because major legislation would be delegated to more committees, multiple referrals would serve members' power-base interests by broadening their jurisdictional claims (Schickler 2001, 201–202).

The Democratic Caucus adopted another set of rule changes in 1974, as well. The caucus expanded the Ways and Means majority membership to thirty-seven from twenty-five, gave the Speaker the power to nominate the Democratic members of the Rules Committee, and required that Appropriations Committee subcommittee chairs be elected by the full caucus (Deering and Smith 1997, 36–38). The caucus also transferred control over member committee assignments to the recently created Steering and Policy Committee. The Steering and Policy Committee was a large, diverse committee by design. Barbara Sinclair (1995) argues that reformers hoped that this design would prevent any single faction from controlling the assignment process. However, because of its size and diversity, the committee found it more difficult to reach consensus, and the party's leadership had more difficulty shaping outcomes.

Burdett Loomis observes, "If the [Speaker Sam] Rayburn-era House artificially retarded members' growth and development," the post-reform House "acted like a hothouse to stimulate career advancement" (1984, 181). Congressional workloads increased tremendously in the 1960s and 1970s. Steven Smith (1989, 7–8) notes that in the 1950s, Congress enacted an average of 1,908 pages into law during each two-year session. This figure increased to 2,439 in the 1960s and to 4,049 in the 1970s. Floor sessions expanded in hours as the workload increased. During the 1950s, the House averaged 1,064 hours of floor time during each two-year session of Congress. Average hours increased to 1,447 in the 1960s and to 1,695 in the 1970s. Increased workloads forced House members to restructure their schedules. Most members in the pre-reform era had done their own legislative research and preparation for committee hearings and floor debate. But as constituency demands and policy issues expanded, members began to "committee-hop," spend less time on the House floor, and rely more heavily on personal and committee staff for policy information and voting cues (Davidson 1981, 112–113). All of these changes altered the structure of opportunities available to junior House members; as a result, the political environment in the House became more competitive as members looked for ways to climb the chamber's power ladder. Redistributing money to colleagues would eventually become one strategy for advancement.

Out with the Old and In with the New

In November 1974, right on the heels of the reforms just discussed, seventy-five new Democrats were elected to the House. They constituted more than one-quarter of the party's full membership in the 94th Congress (1975–1976). Indeed, of the Democrats serving in the 94th Congress, 44 percent were serving their first, second, or third terms; that figure rose to 51 percent in the 95th Congress, and to 53 percent in the 96th Congress (Sinclair 1983, 7). In 1971, the ratio of newcomers (two terms or fewer) to veterans (ten terms or more) was 1.2 to 1; by 1979, the ratio had more than doubled to 2.5 to 1 (Ornstein 1981, 374).

Aside from marshaling in an unusually large freshman class, the 1974 congressional elections signaled the arrival of a new political era. Many of the Democrats who were elected to the House in 1974 were liberal activists who were highly critical of both the chamber's conservative bias and its rigid institutional norms, which favored senior members. Most were younger than their senior colleagues, and many had acquired and honed their political skills during the tumultuous 1960s. While these members embraced the new House reforms, they did so "as foot soldiers not as generals" (Sinclair 1983, 8). Challenges to the House's power structure were well under way when these members were elected, and many of the approved rule changes were already in place. Having never worked within the confines of the House's old institutional arrangements, these members were not inclined to patiently learn the legislative ropes before moving to make their mark in the chamber. They were not accustomed to being deferential, they did not depend on their party for help in getting elected and reelected, and they were independent-minded. Then House Speaker Tip O'Neill said these

> Watergate babies were highly sophisticated and talented . . . and independent, and they didn't hesitate to remind you that they were elected

on their own, often without any help from the Democratic party. They were not steeped in the old traditions of, you know, by your grace and favor, Mr. Chairman. Senior House members referred to them as "outsiders" because they had not come up through the state and local political systems. They had never "rung doorbells, or driven people to the polls, or stayed late stuffing envelopes at campaign headquarters." (Remini 2006, 446–447)

O'Neill was struck by how many of these newcomers had decided to run because of Vietnam, Watergate, or environmental issues: "They said they had no interest in politics until Robert Kennedy ran for office in 1968." After winning seats in Congress, many immediately began participating in the business of both policymaking and self-promotion. The reforms gave these new members the opportunity to advance their own interests in ways that would have been impossible just a few years earlier. In creating a more democratic chamber, the House reformers had paved the way for their more junior and more aggressive colleagues to pursue power in the chamber.

The arrival of new House members in 1974 inevitably coincided with the departure of many of the chamber's more senior members. During the 1970s, the rate of voluntary retirements increased by 77 percent (Hibbing 1993). Between 1969 and 1979 (91st–95th Congresses), 232 members retired from the House; in the prior decade, 194 House members had retired. Not only did voluntary retirements replace electoral defeat as the primary cause of member turnover in the 1970s, but they also gathered momentum as the decade went on. The numbers of voluntary retirements for the five sessions of Congress seated in the 1970s were 35, 44, 47, 51, and 55, respectively (Cooper and West 1981, 84). The unusually high rate of House retirements throughout the 1970s has been attributed to a number of factors, including age, changes in the pension system that made retirement more attractive, political vulnerability, and higher political ambitions. Joseph Cooper and William West (1981, 85) argue that "disaffection with House service" was the driving force behind the growth in voluntary retirements. Too many high costs were associated with the job, and the rewards had become largely insufficient. John Hibbing further describes the surge of House retirements in the 1970s as "an explainable aberration caused by demographics and reforms targeted against senior members already likely to retire" (1993, 70).

The reforms and the large influx of new, more liberal members were almost certainly unsettling for members who were long accustomed to institutional predictability. Many were unsure about where they fit into the new order. This sense of uncertainty was likely reinforced in January 1975, when the 1974 freshmen took the unusual step of inviting prospective committee chairs to address them. The prospective chairs answered questions about legislative matters and responded to various complaints. Some made good impressions, while others offended the freshmen by evading questions or being condescending. Soon after these interviews, the Democratic Caucus voted to unseat three of the chamber's most senior committee chairs (Rohde 1991, 22–23). This action put all committee chairs on notice: If they wanted to keep their posts, they would have to respond to the wishes of the Democratic majority.

The Democratic class of 1974 entered Congress at a time of unparalleled change. Many immediately took advantage of the new opportunities before them and moved quickly into positions of influence. Between 1955 and 1987, the average number of committee assignments for each House member grew from 1.2 to over 1.7, and the average number of subcommittee assignments increased from 1.6 to 3.8. The expansion of the number and average size of the House subcommittees also created new opportunities for members (Smith 1989, 9). By 1981, only 3 of the 44 remaining House Democrats elected in 1974 neither chaired a subcommittee nor sat on one of the chamber's power committees (Loomis 1988, 46). For Democrats elected in 1974, advancement to a position of power was nearly automatic by the fourth term. These members also benefited from the large number of retirements coinciding with their arrival in Congress. By the time the Democratic class of 1964 had reached their fourth terms, they still ranked behind 150 other House Democrats in seniority. When the 44 remaining members of the Democratic Class of 1974 began their fourth terms, they ranked behind only 95 other Democrats (Loomis 1984, 182–184).

While decentralizing power in the House had been a goal of the reformers, decentralization brought a new set of challenges. The increase in committee and subcommittee seats intensified policymaking inefficiencies. As members took on more committee and subcommittee assignments, their schedules became increasingly difficult to manage. Committee hearing schedules often overlapped, preventing members from fully focusing on any one hearing. Committee quorums were difficult to achieve in the postreform House and many hearings featured the chair and only one or two other committee members. Of course, hearings would have been quite difficult to manage if all the committee members actually attended and participated; many committees had become too large for substantive discussion and debate.

In addition to expanding the number of committee seats, party leaders accommodated member preferences in the committee assignment process. And because members gravitated toward committees that would help them pursue their personal ambitions, committee-passed policies tended to be biased toward the committee members' interests rather than impartial. This arrangement also reinforced the long-standing relationships many committee members had with clientele groups that fell under their committee's jurisdiction. These biases also led to inefficiencies in the policymaking process (Davidson 1981, 112–113).

The rise of subcommittee government led to a system with a "surfeit of chiefs and a shortage of Indians" (Fiorina 1989, 60). Morris Fiorina suggests that internal democratic reforms have in part led to inefficiency and "foot dragging" in policymaking, mainly because numerous subcommittees can—and do—claim jurisdiction over a vast array of issues. When responsibility for one issue is spread over several committees, turf battles easily supplant joint efforts because each committee wants to claim full credit for policy outcomes. Because decentralization increased the "number and variety of important legislative players in the House," individual members were less beholden to any one leader (Loomis 1988, 25). Rather than abide by leadership directives as a matter of routine, the House's newer members tended to think and act in their own self-interest. Eric Uslaner attributes the late 1970s waning of "comity on Capitol Hill" to the class of 1974 and suggests that these members were less committed to "core legislative values such as compromise and civility" (quoted in Loomis 1988, 47).

For many House members, decentralized power was something of a mixed blessing. This was particularly true of Democratic House leaders,

whose powers in the House were strengthened while their ability to enforce party discipline was not. Because power was dispersed throughout
the chamber and members were more entrepreneurial, coalition building became much more challenging. Newer members were less loyal to
the party and very active in both the committee and floor stages of the
policymaking process. Younger members were also less likely to defer to
the committees on policy matters and preferred to "legislate on the
floor" (Sinclair 1981, 392–394). As a result, more members had to be accommodated at more points along the way; committee chairs were less
able to broker compromises in committee; and subcommittee chairs,
who assumed more responsibility for managing legislation on the floor,
were often inexperienced and lacked the political clout needed to be effective. The number of unanticipated and unfriendly floor amendments
proliferated as members began to view the floor as a place to challenge
committee decisions and to make a name for themselves. As a result, decision making became much more unpredictable, and House politics
became much more fluid (Smith 1989, 9–15).

The number of voting-bloc groups (otherwise known as *caucuses*)
also began to expand in the postreform House. Before the 1970s, the
only groups of note were the DSG, the liberal Republicans' Wednesday
Group, the Members of Congress for Peace through Law, and several
informal Republican organizations, most notably the Republican
Study Group (RSG), which had formed as a counterweight to the DSG.
But by the end of the 1970s, there were more than fifty caucuses, which
focused on diverse regional, policy, and political issues. Caucuses
flourished because they offered services that were very useful to members, including tailored policy information, voting recommendations,
connections to organized interests, policy proposals, and planning and
mobilizing strategies. Caucus memberships also provided electoral
benefits, as members could tout their affiliations and frequently receive campaign assistance in return. Many of these caucuses offered
partylike services to their members, yet most operated independently
of the party organizations (Davidson 1981, 128–130).

Despite the many challenges they faced in the postreform House,
committee chairs were not entirely undermined. They still retained
day-to-day control of committee agendas, had access to large staffs,

and maintained strong political and policy connections. Committee chairs could also challenge the recommendations of subcommittee chairs at the full committee level (Smith 1989, 47).

Democratic House leaders also found ways to use their enhanced powers. Barbara Sinclair (1981, 412) argues that leaders in the post-reform House followed two major patterns: They became increasingly oriented to providing services for members, and they involved as many House Democrats as possible in coalition building. For example, Democratic leaders brought many junior members into the leadership on an ad hoc basis by expanding the Whip system and by increasing their use of legislative task forces. Put simply, they created more opportunities for junior members to participate in the leadership structure. The 92nd Congress (1971–1972) had a total of 24 Democratic leadership positions. By the 97th Congress (1981–1982), there was a total of 57 Democratic leadership positions under a restricted definition, and 100 under an expanded definition including members of the Budget and Steering and Policy Committees (Loomis 1984, 186). The leadership strategies were designed to increase the involvement of junior members and to cope with the heightened procedural and political uncertainties that the reforms had created.

Political Change and the Rise of Entrepreneurial House Members

Throughout the 1970s, wholesale political and social change was taking place outside Congress as well, contributing indirectly to the rise of member-to-member giving. The civil rights movement of the 1960s triggered gradual increases in black enfranchisement and also contributed to party realignment in the South (Price 1992). The women's movement grew in strength with the push for an Equal Rights Amendment to the Constitution. Hispanic and Native American organizations also began promoting their own minority rights agendas. The Vietnam War and Watergate were particularly instrumental in prompting the public and federal lawmakers alike to reassess the role of Congress vis-à-vis the executive. The federal government's handling of the Vietnam

War made clear that Congress lacked the power to significantly impact foreign affairs, and Watergate demonstrated the ease with which the executive could circumvent congressional oversight and commit numerous illegalities. Watergate also clarified the need for stricter campaign finance laws. Congress faced, as well, criticism for not responding adequately to growing national problems such as crime, poverty, inflation, unemployment, and environmental degradation. While these events and issues inspired greater public activism, they also soured the public's opinion of government institutions—particularly Congress (Rieselbach 1977). Public confidence in Congress dropped dramatically; before the 1974 elections, only about one in four persons gave Congress a positive rating (Loomis 1988).

The public's unfavorable opinion of Congress contributed in part to the rise of entrepreneurial politicians. Formerly eschewed by the chamber's party-bound membership, individualistic behavior became acceptable in the 1970s, and House members who exhibited such behavior tended to be favored electorally. Burdett Loomis (1988, 22) argues that "societal fragmentation affects politicians through partisan dealignment and decomposition" and notes that very few members who entered Congress in the 1970s came from strong party backgrounds. Between 1961 and 1968, House Democrats had an average party unity score of 79.3, and House Republicans had an average score of 80.5. Between 1969 and 1976, the average party unity score for House Democrats was 71.8, and for House Republicans, it was 73.9[1] (Sinclair 1981, 180). Roger Davidson (1981, 107) notes that grassroots party organizations had declined in many districts and no longer sponsored candidate and member careers. Therefore, in many cases, politicians became entrepreneurs out of necessity and relied on their own resources to build support networks in their districts. The new House members were also not inclined to hold the institution of Congress in high regard. While spending time with House members in their home districts during the 1970s, Richard Fenno (1978) documented the then-surprising frequency with which members engaged in Congress-bashing. Today, running for Congress by running against it is nearly the norm, but in the 1970s, the strategy was unusual.

The 1970s trend toward individualistic behavior in the House can be explained partially by the parallel expansion of social movements and the interest group community. As the economy grew and became increasingly diversified, and as communication and information technologies became more advanced, policy issues became more specialized. The surge in interest group growth and activity led to an increasingly crowded legislative agenda. In the early 1970s, about 20 percent of all national nonprofit organizations were headquartered in Washington. Groups including the Antinuclear Campaign for Safe Energy and the National Welfare Rights Organization had a major impact on the Democratic Party, while the Pro-Life Impact Committee and the Moral Majority wielded strong influence on the Republican Party (Cigler 1993, 418). During the decade, more nonprofits opened DC offices, and by the early 1980s, about 30 percent of all nonprofit U.S. organizations were based in the city (see Figure 3.1). At the same time, corporations and state and local governments were also expanding their presence in

Figure 3.1 Trends in the Number of Washington-Based Organized Interests, 1900–1998

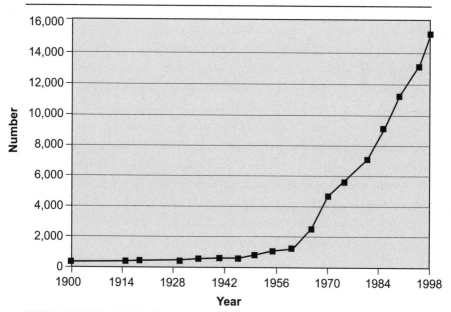

Source: Anthony J. Nownes. 2001. *Pressure and Power: Organized Interests in American Politics.* Boston: Houghton Mifflin.

Washington (Smith 1989, 7). The number and diversity of these groups, along with their general unwillingness to let the parties do their bidding, encouraged members to form "factional allegiances" (Davidson 1981, 130). Organized interests sought out members who could help them achieve their policy goals in Congress, and their criteria had less to do with members' party affiliation than with members' policy expertise and committee assignments. Sunshine reforms opened committee meetings and hearings to the public and increased the presence and participation of organized interests. As a result, House members were under more pressure to respond to the requests of outside groups that had committee-based interests. In return for their help, these organized interests could offer members access to policy information, as well as organizational and financial campaign assistance.

As House members expanded their entrepreneurial activities, they sought out new resources for self-promotion. Congressional staffs grew at record rates throughout the 1970s (see Table 3.1). The cap on personal staff allotments in the House increased from ten in 1965 to eighteen in 1975.[2] Most of the personal staff persons hired in the 1970s were brought on board to help House members with constituency-related services. Increases in committee and subcommittee staff also helped members manage their legislative responsibilities. By the late 1970s, many subcommittee staffs were as large as full committee staffs had been in the 1960s (see Table 3.2). Committee staff also shifted away from the nonpartisan model of the 1950s and 1960s and moved to a system where staff were hired by and worked for the chair of the committee or the ranking member. All House members were also granted expanded access to the services provided by the Congressional Research Service, the General Accounting Office, and other congressional support units. These support agencies grew during the 1970s as well; between 1970 and 1976, the Congressional Research Service's staff grew from 332 to 806 (see Table 3.3). Enhanced staff and research services helped members prepare legislation, floor amendments, and points of debate, as well as publicize and solicit support for their actions. A 1975 study estimated that 63 percent of the Congressional Research Service's staff and 71 percent of its budget were devoted to assisting members of Congress with policy analysis and research (Malbin 1981, 140–144; Smith 1989, 10).

Table 3.1 Staffs of Members of the House, 1891–1999

Year	Employees in the House	Year	Employees in the House
1891	n.a.	1984	7,385
1914	n.a.	1985	7,528
1930	870	1986	7,920
1935	870	1987	7,584
1947	1,440	1988	7,564
1957	2,441	1989	7,569
1967	4,055	1990	7,496
1972	5,280	1991	7,278
1976	6,939	1992	7,597
1977	6,942	1993	7,400
1978	6,944	1994	7,390
1979	7,067	1995	7,186
1980	7,371	1996	7,288
1981	7,487	1997	7,282
1982	7,511	1998	7,269
1983	7,606	1999	7,216

Source: Norman Ornstein, Thomas E. Mann, and Michael J. Malbin. 1999. *Vital Statistics on Congress.* Washington, DC: American Enterprise Institute.

Note: The totals are of full-time employees; n.a. = not available.

Member offices also benefited from the addition of modern conveniences like Wide-Area Telecommunications Service (WATS) lines (which provided offices with free long-distance calling), computers, and automated communication systems (Loomis 1988). Members traveled back to their districts more frequently and kept in constant touch with their constituents through personal appearances, newsletters, mailings, and staff outreach. All of these institutional benefits helped members gain visibility in their districts and put them at an electoral advantage (Hernnson 1998). However, these benefits also contributed to gradual fragmentation. As members consolidated power and increased their autonomy, they relied less on their parties.

Table 3.2 Staffs of House Standing Committees, 1891–1999

Year	Employees in the House	Year	Employees in the House
1891	62	1981	1,843
1914	105	1982	1,839
1930	112	1983	1,970
1935	122	1984	1,944
1947	167	1985	2,009
1950	246	1986	1,954
1955	329	1987	2,024
1960	440	1988	1,976
1965	571	1989	1,986
1970	702	1990	1,993
1971	729	1991	2,201
1972	817	1992	2,178
1973	878	1993	2,118
1974	1,107	1994	2,046
1975	1,460	1995	1,246
1976	1,680	1996	1,177
1977	1,776	1997	1,250
1978	1,844	1998	1,305
1979	1,909	1999	1,238
1980	1,917		

Source: Norman Ornstein, Thomas E. Mann, and Michael J. Malbin. 1999. *Vital Statistics on Congress.* Washington, DC: American Enterprise Institute.

Note: The totals are of full-time employees.

The Money Chase Begins

Campaign finance reform in the 1970s also contributed to the rise of individualism and political competitiveness in the House. As noted in chapter 1, the number of registered PACs grew rapidly following the 1974 passage of the FECA amendments, and PAC contributions to congressional candidates mushroomed. By encouraging PAC forma-

Table 3.3 Increases in Support Agency Staff, 1946–1979

Year	Library of Congress	Congressional Research Service only[a]	General Accounting Office[b]	Congressional Budget Office	Office of Technology Assessment
1946			14,219		
1947	1,898	160	10,695		
1950	1,973	161	7,876		
1955	2,459	166	5,776		
1960	2,779	183	5,074		
1965	3,390	231	4,278		
1970	3,848	332	4,704		
1971	3,963	386	4,718		
1972	4,135	479	4,742		
1973	4,375	596	4,908		
1974	4,504	687	5,270		10
1975	4,649	741	4,905	193	54
1976	4,880	806	5,391	203	103
1977	5,075	789	5,315	201	139
1978	5,231	818	5,476	203	164
1979	5,390	847	5,303	207	145

Source: Michael J. Malbin. 1981. Delegation, Deliberation, and the New Role of Congressional Staff. In *The New Congress*, Ed. Thomas E. Mann and Norman Ornstein, 134–177. Washington, DC: American Enterprise Institute.

[a] Legislative Reference Service through 1970. The totals reflect the number of Library of Congress employees who worked for the Congressional Research Service, which is a part of the library.

[b] Before 1950, the GAO was responsible for auditing all individual federal transactions and keeping a record of them; 1950 legislation transferred these responsibilities to the executive branch. The staff reductions through 1965 resulted from this change.

tion, the reforms shifted the balance between the political parties and organized interests, inadvertently decreasing the role the parties played in providing campaign assistance to candidates (Cigler 1993, 419). The reforms made candidates responsible for reporting their campaign contributions and expenditures to the FEC, and candidates' campaign

documents became a matter of public record. The new provisions sub-
jected candidate campaign finances to the scrutiny of the public, the
media, and campaign opponents and made the members fully responsible for any discrepancies or illegalities (Loomis 1988; Rieselbach
1995). As a result, members who chose to accept potentially controver-
sial donations had to respond to their critics.

Campaign finance reform also increased the financial autonomy of
the congressional campaign committees (CCCs). During the 1960s and
early 1970s, the CCCs operated behind the scenes and focused mainly
on channeling earmarked funds to individual members. In addition to
acting as conduits for major contributors, the committees arranged for
campaign speakers to make district appearances and help candidates
raise money. The 1971 FECA and the 1974 amendments did not have
much impact on the CCCs, requiring only that they disclose contributions and inform candidates of the new reporting requirements. When
the U.S. Supreme Court determined that congressional spending limits,
as set forth in the 1974 FECA amendments, were unconstitutional, the
CCCs—particularly the Republican committees—were newly motivated to raise more money for their candidates. Representative Guy
Vander Jagt, who became chair of the NRCC in 1974, asked President
Gerald Ford to sign a fundraising letter for the committee's efforts in
the 1976 House elections; this marked the beginning of the NRCC's
direct-mail solicitation efforts. The DCCC and the NRCC provided basic services to their candidates in 1976, including resource materials,
challenger voting records, and campaign seminars. The NRCC stepped
up its efforts for the 1978 midterm elections and raised $14.1 million,
enough to engage in more aggressive candidate recruitment and to provide early support for its most vulnerable candidates. The DCCC raised
$2.8 million and concentrated its support on first- and second-term
incumbents. House Republicans picked up fifteen seats in 1978, but
the Democrats maintained a healthy majority and worried little about
the Republicans' strong financial showing (Kolodny 1998, 126–136).

As the CCCs honed their campaign operations, nonparty money
continued to flow into political campaigns. Self-oriented House members began to hire campaign professionals to help them convey their
unique message and image to voters. Under the guidance of these pro-

fessionals, campaigns became much more sophisticated and made heavy use of television, radio, public opinion polls, and direct mail. These new technologies and services were well suited to candidate-centered campaigns because they could be purchased directly by the candidates and their campaign teams. Candidates were afforded greater flexibility in assembling campaign organizations that fit their individual needs without having to request help from their party organizations (Herrnson 1998).

To pay for the services these professionals provided, House members had to devote increasing amounts of time to raising money. They began to solicit donations more actively from PACs, which can contribute more money to candidates than can individual donors. By 1978, PAC contributions made up almost one-third of House members' total campaign funds whereas contributions from the party committees amounted to only 7 percent (Cigler 1993, 420). The tremendous rise in PAC activity in the wake of campaign finance reform illustrates how political actors (in this case, members, parties, and PACs) can exploit reforms in ways that advance their own agenda. While the reforms were in part intended to curtail the influence of organized interests, they arguably increased their power in electoral politics.

Given the remarkable degree to which campaign fundraising activities were emphasized during the 1970s, John Wright (2000) suggests that the House reforms were primarily driven by the Democrats' desire to raise money. In marked contrast to most scholarly accounts of the 1970s congressional reforms, Wright argues that the reforms were consistent with the electoral ambitions of the House's Democratic members. Democrats, according to Wright, implemented the reforms "as a way to accommodate and appeal to organized interests whose financial resources were essential to the maintenance of their majority status" (2000, 221). While Democratic and Republican House members were equally subject to the increasing cost of running for office, Republican members benefited from party-sponsored direct-mail fundraising efforts and from the growing number of nonlabor PACs. At the same time, campaign contributions from labor PACs, which tended to favor Democratic members, waned considerably (Jacobson 1984). As the number of registered PACs increased over the 1970s, a distinct pattern developed: Nonlabor

PACs, which contributed more money than labor PACs, gave more to members of committees with jurisdiction over their policy issues. Two of these three trends in campaign financing—individual contributions via direct-mail solicitations and contributions by the expanding number of nonlabor PACs—clearly favored the Republicans. To tap into the campaign funds that nonlabor PACs could provide, the Democrats had to expand their "presence and participation" on committees of key interest to nonlabor PACs. Wright (2000, 222–225) argues that the Democrats found it necessary to reform the committee system and redistribute power throughout the chamber in order to ensure that Democrats— particularly electorally vulnerable members—would receive PAC contributions. This strategy would increase the party's chance of maintaining its majority standing.

While the need to restrict campaign spending and strengthen the reporting requirements is frequently cited as the primary reason behind the 1971 and 1974 FECA provisions, a growing concern among Democrats that they were losing the money chase to Republicans also helped fuel congressional support for the act. Following Hubert Humphrey's failed bid for the presidency in 1968, the Democratic Party was more than $6 million in debt. Democrats had long relied on their ability to raise money through party networks in urban centers, but as Congress entered a period of reform, Democratic leaders began to fear that the party's old fundraising connections would not support the new crop of candidates. Meanwhile, the Republican Party was successfully building up its party coffers, mainly through extensive direct-mail campaigns. Although the FECA's intent was to rein in spiraling campaign costs for all political candidates, the Democratic Party, which lagged far behind the Republicans in fundraising, stood to benefit more from the act's passage (Sorauf 1992).

Though it is difficult to determine precisely the degree to which growing campaign costs contributed to the push for congressional reform in the 1970s, it is clear that the increasing cost of running for office began to weigh heavily on the minds of House members. The increased number of voluntary retirements throughout the 1970s has been attributed, in part, to a shifting political environment that included growing campaign costs (Hibbing 1993). As their electoral independence increased over the 1970s, members became increasingly concerned about keeping their campaign coffers full, both to ward off potential challengers and to have money readily available come election season. Fundraising was a constant focus, especially of newer members, who lacked the name recognition and influence necessary to attract broad financial support. While the decentralization of power in the House helped to level the playing field between junior and senior members, the chamber's more senior members remained at a clear advantage when it came to fundraising: They had been in office long enough to earn the visibility and political clout that campaign donors find appealing.

As members began to direct more of their attention to fundraising, House leaders began focusing on ways to help members achieve reelection. Campaign money had become the most sought-after commodity on Capitol Hill, and House leaders were able to rake it in better than most of their colleagues. By helping members raise campaign funds, they could expect that, in return, those members would support the leadership's agenda. According to David Rohde, "Members knew that if they wanted leadership help, they had to help the leadership" (1991, 91). This arrangement also provided House leaders with a way to promote their own self-interests. They were interested not only in controlling the legislative agenda, but also in maintaining their leadership posts or advancing up the leadership ladder. While successfully promoting and passing policy is one way to demonstrate leadership prowess, another way is to raise surplus campaign money—enough to contribute to more needy colleagues. Member-to-member contributions in the 1970s gradually became more structured and more deliberate in form as the chamber's political climate changed. The atmosphere was more competitive and the political stakes were higher for members who aspired to committee chairs or other leadership posts. The 1976 race for House Majority Leader illustrates how both political connections and campaign money can aid leadership candidates.

Once it became clear that Tip O'Neill would be elected House Speaker in January 1977, he involved himself in the race for Majority Leader, reasoning that his job would be less difficult if he actually liked his second-in-command. O'Neill did not like any of the three candidates who had thrown their hats in the ring: Phil Burton of California,

Richard Bolling of Missouri, and Majority Whip John McFall. O'Neill did not trust Burton and thought he was "crazy" and a "revolutionary." He thought that Bolling was much too aloof and that McFall was a good candidate but did not have the votes to win. So he decided to find a better candidate. O'Neill asked his close ally Dan Rostenkowski, chair of the Ways and Means Committee, to find someone who could beat Burton (who was leading the race at the time), and Rostenkowski suggested Jim Wright of Texas. Wright, a well-respected orator and floor manager, agreed to run for the post and began working with Rostenkowski to rack up supporters, both in and outside the House. Burton was the first of the Whip candidates to make contributions to other House members; once it became clear that support for his candidacy was tied to these contributions, Wright and Bolling began assisting their colleagues with campaign money. By the time the Democratic Caucus convened in January 1977 to choose its leaders, the bitterness between the Majority Leader candidates was almost unbearable. McFall was knocked out on the first ballot, and Bolling finished last on the second ballot. The third ballot pitted Wright against Burton, and Wright won on a hotly contested 148–147 vote. In the end, O'Neill got his way and rewarded Dan Rostenkowski with the post of Deputy Whip (Remini 2006, 450–451). Although Wright won the race, Burton was credited with establishing the new precedent of contributing money to colleagues in expectation of their support (Baker 1989).

Member support for party leaders became progressively important in the allocation of committee assignments in the postreform House (Rohde 1991). The reforms gave Democratic leaders a weighted presence on the party's Steering and Policy Committee, so members who wanted seats on specific committees had to demonstrate their support for the leadership. By the late 1970s, party leaders were bringing party vote scorecards to Steering and Policy Committee meetings so that they could weigh members' committee requests against their support for the party. Over the next few years, leaders continued to play a more active role in guiding committee assignments. They made clear that loyalty was a criterion (Sinclair 1995).

At the same time, some leaders began using campaign money to encourage members' political support. By making contributions to their colleagues' campaign committees, leaders could more easily round up member support for the party's agenda and for their own leadership goals. The strategy was mutually beneficial: Members could raise campaign money while demonstrating support for the leaders, who, among other things, controlled their committee assignments and scheduled their bills for floor action. What had once been considered a friendly gesture thus took on the air of a quid pro quo.

Before long, ambitious members took a cue from their leaders and also began spreading the wealth. In the postreform House, members who were interested in moving up the chamber's power ladder focused on building colleague support rather than years of service. As described in chapter 1, this strategy was aptly demonstrated by Henry Waxman, a two-term Democrat from California who in 1979 secured the chair of the Health and Environment Subcommittee of the Energy and Commerce Committee. Waxman won the subcommittee chair after distributing campaign contributions from his leadership PAC to many of his Energy and Commerce Committee colleagues. Waxman's victory signaled a dramatic shift in House norms; seniority, along with policy and political expertise gained through long service, was no longer a leadership prerequisite (Sinclair 1983).

Conclusion

The House reforms of the 1970s helped to create a political environment that fostered the growth of member-to-member giving. While campaign finance reforms regulated the raising and spending of funds, they also encouraged PAC formation. And while institutional reforms weakened the seniority rule and redistributed power in the chamber, they also encouraged self-oriented, entrepreneurial members to use the new system for personal gain. Reforms are "imperfect compromises" that inevitably have unexpected consequences. During the 1970s, member-to-member giving was one such consequence. Though House members (namely, leaders) had redistributed money to their colleagues for decades, they did so for the purpose of helping colleagues in need. The 1970s marked the first time House members redistributed money for the purpose of "buying" colleague support. This postreform strategy continued in the 1980s. But as party leaders began to exercise more control over the chamber, and as the congressional parties became more cohesive, new strategies for redistributing campaign money emerged.

Notes

1. A member's party unity score is the percentage of the times the member voted with a majority of her or his party in roll call votes pitting a majority of Democrats against a majority of Republicans.

2. Personal staff work in members' Washington and district offices.

4

The 1980s

New Directions in Campaign Funding

When California Representative Tony Coelho took over the Democratic Congressional Campaign Committee (DCCC) in 1981, things were not looking up for House Democrats. Ronald Reagan had just won the presidential election by a landslide, and Republicans had just taken control of the Senate for the first time in twenty-six years and had picked up thirty-three seats in the House. Indeed, the 1980 elections brought Republicans within twenty-six seats of majority control of the House. The National Republican Congressional Committee (NRCC), chaired by Michigan Representative Guy Vander Jagt, was raising millions of dollars through direct-mail solicitations while the DCCC was languishing in debt. First elected in 1978, Coelho was a Hill staff veteran and well schooled in the California fundraising tradition. His decision to build a war chest that would rival the Republicans' was welcomed by his colleagues, but his decision to solicit campaign funds from nontraditional sources—mainly corporate—was less popular. Coelho also took the extraordinary step of telling incumbent members from safe districts not to expect campaign assistance from the DCCC. Under the leadership of Representative James Corman, Coelho's predecessor at the DCCC, the committee had directed contributions to incumbent members whether they needed the help or not. But Coelho established a new standard for the DCCC; in addition to turning the committee into a state-of-the-art campaign machine, he turned the committee chair post into a formal part of the House's leadership structure (Babson 1994; Kolodny 1998).

The decade following the 1970s House reforms saw major changes in how the parties competed for majority control. The national party organizations, and particularly the congressional campaign committees (CCCs), expanded their candidate-oriented services and began to concentrate on fundraising as a means of maintaining or gaining majority control. Money emerged "as the first and most essential element in political party activity and effectiveness in the 1980s" (Adamany 1984, 105). At the same time, the parties became more ideologically polarized in Congress. Democrats continued to expand the leadership structure and enhance the powers of their leaders. Texas Democrat Jim Wright's election to the Speakership of the House in 1987 marked a new era in aggressive leadership. Wright took the lead in setting the chamber's legislative agenda, used his organizational powers to exert influence over the Democratic Caucus, and used the House rules to protect his party's agenda. House Republicans were unified in frustration over their minority status, but they disagreed about how to challenge the majority. The more traditional Republicans believed that party members should seek to participate in the legislative process and build records that would appeal to voters. The new conservatives, who tended to be much more assertive, thought that the party should confront and challenge the Democrats, to show voters where they stood on the issues (Rohde 1991).

Changes in the party's electoral and governing strategies affected how House members redistributed money to their colleagues. While leadership PACs were established by some Republicans during the 1980s, most were operated by Democratic members who either held leadership positions or had leadership aspirations. As House leaders were granted more power, leadership posts became more attractive. And because seniority was no longer the sole criterion in determining which members would become leaders, the leadership races became much more competitive. While members vying for leadership posts still emphasized their experience, skill, and policy expertise, many also highlighted their fundraising abilities: "Campaigning and raising money is a traditional role for leaders and senior members . . . but in the 1980s, leadership elections suddenly looked like bidding wars as members eager to move up handed out campaign funds" (Alston 1991, 2763). More members were giving out more money in the 1980s than in the 1970s, but not all of them were leaders or leadership aspirants. According to Minnesota Democrat Martin Olav Sabo, "All of us in the majority have benefits from being in the majority." Giving money to colleagues, in Sabo's view, was an "obligation" because it would help Democrats get elected and maintain the Democratic majority (Alston 1991, 2763). Member contribution strategies in the 1980s emphasized both personal goals and collective party goals.

Party Campaign Strategies in the 1980s

David Adamany claims that "the story of political parties in 1980 was a tale of one party that has been successfully making the transition to the 'cash economy of the new . . . politics' and of its rival that has not" (1984, 75). During the 1979–1980 campaign, the Republican national party raised $130.3 million while the Democratic Party raised approximately $23 million.[1] The vast disparity between the two parties reflected the Republicans' advanced fundraising techniques, which centered on mass direct-mail and small-donor solicitation programs that generated 70 percent of the party's 1980 election cycle receipts. The Republicans had been building their small-donor roster since 1964, when supporters of Barry Goldwater began mailing contributions to the party. In 1977, the Republican National Committee (RNC) claimed a list of 350,000 contributors, and by 1980, the list had expanded to over 1.2 million contributors, who gave between $25 and $30 on average. The Republicans also increased their large-contributor base: The Eagles Program, which solicited contributions of $10,000, grew from 198 donors in 1975 to 865 donors in 1980, and the Victory 80 program, which also solicited large contributions, raised $1 million in 1980. Republicans also benefited from fundraising dinners and from PAC-sponsored breakfast and lunch policy briefings. The national party committees avoided soliciting campaign contributions from PACs and instead encouraged them to contribute directly to Republican candidates (Adamany 1984, 76).

Former Senator Bill Brock was named chair of the RNC in 1977 and is credited with reviving the party organization. Brock believed that modernizing the national Republican Party committees was the key to electoral success, and he focused on raising the money needed to realize this goal. He envisioned the national party committees as political action groups that would offer financial, technical, and campaign-planning assistance to other Republican Party groups, particularly those at the state and local levels. By 1979, the RNC had expanded its financial assistance to local and state candidates, extended its mass direct-mail fundraising programs, and initiated a number of technical assistance programs (Adamany 1984, 78–79).

The NRCC, which began to operate independently of the RNC in the late 1970s, followed the model Brock had established for the national committee. During the 1979–1980 election cycle, it raised $28.6 million, most of which came from a contributor base of about 300,000 donors who gave an average of $23. The committee also established a Republican Congressional Leadership Council, made up of about 400 members who were invited to participate in special briefings with the Republican leadership in exchange for contributions of $2,500 each. During the 1980 election cycle, the NRCC's fundraising efforts made it possible for the committee to support a number of campaign activities, including candidate recruitment, party worker training, voter mobilization, research support for candidates, polling and media assistance, and campaign fund contributions. NRCC chair Guy Vander Jagt helped to persuade over 100 Republicans to run for House seats in 1980 and targeted 138 potentially competitive districts for technical and financial assistance (Conway 1983, 6–10).

While the Republicans were raising unprecedented amounts of campaign money, the Democrats were struggling to pay off debts. In 1968, the party absorbed $9.3 million in debts from Hubert Humphrey's presidential campaign and from Eugene McCarthy's and Robert Kennedy's primary challenges. By 1976, the party had reduced its debt to about $2.5 million by negotiating a lower debt payment rate and by staging a series of telethons and mass mailings. However, the new campaign finance laws made it illegal for the parties to borrow large sums of money; as a result, Democrats were unable to obtain start-up funds for more debt reduction programs. John White, who was named Democratic National Committee (DNC) chair in 1977, vowed to pull the party out of debt and began by slashing the committee's operating budget by $3 million over three years. For the 1980 election cycle, the DNC raised just over $15 million and ended 1980 with about $1 million in debts. Most of the money the party raised had come from fundraising events and from moderate to large donors; small-donor contributions totaled just $2.5 million (Adamany 1984, 77).

The DCCC raised approximately $2 million in the 1980 election cycle but did not engage in any small-donor or mass direct-mail solicitations. Unlike the NRCC, the DCCC did solicit PAC contributions. The committee also relied on transfers from the Democratic House and Senate Council, a separate fundraising committee that maintained a list of donors who gave at least $1,500 each in exchange for newsletters, congressional briefings, and private dinners. In addition to lackluster fundraising, the DCCC suffered from the effects of incumbency. Democratic incumbents had access to organizational and funding support, and they used this access to benefit themselves; money was not a problem for Democratic incumbents, but it was for Democratic challengers. PACs opted to give directly to incumbents rather than to the DCCC or to challengers. Democratic incumbents also had staff resources, which weakened the need for party-provided field services and put Democratic challengers at a disadvantage (Adamany 1984, 78–87). Heading into the 1980 elections, many House Democrats did not realize that they were unprepared for tough campaigns. It simply had not occurred to them that the Republicans could pose a threat to their majority status. As they consolidated power and autonomy, House Democrats had become more disconnected from their party, and it drifted toward fragmentation.

In 1981 a U.S. Supreme Court decision clarifying FECA's provisions on coordinated expenditures allowed the CCCs to become more active in financing House candidates following the 1980 elections. Coordinated expenditures pay for campaign activities initiated by the party committees, with the candidates' knowledge and approval. FECA allowed the national party committees and the state party committees to make coordinated expenditures on behalf of congressional candidates, expenditures that were intended to strengthen the parties by allowing them to determine and pay for the activities or services that they thought would best benefit a candidate's campaign.[2] For House and

Senate candidates, the problem was that the national party committees were focused primarily on helping presidential candidates, and the state parties were interested in helping candidates for state-level office. In addition, enforcement of the disclosure laws and limits on contributions had made fundraising more difficult for congressional candidates. Before the 1981 Court decision, the law prohibited the CCCs from making coordinated expenditures, preventing them from offering much in the way of assistance.

The Court's 1981 ruling held that the national party committees and state party committees could designate other committees as agents and allow them to make coordinated expenditures on the party committees' behalf (*Federal Election Commission v. Democratic Senatorial Campaign Committee et al.*). "In finding these agency agreements to be legal, the Court led the way for the CCCs to increase their financial involvement in congressional campaigning" (Kolodny 1998, 141). As a result of the Court's decision, the CCCs achieved greater financial autonomy and operational independence. It was not difficult for the CCCs to convince the national and state party committees to enter into these agency agreements as they did not have time for or interest in congressional campaigns. Coordinated expenditures gave the CCCs the ability to help incumbents deal with contribution limits and the financial demands of new campaign technologies. In addition, the ability to make such expenditures forced the CCCs to set funding priorities: Now that the committees could legally provide more than direct contributions, more candidates expected to reap the benefits (Kolodny 1998, 136–143).

After the 1980 elections, the House campaign committees determined that their incumbent candidates needed to understand and use new campaign technologies and that more attention needed to be directed to attractive outside challengers. While the DCCC sought to recruit strong challengers for open-seat and competitive races, the Republicans focused even more heavily on this task as they were trying to gain majority status. Tony Coelho's main duty as DCCC chair was to protect incumbents, but he also wanted to recoup some of the losses House Democrats had suffered in 1980 by helping strong challengers for seats currently held by Republicans. His strategy was twofold: He would increase the Democrats' majority and he would show senior incumbents the value of learning new campaign techniques. Coelho also decided that marginality would be the determining factor in whether incumbents received financial assistance from the committee (Kolodny 1998, 146–148).

Recruiting and financing strong challengers was particularly important to Republicans. Until the early 1980s, the NRCC's policy was to give the maximum allowable contribution to each incumbent, but to forgo coordinated expenditures. But in 1982, the committee was flush with money—a fact that did not go unnoticed by electorally insecure incumbents. Believing (rightfully) that the NRCC's mission was to support incumbents, these members requested additional financial assistance. Vander Jagt knew that the NRCC could not afford to provide coordinated expenditures to all Republican incumbents and still have the money to support challengers for competitive seats, so he created an Incumbent Review Panel. The panel, which consisted of three incumbent members, the NRCC chair, and the NRCC executive director, heard requests from members who wanted full coordinated expenditures. The panel then determined whether the requests were genuine or frivolous and awarded money accordingly. Strong consideration was given to whether members had attempted to use new technologies and whether they had truly exhausted their fundraising potential; these announced criteria required members to think carefully about whether to make a request of the panel (Kolodny 1998, 148–149).

The parties always want to maximize their number of seats, and in the abstract, they do not care which candidates win, only that as many as possible do. However, individual candidates, of course, care tremendously who wins. In the early 1980s, these clashing perspectives caused conflict between the CCCs and incumbent members over how campaign resources should be distributed. Most incumbents did not face strong challengers, so any redistribution of campaign resources from stronger to weaker candidates would come almost entirely at the expense of incumbents (Jacobson 1985–1986, 604–605). Thus the CCCs faced the daunting task of convincing their members to look beyond their individual campaigns and consider the good of the whole.

Although the DCCC did not establish a formal review panel, Coelho considered the merits of incumbent requests using criteria similar to those of the NRCC. Accustomed to getting what they wanted from the DCCC, Democratic incumbents were displeased by Coelho's "need-based" approach to awarding funds. But during Coelho's tenure, the DCCC became competitive again. Robin Kolodny notes that "when the CCCs were less money oriented, they would not have been able to confront Republican and Democratic incumbents in such an abrupt manner. Instead, as campaigning changed . . . incumbents learned that it is in their best interests to be led by the CCC's technological expertise" (1998, 155). Coelho formed close alliances with business PACs, constantly reminding them that the Democrats controlled the legislative process in the House (Kolodny 1998, 149–150). He understood that many of these PACs leaned toward the Republican Party, but he advised them "not to let your ideology get in the way of your business judgment" (Sabato 1990, 199). In 1986, Coelho used his successful chair post at the DCCC to launch a winning bid for the position of House Majority Whip. Representative W. G. Hefner, one of Coelho's opponents in the Whip race, observed, "Money, whether we like it or not, is a pretty powerful tool." Coelho's other opponent, Representative Charles Rangel, noted that Coelho "was the man who signed the checks" (Canon 1989, 427). When the Democratic leadership decided to make the DCCC chair an official leadership post, Coelho's aggressive fundraising style was legitimized.

Both parties gained greater financial and organizational strength during the 1982 election cycle. The NRCC's staff grew to eighty-four, while the DCCC maintained a much smaller staff of thirty-two. Republicans continued to reach out to small contributors, reportedly contacting more than 40 million households and expanding their active contributor list to approximately 2 million. Republican House candidates received $4.6 million in party contributions and an additional $5.3 million in coordinated expenditures during the 1982 cycle—$4.2 million over the 1980 funding levels. The national party also funded preelection research, gave legal assistance to the state parties for their district apportionment efforts, and paid for national advertising campaigns attacking the Democratic Party leadership. To mobilize support for President Ronald Reagan's tax and budget plans and to put pressure on the Democratic members of Congress, Republicans also undertook grassroots efforts (Adamany 1984, 96–99). The party's ability to offer financial and campaign resources helped it recruit strong candidates for the 1982 campaign. In addition to providing campaign assistance to candidates, the NRCC worked to persuade 225 PACs to make the maximum contribution to forty Republican candidates (Conway 1983, 7).

As a result of the Republican Party's superior fundraising and organizational efforts, Democrats were not expected to fare well in the 1982 elections. Although the Democratic Party had made modest improvements over its 1980 fundraising levels, it managed only to pay off the debt it had been carrying since 1968. The Democrats had also developed a successful direct-mail program and claimed a contributor list of 220,000. In 1982, party contributions to Democratic House candidates totaled $1 million, and coordinated expenditures amounted to $689,000. While Democrats funded their House candidates at much lower levels than the Republicans, the party's 1982 candidate contributions were an improvement over its 1980 numbers. The Democrats also undertook a national advertising campaign, but their $1-million budget was considerably lower than what the Republicans spent. Also, although the party invested in candidate recruitment and campaign assistance, its efforts did not match those of the Republicans. Despite the party's comparatively weak financial and organizational performance in 1982, Democrats held on at the polls, and the Republicans lost twenty-six House seats, in part because the party was blamed for the nation's failing economy (Adamany 1984, 96–101). Because many Democratic incumbents were still in shock over the party's losses in 1980, they had focused on raising as much money as possible for their own campaigns. According to Martin Franks, then director of the DCCC, "Panic is not too strong a word to describe it. Even people who were traditionally safe went out and really raised money in Washington and around the country in a way that they haven't before" (Jacobson 1985–1986, 615). When election day arrived, many of these incumbents had large amounts of unspent funds in their campaign accounts.

While these excess funds might have helped some of the party's promising challengers, the Democrats had no system in place for encouraging the redistribution of campaign money. By the summer of 1982, Democratic incumbents had raised on average seven times as much money as Democratic challengers (Jacobson 1985–1986, 615).

By the mid-1980s, the CCCs had moved out of government build-
ings and into permanent nongovernment offices, built up their staffs,
diversified their functions, and raised increasing amounts of money.
The committees began providing services that rivaled those offered by
professional consultants, including "campaign management, communications, fundraising, and some traditional local party activities"
(Herrnson 1988, 81). Both the DCCC and the NRCC furnished their
candidates with lists of campaign managers, media consultants, pollsters, and direct-mail specialists. The committees also began to pur-
chase blocks of campaign services from consultants and either gave
them to candidates as in-kind contributions or sold them to candidates
at well below their market value. Both CCCs also provided media advertising and fundraising assistance as direct services to their candidates. They taught incumbents how to run competitive campaigns and
how to use new campaign technologies, and they provided newly
elected members with extensive orientation services. During the 1970s,
members had relied heavily on nonparty contributions (namely, from
PACs) to pay for these kinds of services, which were offered only by
professional campaign consultants. But as the campaign services offered by the CCCs became more sophisticated, members came to expect the committees to assist them in their reelection efforts. These new
pressures created tension between the CCC chairs, who wanted to focus
on the collective goal of winning majorities, and the incumbent members, who wanted "free" campaign assistance.

Paul Herrnson (1988, 30–44) argues that by the mid-1980s, the
national party committees (including the CCCs) had taken on a new
role, as intermediaries between candidates and campaign resources.
While the CCCs had long channeled contributions to candidates (see
Kolodny 1998), they became major brokers between the PAC community and political candidates during the 1980s. Both parties helped
PACs direct contributions to particular campaigns and helped candidates solicit funds from potential PAC donors (Cigler 1993, 424). Although the NRCC's PAC division was larger and more elaborate than
the DCCC's, both parties were able to direct large amounts of PAC
money to their candidates throughout the 1980s (Herrnson 1986,
592–594). Indeed, the CCCs seemed to turn the "PAC threat" of the

1970s to their advantage, changing a conflictual relationship into a generally cooperative one. One disadvantage of these alliances was that the parties risked becoming "creatures of the PACs, serving primarily as a conduit for their funds" (Conway 1983, 15). These newly formed alliances did not altogether alleviate the tensions between parties and PACs; some PACs continued to "jealously guard their independence" and others continued to compete directly with the national parties. Tensions between closely aligned PACs and parties also continued to crop up, particularly when the party's broad, diversified message clashed with the PACs' more narrow agenda (Cigler 1993, 424).

In 1986 and 1988, the reelection rate for House incumbents was 98 percent, which suggested that fewer and fewer outside challengers were able to raise the amount of money needed to run competitive campaigns (Jackson 1990, 5). The original mission of the CCCs was to pursue majority status; for the Democrats, this meant primarily protecting marginal incumbents, and for the Republicans, it meant protecting at-risk incumbents and supporting strong challengers. But because of the changes in how campaigns were financed and run, the CCCs found that *all* of their incumbent candidates expected considerable assistance (Kolodny 1998). Gary Jacobson (1985–1986, 611) suggested that the CCCs were not free to pursue the party's collective interests because they were controlled by members of Congress who were expected to take care of their colleagues. In 1982, for example, the Democrats contributed nearly one-third of their funds to incumbents who won with more than 70 percent of the vote. Jacobson argues that from the party's perspective, this money was "almost completely wasted," especially because 1982 was a year when Democrats should have been on the offensive, going after seats held by marginal Republicans. Republicans contributed 13 percent of their funds to incumbents who won with more than 70 percent of the vote in 1982—less than the Democrats, but still wasted money. This collective action dilemma is particularly difficult for the minority party, which must choose between supporting incumbents and pursuing majorities.

Members who value independence from the party organization must consider the financial retribution they may face if they choose not to support the policies or programs preferred by those who control the

CCCs (Conway 1983, 15). While the CCCs did not routinely punish disloyal members in the 1980s, they did begin to reward loyalty in the 1990s. However, the rewards dispensed had more to do with power in the chamber than with financial support.

The Resurgence of
Strong Leaders and Party Cohesion

Major changes in House electoral activity during the 1980s were accompanied by changes within the congressional party organizations. These transformations contributed to an increased emphasis on campaign money, and to the growth of member-to-member and member-to-party giving.

Factional divisions within the Democratic Party were a major cause of the 1970s House reforms. Southern conservatives routinely voted in opposition to the party during the 1960s, when social welfare issues, civil rights, and the Vietnam War regularly topped the policy agenda. Their party opposition scores remained high until the 92nd Congress (1971–1972), when the proportion of southern Democrats who supported the party's agenda began to increase. Changes in electoral coalitions during the 1970s allowed southern Democrats to vote with their northern colleagues without fear of retribution at the polls. As more black voters joined the Democratic Party and as more conservative members and voters left, the party gradually shifted to a more liberal position. Conservative Democrats became increasingly frustrated by their lack of influence and began to pressure the House leadership to accommodate their views. Following the 1980 elections, the Democrats had a much smaller majority (243–192), and Speaker O'Neill recognized that he could not afford to ignore his party's conservatives, who numbered somewhere between 30 and 40 members. He agreed to add 3 conservatives to the Steering and Policy Committee, and to appoint several others to the chamber's power committees. Only a few southern Democrats lost to Republicans in the 1982 and 1984 elections; some of the electoral threat that these members might have felt was thus reduced, and collaboration between conservative and liberal

Democrats became more common. All of these changes helped to minimize the differences between the party's southern conservatives and liberal northerners (Rohde 1991, 45–48).

Other factions within the Democratic Party included the neoliberals, the traditional liberals, and the deficit hawks. Most of the neoliberals were elected in 1974 and 1978 and were more supportive of strong defense programs and alternative economic policies than were the traditional liberals. Many deemed social welfare programs inefficient and forced significant compromises within the party on budgetary policy. These members also were quite ambitious; a number of them successfully sought leadership positions and higher office (Rohde 1991, 48–49).

The traditional liberals dominated legislative outcomes in the House through the mid-1970s, but they lost some of their power after the 1980 elections and as economic pressures put a damper on the big government initiatives they favored. *Liberal* also became a politicized term during the 1980s, and many Democrats—especially marginal members—avoided the label. But as ideological homogeneity increased within the caucus during the 1980s, liberals found the balance of party opinion tipped in their favor.

The Democratic class of 1982 contained a number of deficit hawks. Many of these members held liberal positions on other issues but saw reducing the deficit as the way to afford new programs. Their entry into the party made the deficit an even more salient issue for the Democrats. And because they tended to be liberal on other issues, these members also provided the votes needed to block President Reagan's agenda (Rohde 1991, 45–50).

Throughout the 1980s, factional change within the Democratic Party, together with shifts in the political environment, provided the basis for greater Democratic cohesion. David Rohde's (1991, 50–58) detailed analysis of party unity scores from the 1950s through the 1980s reveals a considerable increase in Democratic Party unity and cohesion in the postreform House. Rohde attributes most of this increase to major declines in factional divisions among Democrats in the postreform years. While Democratic House members certainly did not unite on everything, they did display a greater homogeneity on policy matters that enabled the development of a party position on a range of issues.

In addition, "the 1980s political environment, especially the deficit, made free-lance policy entrepreneurship, as practiced in the 1970s, much less feasible for moderates and liberals" (Sinclair 1992, 659). The policy divisions between President Reagan and House Democrats were extensive, and huge budget deficits made it difficult for Democrats to pass legislation that they found acceptable. Most of the battles centered on budget resolutions and omnibus measures that addressed major policy priorities for the Democrats. Passing these bills required Democratic leaders to tightly coordinate the legislative agenda and enforce strict party loyalty.

House Republicans were not as fractious as House Democrats throughout the 1960s and 1970s, but there were divisions within the party. The traditional conservatives were the largest and longest-standing faction within the party. They opposed most Democratic policy initiatives and often worked with Democratic conservatives to oppose the liberal majority. The Republican conservatives shared President Reagan's strict conservative views and pressured Republican leaders to advocate a more limited role for the government domestically and a strong defense effort to counter the Soviet Union. During the late 1970s, a more activist faction of the conservative wing had formed. This group, which was started by thirty-five members of the class of 1978, did not conflict much with the party's senior conservatives over policy matters; rather, disagreements between the two groups centered on what goals the party should pursue and what tactics it should use. The new conservatives believed that their senior colleagues had settled for minority status. They, by contrast, wanted to move Republicans into the majority and pushed for a much more activist approach. In 1983, a small group of neoconservatives formed the Conservative Opportunity Society (COS) and named Georgia Representative Newt Gingrich chair. Members of the COS aggressively challenged the majority and used tactics designed to provoke the Democratic leadership. While conservatives dominated the House Republicans, a significant number of moderates and even a few liberals also populated the party. These two factions saw themselves as the counterweights to the party's conservatives, and they pushed for a more moderate agenda, which they believed would broaden the Republicans' electoral base (Rohde 1991, 120–126).

Until the 1980s, party unity scores for House Republicans had followed a pattern of decline and resurgence that was similar to House Democrats' scores. Throughout the Reagan years, as Democratic cohesion increased, party unity scores for House Republicans returned to a level comparable to that of the 1960s. Cohesion remained strong, but it did not approach the levels that Democrats achieved in the mid- and late 1980s. While House Republicans were not as internally divided as the Democrats, they also did not experience the same increase in homogeneity (Rohde 1991, 125–127).

As Democratic cohesion intensified during the 1980s, strong House leadership emerged. Barbara Sinclair (1992, 658) argues that changes during the 1980s reduced the costs of strong leadership and allowed Democratic leaders to be more active and decisive in organizing the party and the chamber, in setting the House agenda, and in shaping legislative outcomes. The 1970s reforms increased the vulnerability of legislation on the House floor, and constraints in the 1980s—including divided government and huge budget deficits—made enacting legislation even more difficult. Policy entrepreneurship was much less feasible in this environment, especially for members promoting costly new programs. Democratic leaders had the resources to shape legislative outcomes (for example, control over the Rules Committee and the floor schedule) but needed their members to show restraint in pursuing their personal agendas and instead support the party's collective agenda. This task was made easier as the party grew more homogeneous. When party leadership agendas conflict with members' reelection goals, members resist strong leadership, but by the late 1980s, no significant segment of the Democratic majority had to worry about the leadership's agenda interfering with their reelection goals. The potential costs of strong leadership decreased as battles between committees and Democratic Party factions grew rare, as major legislation split Democrats and Republicans rather than northern and southern Democrats, and as the political environment decreased opportunities for freelance entrepreneurship (Sinclair 1992, 674).

One consequence of greater cohesion among House Democrats was increased pressure on party leaders to share the views and policy positions of the majority of caucus members. Members began calling caucus meetings by petition for the purpose of pushing specific issue positions and pressuring party leaders to move majority-backed bills. House Democrats also began to pressure their leaders to expand the leadership structure to accommodate the various positions within the party. Speaker O'Neill acquiesced and appointed a six-member Speaker's Cabinet to provide policy advice to the leadership and the major committee chairs. Then, in 1985, the caucus adopted a rule making the party Whip an elective rather than appointive post; the intent was to give the caucus control over the choice of a leader who would speak for the party and who might one day rise to the Speakership. In 1986, Representative Tony Coelho became the first elected party Whip. The caucus also began to play a more active role in controlling committee chair appointments and member committee assignments (Rohde 1991, 69–77). Despite the fragmentation of authority throughout the caucus, the party was cohesive.

The Democratic Whip system became more elaborate and Whips became more prestigious during the 1980s. Democratic leaders expanded the number of appointed Whips as the number of decision points in the legislative process grew. The leadership chose Whips who would represent different factions within the caucus and assigned them the tasks of gathering vote information and persuading colleagues to support the party line. The prestige of Whips was enhanced when the Whip and Deputy Whips were placed on the Steering and Policy Committee and when the Whip's office was given more staff and a higher budget. In 1981, the Democratic Whip organization included 18 percent of the Democratic Caucus members, and by 1989, 40 percent of the caucus members were part of the Whip organization.

The Democrats also greatly expanded their task force operation during the 1980s; task forces were organized around ongoing issues as well as particular bills. With so many members participating in the process of informing and persuading, House Democrats were able to push their agenda quite efficiently (Rohde 1991, 84–88). Expanding the Whip system was also part of the Democrats' "strategy of inclusion." By allowing more members to participate in the process, leaders extended their resources and gave independent-minded members a chance to shape policy (Sinclair 1983). As a result of the expanding leadership structure, the operating funds allocated to House leadership offices grew tremendously during the 1980s: from $482,850 in 1968, to $2,343,225 in 1974, to $6,755,468 in 1986 (Canon 1989, 431).

The revival of a strong House Speakership in the late 1980s highlighted the Democrats' party-building efforts. While Tip O'Neill had begun strengthening the Speakership, Jim Wright's leadership in the 100th Congress (1987–1988) set a new, aggressive tone in the House. As Democrats bonded over their policy preferences and their opposition to President Reagan's agenda, they came to see strong leadership as necessary. Although Democrats had increased the Speaker's powers through a series of rules changes in the 1970s and 1980s, Wright was the first Speaker to take full advantage of the office's enhanced resources. Changes in the political environment—particularly greater party cohesion—allowed Wright to exercise power with the support of his party. O'Neill had elevated the public profile of the Speakership, but Wright pushed his powers to levels not seen since Joe Cannon's turn-of-the-century reign. Wright set the legislative agenda and did not hesitate to intervene in the committee and rules processes. He also threatened retribution (and made good on his threats) when members were uncooperative. Under Wright's Speakership, the House became much more partisan; by virtually shutting Republicans out of the process, he provoked their intense opposition (Schickler 2001, 238–242). Anger and resentment rose to new levels; Wyoming representative Dick Cheney angrily proclaimed that Wright "will do anything he can to win at any price, including ignoring the rules, bending rules, writing rules, denying the House the opportunity to work its will. It brings disrespect to the House itself. There's no comity left. Why should you, if you are a Republican, and given the way Republicans are treated, think of a Democrat as a colleague? They aren't colleagues" (Remini 2006, 473–474).

Wright's aggressive leadership style served to galvanize House Republicans around activist tactics. Pennsylvania Republican Bob Walker, a member of Newt Gingrich's COS, claimed that Wright "really became a catalyst for bringing the whole Republican party over to our [Gingrich's] side" (Remini 2006, 473). According to Eric Schickler, the "COS gave organizational form to the so-called bombthrower wing of the Republican party" (2001, 242). Its members were not content to work quietly within the system; they preferred to obstruct business and publicize Democratic misdeeds. As Republicans grew more frustrated by Democratic mistreatment, their support for the confrontational tactics that the COS promoted increased. Republicans were particularly resentful of the majority party's use of special rules. Mississippi Representative Trent Lott charged that "the Democratic leadership . . . now has set a formula for these rules: the restrictiveness of a rule is in direct relation to the importance of the legislation it makes in order" (Rohde 1991, 133). Because rules are approved by majority vote, Democratic cohesion kept the Republicans from having any impact once the rules reached the House floor. Republicans came to believe that their only course of action was to publicize the sharp increase in restrictive and closed rules. They organized media events and provided the text of prepared speeches, along with statistical evidence, to the media and congressional scholars. During the late 1980s, the Republican Conference also passed a series of centralizing reforms designed to make Republican members who were in positions of power more accountable to the party. The House Republicans also adopted rules that gave Republican leaders more influence over the conference. These reforms were modeled on the DSG-sponsored reforms of the 1970s; Republicans believed that centralizing power had helped the Democrats gain control over the legislative agenda, and they wanted to achieve the same control (Rohde 1991, 132–138).

Television coverage of the House was central to the Republican protest movement. COS members were the first to take advantage of C-SPAN, which allowed them to speak directly to their constituents and to the public at large. They used the Congress "largely as a prop to frame issues for the media" and to draw attention to themselves and the conservative agenda (Schickler 2001, 244). Robert Remini observes that C-SPAN was especially useful for Newt Gingrich: "I figured it out," Gingrich declared, "if I could start making speeches on C-SPAN, then I would reach a dramatically bigger audience than people who flew five hundred miles to speak to a Kiwanis club" (2006, 463). Gingrich and the other COS members would take one-minute jabs at the Democrats in the morning and give longer "Special Order" speeches in the evening. All of these speeches were designed to provoke the Democrats— especially the leadership—into confrontation, preferably in front of the television cameras. By 1986, many House Republicans were looking to

Newt Gingrich to provide the party's plan of action rather than to Minority Leader Bob Michel, who was uncomfortable with the neoconservatives' confrontational style (Remini 2006, 470).

Newt Gingrich believed that Republicans essentially needed to destroy the system that the Democrats had created and build a new one from scratch (Evans and Oleszek 1997). By drawing attention to Democratic abuses, Republicans could claim the high ground and win majority control. The COS also believed that a strong conservative platform was the key to winning majority control, and they worked to build coalitional support for their ideas. Many senior Republicans disapproved of the COS's tactics and feared that such an aggressive strategy would backfire. But times were changing, and in 1989, Newt Gingrich was elected Republican Whip. Soon after winning the Whip post, Gingrich toured the country, calling Jim Wright a crook and demanding an investigation into Wright's personal finances. He then filed charges against Wright with the House Ethics Committee, claiming that Wright had violated the House's gift and income rules. The committee investigated and charged Wright with violating House rules in sixty-nine separate instances, mostly involving a sweetheart deal with the publishers of his book, *Reflections of a Public Man*. The Republicans accused Wright of even more ethics violations, and the Democrats, worried about public opinion, began to back away from the Speaker. Abandoned by many members of his own party, Wright resigned his seat and, in an emotional floor speech, urged that members of both parties "resolve to bring this period of mindless cannibalism to an end" (Remini 2006, 474–476). Wright was replaced by Washington representative Tom Foley.

As the Wright scandal unfolded, Majority Whip Tony Coelho announced that he would resign rather than face an investigation into some questionable financial transactions that were first reported in *Newsweek* magazine. He was replaced by Representative Bill Gray in June 1989.

Patterns of Member-to-Member Giving

During the 1980s, the CCCs greatly expanded their campaign fundraising efforts and began offering their candidates more campaign resources and services. The congressional leaders were extended more power by their parties as policy disputes became more heated and as the political environment grew more partisan. Democrats also expanded their leadership structure, offering more caucus members a role in shaping policy outcomes. These dynamics afforded ambitious members not only more opportunities but also the means to use them. Redistributing campaign money to colleagues was one strategy members could use to build support for their ambitious pursuits.

Seniority was no longer the sole criterion in determining which members would become leaders, but both parties still tended to "promote from within." David Canon argues that a leadership structure that promotes from within "is more likely to recruit ambitious, high-quality members . . . because the thankless task of party whipping or floor coverage may have some payoff. A [member] who is elected majority leader without 'serving time' in a lower leadership position undermines members' incentive to sacrifice other options for a position that has no power and little prestige" (1989, 434). In the House Democratic Whip system, for example, the expectation was that members who served as Whips would have a leg up to leadership. This expectation, in turn, influenced the type of member who wanted to become part of the Whip structure. Leadership systems with clearly delineated lines of advancement are more likely to turn out leaders who have demonstrated their commitment to the party. According to Speaker Jim Wright, leadership ladders produce "people who understand the institution and the problems, and who have seen Congress grapple with things, succeed and fail" (Canon 1989, 435).

Members want leaders who can help them achieve their individual and collective goals. They want leaders to support their efforts to attain committee assignments, bring bills to the floor, attract campaign resources, and provide institutional perks that will help them get reelected. Members also want either to maintain or to gain majority party status, and they expect that their leaders will support that goal by effectively promoting the party's agenda and building party cohesion. The challenge for leadership aspirants is to convey to their colleagues their ability to handle these tasks.

In several leadership races in the 1980s, the candidates were part of the leadership system and hoped to advance further up the ladder. For many of these challengers, giving campaign money to colleagues was an important way to demonstrate commitment to both the party and its members. Clyde Wilcox (1989, 400) found that, increasingly, during the early 1980s, members of Congress began to use their leadership PACs and personal campaign committees in their pursuit of party leadership posts. Contributions were directed primarily to incumbents and to challengers, rather than to the CCCs. This strategy allowed House members to decide which candidates needed financial help, as well as which candidates might help them achieve their own leadership goals. In 1988, twenty-seven House members (seventeen Democrats and ten Republicans) had registered leadership PACs with the Federal Elections Commission. While this number represents a small percentage of the chamber, the amount of money these PACs distributed was not inconsequential. Although relatively few House members had established leadership PACs, nearly half of all members of Congress contributed money to their colleagues. During the 1984 election cycle, for example, House Democrats gave $623,700 out of their leadership PACs and $593,103 out of their personal campaign committees. House Republicans gave $290,897 out of their leadership PACs and $306,934 out of their personal campaign committees (Wilcox 1989, 390).[3] In 1986, House Democrats collected $935,897 from leadership PACs, while their Republican counterparts collected $95,049. Perhaps more important than the amount of money that was redistributed in the 1980s is the precedent that such transactions set. Member-to-member giving had become the norm by the late 1980s and played a significant role in several leadership races. With the exception of Clyde Wilcox (1989) and Ross Baker (1989), scholars did not focus on the redistribution of campaign money during the 1980s; most detailed accounts of member-to-member giving come from congressional journalists, who began to pay more attention to these transactions in the 1980s.[4]

When Representative Charles Rangel ran for Majority Whip in 1986, he established a leadership PAC solely to support his campaign for the post. "I would never have any other reason for a PAC," he said. Rangel claimed that he did not want to be "thrown into the money-raising market," but that the nature of the competition forced him to do just that. His main challenger was DCCC Chair Tony Coelho, who not only outraised Rangel but also won the race. Coelho contributed $570,000 to his colleagues—more than double what Rangel contributed—and gave to twice as many candidates. Rangel initially doubted that his campaign for the Majority Whip post would benefit much from setting up a leadership PAC because he was running against one of the chamber's most prolific fundraisers. Representative Martin Sabo and Representative Norm Mineta, two other Whip candidates, had also contributed money to their Democratic colleagues; if Rangel opted out of the "money-raising market," he risked appearing unwilling or—even worse—unable to raise and distribute campaign funds. In 1984, Rangel had contributed a relatively small amount of money from his personal campaign committee, and 74 percent of his contributions went to black candidates. His 1986 contributions went to a much larger and much more diverse group of Democratic candidates. Coelho and Sabo contributed to candidates across the party's ideological spectrum as well (Benenson 1986; Wilcox 1989).[5]

Rangel was also running from outside the official leadership system, whereas Coelho was running from within. At Coelho 's insistence, the Democratic leadership had made the DCCC chair part of the leadership structure, so he had a leg up the ladder in his Whip campaign.

Tip O'Neill's retirement as Speaker in 1987 allowed two other "insiders" to move up the leadership ladder. Jim Wright moved from Majority Leader to Speaker and Tom Foley moved from Majority Whip to Majority Leader. Although neither faced competition, both contributed money to their Democratic colleagues nonetheless. Wright gave through his leadership PAC and his campaign committee, and Foley gave through two campaign committees. Both favored incumbent candidates and contributed across a range of ideologies. In 1988, Representative William Gray campaigned for the Democratic Caucus chair from his position as chair of the House Budget Committee. The Budget Committee chair is an elected post with a two-year term limit, so it is part of the official leadership structure. Gray was no stranger to the money game; in 1984, when he ran for the Budget Committee chair, he had established a leadership PAC and contributed $27,000 to seventy-five of his colleagues. After announcing his candidacy for the caucus chair, Gray distributed just over $35,000 to his colleagues, using money left over from his committee chair race. He then formed a new leadership PAC and began to actively solicit money and support from lobbyists and other outside interests for his campaign for caucus chair—a new strategy in House leadership races. A letter mailed by Gray's leadership PAC to potential contributors said, "If you believe as I do that we should encourage new and creative leadership within the Democratic Party, then I need your active help. I need to raise funds to pursue this new challenge. I would appreciate your sending me a check for $500 to $1,000 so that I can begin to build the active support within the Democratic members of Congress to win this key leadership position" (Kenworthy 1988, A9). The implication, of course, was that Gray would use the money to make donations to other Democratic candidates in an attempt to build support for his caucus chair bid. Though Gray insisted that his fundraising efforts had nothing to do with the caucus race and were consistent with his previous work to build a strong majority, his rigorous campaign efforts enabled him to shower his colleagues with contributions and to secure the caucus chair. Representative Mary Rose Oakar, one of Gray's challengers in the caucus chair race, said of Gray's fundraising efforts, "I think it sets an unfortunate precedent. It's an internal race, and you ought to be able to do it without money and lobbyists. To my knowledge, they don't vote [for caucus chair]" (Kenworthy 1988, A9).

Clyde Wilcox (1989) suggests that member contributions can be viewed as a form of instrumental behavior, where members give for the purpose of achieving their individual goals.[6] He also suggests that contributions can be viewed as a form of noninstrumental behavior: Members may respond to solicitations from colleagues or may be pressured by the leadership to give. Majority party leaders tend to give a higher proportion of their contributions to incumbents because they want to maintain the party's majority status. And because they must build coalitions to move legislation through the chamber, majority party leaders also tend to contribute across a wider ideological spectrum. One month before the 1984 elections, Speaker Tip O'Neill's leadership PAC gave $500 each to forty-eight Democratic House candidates, including a few outside challengers. As Speaker, O'Neill was obviously not looking to move up the House's leadership ladder, but he was interested in helping Democratic candidates who needed help and in fostering support for the party's agenda. Democratic leaders who were attempting to climb the leadership ladder in the 1980s took a similar approach and directed their contributions to a broad range of their incumbent colleagues. This strategy served the collective goal of helping to maintain the party's majority status and the individual goal of building support in the chamber for one's personal goals.[7]

While Democratic members who aspired to leadership posts during the 1980s tended to contribute to a broad range of incumbents, Democrats who were interested in maximizing their influence on House committees tended to use different contribution strategies. Clyde Wilcox (1989, 397) found that during the 1984 election cycle, fifteen House Democrats gave significant portions of their overall contributions to members of specific committees, and that nine of these fifteen members were committee or subcommittee chairs. In many cases, these contributions went to committee colleagues who were in close races. But need was certainly not the decisive factor in every case. Representative Dan Rostenkowski, chair of the House Ways and Means Committee, gave to thirteen incumbents on his committee, ten of whom won reelection with more than 60 percent of the vote. Rostenkowski's leadership PAC, America's Leaders Fund, contributed a total of $38,000 in 1984 but then raised more than $700,000 for the 1986 election cycle. Representative Stephen Solarz gave close to $10,000 to eleven of his House Foreign Affairs Committee colleagues, most of whom sat on his subcommittee and held safe seats. Representative Henry Waxman contributed nearly $37,000 to his House Energy and Commerce Committee colleagues, almost all of which went to members of the subcommittee he chaired. Waxman's Energy and Commerce colleagues, Representatives Meldon Levine and Howard Berman, also contributed several thousand dollars to their committee colleagues, as did Representative Ed Markey, who contributed to half the members who sat on the Energy and Commerce subcommittee that he chaired. In 1986, Democratic Representatives Marvin Leath and Les Aspin contributed over $100,000 to their colleagues before their contest to chair the House Armed Services Committee. After Aspin was named chair, Representative Charles Bennett, who was third in seniority on the committee and had also challenged for the chair, attributed his defeat to the contributions made by his rivals.

"When I went around and talked to members, asking them to support me, they would tell me that they had been helped financially by Mr. Aspin or Mr. Leath," said Bennett. "One implied that it would all be rectified if I contributed to him too" (Wilcox 1990, 178). According to Wilcox (1989, 398), most of these members explained their contributions as part of their chair responsibilities. However, a committee staff person claimed that chairs contributed to members of their own panels to preempt challenges and to collect chits that they could call in at a later date.

House leaders, committee and subcommittee chairs, and leadership aspirants help themselves by helping their colleagues. During the 1980s, members could comply with the collective goal of majority status by giving to their colleagues and still pursue their personal goals by selecting which incumbents to support. The contribution strategies of committee and subcommittee chairs provide a good example of how this approach works. Members—particularly those outside the leadership system—may also choose to direct their contributions to incumbents who share a similar ideological view. In his examination of member-to-member giving in the 1984 election, Wilcox (1989) found that ideology played a major role in determining contributions. For example, Representative Henry Hyde (R-IL) contributed almost exclusively to anti-abortion candidates, and Representative Ed Markey (R-MA) received contributions primarily from members who were active in the nuclear freeze movement or in the fight against Contra aid, both issues in which Markey was heavily involved. During the 1986 election cycle, Representative Jack Kemp's (R-NY) leadership PAC, Campaign for Prosperity, targeted conservative Republicans who demonstrated "growth-oriented thinking" (Benenson 1986).

While some member-to-member contributions can be understood in terms of the donor's personal goals, others are less clear-cut. Wilcox (1989, 404) found that in 1984, over half of incumbent contributors gave to three or fewer candidates and gave less than $2,000. For these contributors, giving seemed to be less about the pursuit of personal goals and more about supporting candidates in need, geographic colleagues, or friends in the chamber. Small contributors directed about one-third of their money to candidates from their home states and also gave to open-seat candidates and incumbents in close races. Indeed, most of the contributions that House members gave in 1984 went to a short list of about seventy-five candidates who were in close races. Special-election candidates also received a high proportion of member contributions, as did freshman members.

By the late 1980s, contribution patterns showed that recycling campaign money had become "the practice of the many as opposed to an aggressive few looking to secure a present or future in the leadership" (Alston 1991, 2763). While giving by leadership PACs declined in 1989, contributions by personal campaign committees increased. The 1989 departures of Representatives Jim Wright and Tony Coelho, two of the House's most prominent fundraisers, took more than $905,000 out of the system. But when leadership PACs slacked off, rank-and-file members picked up by making large numbers of small contributions from their campaign committees. By 1989, more members had more money to give and got asked for it more often. Members found that by raising excess campaign money, they could offer help to their colleagues in need and simultaneously build goodwill and possible support for their own ambitions. Incumbents who ran in 1989–1990 had more than twice as much in leftover campaign funds as incumbents who ran in 1983–1984. Giving some of these funds away "has almost become a question of loyalty to your party," said Minnesota Republican Vin Weber (Alston 1991, 2763).

Party leaders routinely began to request that safe incumbents help their colleagues in close races. At the same time, members who needed help were less reluctant to ask their colleagues for money. Representative Henry Waxman (D-CA) claimed that such requests had become standard. "You see a colleague in trouble, we all want to help out," he said (Alston 1991, 2763). Waxman contributed more than $152,000 to Democratic candidates in the 1989–1990 election cycle, more than two-thirds of it through his leadership PAC. Indeed, members with excess cash on hand demonstrated a new willingness to spread the wealth. In 1982, at least thirty-two House Democrats had more than $100,000 in leftover campaign funds, amounting to a total of more than $6.3 million. But the party had no system in place to encourage the redistribution of surplus funds. The DCCC asked a number of financially secure Democrats to donate money for the good of the whole, but only two members—Gillis Long of Louisiana and Charles Schumer of New York—responded favorably. "One of the most depressing things," according to one Democratic Party fundraiser, "was the absence of selflessness out there" (Jacobson 1985–1986, 615–617). By the late 1980s, attitudes had changed. When Massachusetts Democrat John Olver ran for a House seat in a 1989 special election, forty-three Democratic incumbents contributed a total of $23,750 from their personal campaign committees, and five incumbents contributed a total of $19,500 from their leadership PACs. When Olver won his race, he returned the favor by contributing $500 to Arizona Democrat Ed Pastor, who also won a House seat in a 1989 special election (Alston 1991).

Not all House members wanted to give money to their colleagues. Some, like Representative David Drier (R-CA), were willing to help promising challengers and open-seat candidates but believed that incumbents were in a position to take care of themselves. Virginia Democrat Jim Olin took the position that his campaign contributions were from people who had given to him, and that his then giving money to other candidates would violate the spirit of his donors' contributions. Some members resolved this dilemma by establishing leadership PACs. When Representative Vin Weber was elected to a junior post in the Republican leadership, he felt obligated to do more for the party but did not want to upset the contributors who had given to his campaign. By establishing a leadership PAC, Weber was able to raise money from contributors who shared his desire to help Republican candidates. Likewise, when Representative Charles Rangel established a leadership PAC to support his bid for Majority Whip, he made certain that potential donors knew how their contributions would be used: "You bet your life, the contributors have to know that money is going to go to somebody they might not even know" (Benenson 1986; see also Alston 1991).

Partisan Politics Heats Up

The 1991 Whip race tapped into widespread discontent within the Democratic Caucus over the makeup of the House leadership. The Whip is the leadership's connection to the rank and file and had become a stepping-stone to the Speakership: Tom Foley, Tip O'Neill, and

Carl Albert had all served as Whip before becoming Speaker. Majority Whip William Gray's decision to step down from a leadership post he had fought so hard to win stunned many of his colleagues; sudden departures were rare for House leaders, as moving up the leadership ladder required long-term commitment. But Gray was less traditional and more in step with the highly ambitious, restless members who were increasingly populating the House.

Shortly after Gray announced that he would step down from the Majority Whip post, Michigan Representative David Bonior contributed $21,000 from his personal campaign committee to twenty-one House Democrats. Bonior, who was the Democrats' chief Deputy Whip, and Maryland representative Steny Hoyer, the Democratic Caucus chair, were the two main contenders in the race to succeed Gray. Hoyer gave $53,000 to Democratic candidates during the 1989–1990 election cycle, while Bonior, who feared a tough reelection race, collected just over $53,000 from his colleagues. If money were the sole criterion, Hoyer would have won the race, but he did not. Bonior, who had run against Gray for Whip in 1989 and lost on a 134–97 vote, had the early edge. After receiving vague indications that Gray might run for the Senate or leave Congress altogether, Bonior began to actively lobby his colleagues. Hoyer chose not to campaign for the position until Gray had made his intentions clear. When Gray announced his resignation, Bonior was counting votes while Hoyer's team was holding its first organizational meeting. In the end, Hoyer conceded that Bonior's early efforts had paid off (Alston 1991; Hook 1991).

Gray's departure came just two years after the resignations of Jim Wright and Tony Coelho; between 1986 and 1991, there was more turnover in House leadership than in the prior fifteen years. These changes made it increasingly difficult for Democrats to forge a common party identity, especially as various factions within the party—particularly women, African-Americans, and southern conservatives—began pushing for representation in the leadership ranks (Hook 1991).

The turn of the decade was tumultuous for the DCCC as well. Reports of lingering debt, fundraising difficulties, high staff turnover, internal strife, and a financial surge at the NRCC greatly concerned the Democratic Caucus. Former Speaker Jim Wright's acrimonious, drawn-out departure seriously impaired the committee's fundraising abilities; in August 1989, the committee's debt stood at $1.6 million. DCCC Chair Beryl Anthony argued that the focus on the committee's debt was misplaced. According to Anthony, the committee had invested heavily in candidates during the 1988 campaign and had also paid for new computer equipment that would enhance the party's direct-mail operation. Despite criticisms of how the DCCC was being managed, Democratic House leaders committed themselves to active fundraising on behalf of the committee and urged their colleagues with excess campaign cash to spread the wealth. The 1990 elections were crucial as they were expected to set the tone for the more critical postredistricting elections in 1992 (Kenworthy 1989). Anthony stepped down from the DCCC chair after the 1990 elections and was replaced by Representative Vic Fazio, a California Democrat with extensive fundraising experience.

House Republicans in 1990 were facing their own intraparty battle over who would lead the NRCC into the crucial 1992 elections. Representative Guy Vander Jagt, who was in his eighth term as NRCC chair, was facing a challenge from Representative Don Sundquist. Unlike DCCC chairs, who were appointed by the party's top House leader, NRCC chairs were elected by a vote of the Republican Conference. Until 1990, NRCC chair elections took place only if the position was vacated. Sundquist's challenge was widely interpreted as protest against Vander Jagt's decision not to support President Bush's budget. Minority Leader Bob Michel and Minority Whip Newt Gingrich both supported Vander Jagt, who won on a 98–66 vote. While the vote was not close, a sizable number of Republican members did vote against Vander Jagt, indicating widespread displeasure with the NRCC's leadership. As chair, Vander Jagt had decided to eliminate automatic contributions to incumbents. Republicans had not picked up seats in recent elections, and according to Vander Jagt, the general consensus was that it was time for change. In 1992, Representative Bill Paxon replaced Vander Jagt as chair of the NRCC. Following Paxon's election, the committee changed its bylaws and made its chair an appointee of the House Republican leader (Kolodny 1998, 187).

After taking over the DCCC chair in 1990, Vic Fazio began a campaign to convince his Democratic colleagues to contribute $5,000 apiece to the committee. The DCCC had been left with a $2.1-million debt following the 1990 elections and Fazio believed that securing contributions from House members would encourage outside contributors to donate. Eight months into the 1992 election cycle, the DCCC had collected $735,000 from over one hundred House Democrats, a sum that surpassed by far the previous record for member fundraising. Fazio's strategy was to constantly remind his colleagues of what was at stake in 1992. "I've put a good bit of time in putting the fear of God into people. I'm a pain," he said (Kenworthy 1991, A17). Fazio believed the practice should be institutionalized and hinted that members looking for choice committee assignments and other institutional perks could be judged on whether they contributed to the DCCC. "I personally would like to think it would become a factor. I don't think we can ask people to make this sacrifice and totally ignore it. It is one way of determining how much effort you are willing to make for the greater whole, the sort of thing that moves people up in committees and the leadership" (Alston 1991, 2763; see also Kenworthy 1991). Writing about the Democrats in 1982, Gary Jacobson claimed that there was an "absence of any tradition of mutual aid among Democratic candidates" (1985–1986, 623), which made it difficult for them to redistribute campaign money. By 1991, it seemed that the Democrats were beginning to establish such a tradition. Jacobson also noted that members might eventually find it possible—and even profitable—to win influence among their colleagues by helping to finance their campaigns. As the decade progressed, this strategy began to take shape.

Following the 1990 elections, the NRCC was about $5 million in debt. Despite the shortfall, the committee was reluctant to engage in nontraditional fundraising efforts. "We very seldom go to our members and we've never gone to them with a general appeal," said Tom Cole, executive director of the NRCC. "We believe that the party exists to elect candidates, not that members exist to fund the party. You pay a price for that sort of thing" (Kenworthy 1991, A17). Under the leadership of Bill Paxon, the NRCC would eventually decide to "pay the price" and ask members to contribute for the good of the whole.

In 1991, the Government Accountability Office (GAO) released a report revealing that 325 sitting and former members of the House had overdrawn on their House bank accounts but had not paid any penalty fines for issuing bad checks. The Republicans moved to exploit the issue, demanding an investigation by the House Ethics Committee. Democrats ignored the Republican outcry, claiming that no federal funds were involved and no crime had been committed. But the Republicans persisted and took to the House floor; with the C-SPAN cameras rolling, they demanded to know who was responsible for issuing the overdrafts. Speaker Foley faced mounting criticism; some members began demanding his resignation. As the attacks grew bitterly partisan, Minority Leader Bob Michel decided it was time for him to leave the House. Michel had always been inclined to work out differences with the other side and felt that the House no longer supported moderate politicians. When Michel left at the end of the 103rd Congress (December 1992), he was joined by many of his colleagues. The 1992 elections produced the largest turnover in forty years: 44 House members were defeated in the primaries or the general election, and over 100 new members were elected; 77 members who had been named in the House bank scandal had been defeated or had retired. The Republicans gained 9 seats, but the Democrats retained control with a 258–176 margin (Remini 2006, 479–480).

Conclusion

During the 1980s and early 1990s, the House moved firmly away from committee and subcommittee government toward conditional party government. House leaders were given expanded powers, and they were increasingly willing to use the institutional tools at their disposal. The Democrats grew more cohesive during the 1980s, while the Republicans gradually united over their inability to participate in the legislative process. Fiercely partisan leaders like Jim Wright and Newt Gingrich, who were polarizing forces in the chamber, drove the parties even further apart. The 1994 Republican revolution would do little to curb these trends.

The political environment that had advanced the growth of member-to-member giving in the 1970s changed during the 1980s, but in ways that continued to encourage the redistribution of money. Although the 1970s reforms had strengthened party leaders, they did not take full advantage of their new powers until the 1980s. The political environment during the 1980s encouraged strong leadership, and as a result, leadership races became more competitive. During the 1980s, member-to-member giving became a common strategy in leadership races. At the same time, more rank-and-file members—encouraged by their party leaders—gave to colleagues in need for the good of the whole. The patterns of member-to-member giving witnessed during the 1970s and 1980s took an entirely new shape during the 1990s and dramatically changed the way House members pursued power and the parties pursued majority control.

Notes

1. The following discussion on the 1980 elections is drawn from David Adamany (1984, 75–87).

2. The law sets restrictions on how much money the parties can spend, per candidate, in coordinated expenditures.

3. Though Wilcox's 1989 study focuses on the 1984 election cycle, he also examined data from the 1980, 1982, and 1986 election cycles to isolate trends and consider changes in the political environment. The data reported from the 1984 cycle in this study are broadly representative of the 1980–1986 period.

4. A number of other scholars have written about leadership PACs, but mainly within the context of larger studies on campaign finance or congressional politics. For example, see Herrnson (1998), Rohde (1991), Brown and Peabody (1992), Sorauf (1984, 1992), Sabato (1984), Corrado (1992), and Alexander (1984).

5. See chapter 1 for a more detailed discussion of this race. There were initially six candidates for the position of Majority Whip: Coelho, Rangel, Sabo, Mineta, Alexander, and Hefner. Coelho and Rangel were considered the top contenders.

6. As explained in chapter 2, Wilcox explores instrumental giving in terms of members' reelection, policy, and power goals. This study does not assign specific goals to members and instead assumes that members' goals reflect their personal ambitions. As the structure of opportunity before members changes, members adjust their goals accordingly.

7. Minority leaders tend to direct more of their contributions to promising challengers because gaining majority status requires them to expand the party's numbers in the House. This strategy will be discussed in greater detail in chapter 5.

5

A Republican Revolution in
Politics and Money

The Gingrich Era

Following the 1992 elections, newly installed NRCC Chair Bill Paxon began an aggressive effort to restructure the committee's fundraising operations. As part of this plan, he directed incumbent members to contribute money out of their own campaign funds to help Republican challengers who were running in 1994. Paxon and his close ally Newt Gingrich reasoned "that the collective goal of majority status was more valuable to these incumbents than the few extra thousand dollars" they were asked to contribute (Kolodny and Dwyre 1998, 289). Gingrich organized teams that determined each member's fundraising capacity, then established a formula for "voluntary contributions" by each incumbent. Unless members were in financial trouble themselves, they were expected to contribute. The strategy was hugely successful. Tony Blankley, Gingrich's press secretary, claimed that "many had never raised money before, except for their own campaigns. One member said, 'I don't know how to do that.' Newt said, 'I'll teach you.' And they sent him over to the RNC. The member came back a while later and excitedly said, 'I just raised $50,000 over at the RNC!' As more members saw we had a chance of winning [the majority] more of them pitched in on the fundraising effort" (Gimpel 1996, 10–11).

Indeed, over one hundred House Republicans contributed a total of $1 million to the NRCC during the 1994 election cycle. This was a major increase from 1992, when only twelve members had agreed to help the NRCC and had raised less than $50,000 in total. The NRCC also successfully convinced members to raise money for the committee's Victory Accounts, which benefited Republican candidates in House members' home states.

In addition to helping the NRCC meet its collective fundraising goals, House Republicans engaged in more personal redistribution efforts in 1994. Republican incumbents donated $0.4 million to each other and $2 million to outside challengers and open-seat candidates. This sum was $1.7 million more than House Republicans had redistributed in 1992 (Bedlington and Malbin 2003).[1] Republicans also initiated a "buddy system" and "adopt a candidate" programs that matched non-incumbent candidates with Republican House leaders and other influential members to raise campaign money (Herrnson 1996). Republican incumbents also campaigned aggressively for challengers and open-seat candidates. This was the first time many of these members had campaigned for a candidate other than themselves. Representative Bob Inglis (R-SC) explained how he "went into [Democratic incumbent] John Spratt's [neighboring] district and toured around with our candidate. This violated a long-standing rule of comity in South Carolina politics but this rule needed to be broken so we broke it" (Gimpel 1996, 11).

Republican efforts to build a sustainable fundraising operation were long in the making. A decade or so before the 1994 Republican revolution, Newt Gingrich had begun to actively recruit and raise money for Republicans under the auspices of GOPAC, his political action committee. GOPAC invested a great deal of time and money in helping Republicans run for local and state office. Gingrich believed that helping these candidates early in their careers would pay off several years down the road, when they could run for federal office as experienced politicians. In addition to raising money and training candidates, GOPAC distributed copies of House Republican floor speeches, along with audiotapes that were designed to "teach a generation of activists how to think and talk about political strategy" (Pitney 1996, 20). During the 1980s, the NRCC played a secondary role to GOPAC in a number of House races.

But in 1994, the Republicans' electoral strategy successfully combined the NRCC's fundraising efforts with GOPAC's candidate support services, and Gingrich's long-term fundraising and candidate investment goals finally paid off.

The 1994 elections "signaled the coming of a Republican revolution both in terms of message and money" (Gimpel 1996, 11). The Republicans' efforts to win a majority in the House were the most ambitious and comprehensive ever undertaken (Kolodny and Dwyre 1998, 289). Using an expansion strategy, House Republicans invested heavily in challengers and open-seat candidates. House Democrats, by contrast, assumed a maintenance strategy and devoted more campaign money and resources to defending incumbents. Democratic House leaders made campaign appearances and helped nonincumbent candidates raise money, but there were no organized efforts in 1994 to help party candidates more broadly. Many rank-and-file members did not believe their majority was at risk and chose not to give to the DCCC or to other candidates. Still, some House Democrats did contribute, giving $0.6 million to the DCCC, slightly more than the $0.5 million they had contributed to the committee in 1992. They also contributed $2.9 million directly to Democratic House candidates, $1.8 million of which went to House incumbents. This marked a $1-million increase over what Democrats had redistributed in 1992 (Bedlington and Malbin 2003). However, Democratic member-to-candidate redistribution was limited. Leadership PACs affiliated with Majority Leader Richard Gephardt (D-MO), Oversight Committee Chair Charlie Rose (D-NC), and DCCC Chair Vic Fazio (D-CA) contributed more than $1.6 million of the $2.9 million that Democrats redistributed in 1994 (Herrnson 1996).

During the 1990s, the amount of money that House members gave to each other, and especially to the CCCs, skyrocketed. After taking majority control in 1995, House Republicans centralized control in the leadership and significantly enhanced the Speaker's powers. They held a twelve-seat margin over the Democrats, and competition between the parties was fierce. The Republicans had to stay unified to pass their policy agenda, so the leaders enforced strict party discipline. The political environment during the 1990s generally inhibited Republican members from acting as independent operators because their ability to pursue their own ambitions was so closely tied to their party's ability to maintain the House majority. Even so, self-oriented members typically need incentives to promote the party's collective goals. Party leaders discovered that by linking members' ability to advance in the chamber to their willingness to help the party pursue its collective goals, they could channel members' entrepreneurial tendencies in ways that would benefit the party. And because the Republican House leaders generally controlled the means by which their members advanced, they emphasized party loyalty in the form of fundraising. In this system, the party benefits as members pursue their own ambitions. By 1996, the Democrats were following the Republicans' example. They had formalized their party-based fundraising programs and had also begun to link Democratic members' ability to advance in the chamber to their willingness to raise money for the party.

The Contract with America

Although the Republicans' remarkable fundraising efforts in 1994 were central to their electoral success, they were widely overlooked. In the aftermath of the 1994 elections, most of the focus was on a public campaign agenda known as the Contract with America. On September 27, 1994, approximately three hundred Republican incumbents and challengers gathered on the steps of the U.S. Capitol and endorsed the Contract with America, a ten-point platform that became the campaign centerpiece for many of the party's House candidates. The Contract represented a major turning point for the CCCs. In the two decades before the 1994 elections, the NRCC had focused on providing highly sophisticated campaign services to Republican House candidates. But in 1994, the committee realized that the only form of campaign assistance that clearly influenced electoral success was money. The committee also realized that its long-standing practice of providing incumbents with campaign services would not move the party into the majority. Fundraising thus became the NRCC's primary focus, and the committee directed its money to competitive challengers and open-seat candidates. The Contract with America, a campaign platform that would bring media attention—and hopefully campaign money—to the party and its candidates, was a part of the committee's fundraising plan. The NRCC's articulation of a national legislative agenda marked a departure from the more traditional view that House elections are local and best run race by race (Kolodny 1998, 197–198). The strategy also marked the first time a party's legislative agenda was used as a campaign tool to secure majority control of the House.

The Contract was developed primarily by Newt Gingrich, Bill Paxon, and Republican National Committee Chair Haley Barbour. Gingrich believed that a Republican House majority could enact a historic program, akin to President Franklin Delano Roosevelt's New Deal agenda, and he pushed for the creation of legislative proposals that Republican candidates could promote. In 1993 and 1994, the Republican House leadership surveyed incumbents and challengers about what issues and common principles they thought were most important. Once the results had been tabulated, incumbents and challengers were surveyed about which items should be included in the Contract. When a final list was determined, working groups of members and staff drafted legislative proposals using information from focus group studies that the NRCC and RNC had conducted to determine the public's reaction to certain phrases and concepts (see Table 5.1). Thus welfare reform was named the "Personal Responsibility Act," and a proposal to cut the capital gains tax and weaken environmental regulations was named the "Job Creation and Wage Enhancement Act." All House Republicans were invited to join the working groups and participate in drafting the Contract, but younger, activist members were more involved in the process than were senior members (Kolodny and Dwyre 1998, 280; Sinclair 1999, 429–431).

Republican candidates used the Contract in accordance with their own electoral needs. Most senior House Republicans made little use of the Contract, or they ignored it altogether. Robin Kolodny (1998, 204) argues that many of these members believed that the Republicans were unlikely to win a House majority in 1994, so they saw no need to promote the Contract. Neither did they believe that endorsement of the Contract would promote their reelection. Because nonincumbent candidates did not have legislative or service records to run on, they were

Table 5.1 Elements in the Republican Contract with America

Title	Bill	Focus of Legislation
Congressional Accountability Act	H.R. 1	Application of antidiscrimination laws to Congress
Line-Item Veto Act	H.R. 2	Enhancement of the president's recision authority
Taking Back Our Streets Act	H.R. 3	Crime control
Personal Responsibility Act	H.R. 4	Welfare reform
Unfunded Mandate Reform Act	H.R. 5	Reduction of the burden of federal mandates on states
American Dream Restoration Act	H.R. 6	Tax code reform
National Security Restoration Act	H.R. 7	Defense/military procurement
Senior Citizens' Equity Act	H.R. 8	Social Security reform
Job Creation/Wage Enhancement Act	H.R. 9	Deregulation and tax code reform
Common Sense Legal Reforms Act	H.R. 10	Product-liability and tort reform
Family Reinforcement Act	H.R. 11	Child support and adoption
Balanced Budget Amendment	H.J. Res 1	Balanced budget
Citizen Legislature Act	H.J. Res 2	Term limits, 12 years for House members
Citizen Legislature Act	H.J. Res 3	Term limits, 6 years for House members

Source: James G. Gimpel. 1996. *Fulfilling the Contract: The First 100 Days.* Boston: Allyn & Bacon.

much more receptive to using the Contract as a source of campaign issue themes. While the Contract espoused a national legislative agenda, most of the candidates emphasized (and localized) just a few specific items that resonated in their districts. The media paid little attention to the Contract, but many of the Republicans newly elected to the House in 1994 credited the Contract with helping them win (Kolodny 1998, 204–205).

The 1994 Republican Revolution

All Republican incumbents were reelected in 1994 and 34 Democratic incumbents were defeated. Republicans won 39 of the 52 open seats, including 21 of the 31 open seats that Democrats had previously held. Of the 73 newly elected House Republicans, 33 were direct beneficiaries of GOPAC efforts; most others were indirectly influenced by GOPAC's activities. Almost all of the incoming freshmen had received contributions or other types of campaign assistance from all the incumbent Republicans in House leadership races, as well as from many rank-and-file members (Koopman 1996, 51–52). Speaker Tom Foley became the first sitting Speaker to be defeated in an election since 1862. Representative Dan Rostenkowski, chair of the Ways and Means Committee, and Representative Jack Brooks, chair of the Judiciary Committee, were also defeated. The 104th Congress, which convened in January 1995, comprised 230 Republicans, 204 Democrats, and 1 Independent. For the first time in forty years, Republicans had gained majority control of the House, and Newt Gingrich was hailed as "the wizard who had engineered this extraordinary victory." Republicans had also captured control of the Senate, 53 to 47 (Remini 2006, 482).

Almost all Republican House members, with the exception of Gingrich and his closest allies, were stunned by the election results (Kolodny 1996, 319). A senior Republican, who expressed the reaction of most of his colleagues, said, "I didn't believe it on election night. I had no remote belief or hope that we would make gains like that. On election night, when I saw 25 I was surprised; then 30; then 35 and my heart skipped a beat; then we were at 40, the magic number, I rubbed my eyes and I told people that I wouldn't believe it until I got up the next morning and read it in black and white." Even optimistic freshmen were shocked. "I never dreamed I would serve in the majority," said one newly elected Republican. "I don't care what those leaders say, they didn't know we were going to win either. If they had, they would have known what to teach us at orientation" (Gimpel 1996, 15). Despite the almost universal proclamations of disbelief, preelection evidence suggested that the Democratic majority was unraveling. For example, the number of Democrats defecting on House rules had increased substantially in 1993. Democratic members had denied their leaders the votes needed to continue funding the Select Committee on Narcotics and the Select Committee on Hunger, Aging, and Children, Youth and Families. Conservative Democrats had defeated a number of special rules to consider legislation in the 103rd Congress, and members had also filed discharge petitions to bypass the Rules Committee's attempts to block certain bills. House Democrats were more frequently choosing to pursue their own agendas rather than the party leadership's agenda. As Democratic unity splintered, the leadership's ability to exercise procedural control and enforce party discipline had declined (Schickler and Rich 1997, 1371–1372).

While the Republicans' superior fundraising, the Contract with America, and a frayed Democratic majority were major factors in the 1994 elections, several other explanations help clarify why the Democrats suffered such a dramatic defeat. In 1994, Democratic president Bill Clinton's approval ratings were dismal. While Clinton's record of passing legislation was impressive, questions about his character and honesty were reinforced by the Whitewater investigation and the resignations of several key administration appointees. The president's unpopularity did not bode well for congressional Democrats, who were already dealing with a hostile electorate. Surveys by the Gallup organization in early 1994 showed that only 18 percent of respondents expressed "a great deal" of confidence in Congress. Republicans capitalized on the general disgust voters felt toward Washington by emphasizing their message of change. Republicans also aggressively pursued the forty-five seats that Democrats had won with less than 55 percent of the vote in the 1992 elections. Twenty-seven Democrats retired in 1994, leaving open a number of seats in districts that had leaned Republican in the 1988 and 1992 presidential elections. For the first time in decades, Democrats had also left more seats uncontested than the Republicans. As Figures 5.1 and 5.2 indicate, Democratic incumbents outspent Republican incumbents, but Republican challengers outspent Democratic challengers. Republicans were much more successful in targeting their money to competitive races. They were also successful in recruiting quality candidates to run in 1994. Almost half of the Republican challengers had prior political experience, and many came from business-oriented backgrounds—an advantage in a year when outsiders were favored (Gimpel 1996, 2–11). And the political

Figure 5.1 Mean Incumbent Spending, 1986–1996

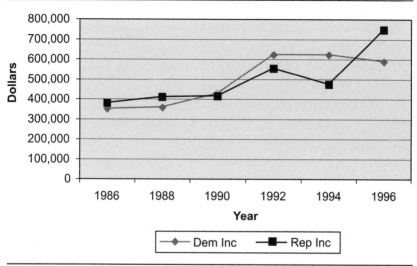

Source: Norman J. Ornstein, Thomas E. Mann, and Michael J. Malbin. 1999–2000. *Vital Statistics on Congress.* Washington, DC: American Enterprise Institute Press.

Figure 5.2 Mean Challenger Spending, 1986–1996

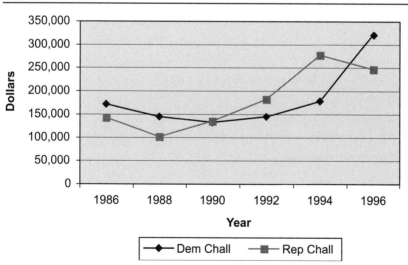

Source: Norman J. Ornstein, Thomas E. Mann, and Michael J. Malbin. 1999–2000. *Vital Statistics on Congress.* Washington, DC: American Enterprise Institute Press.

environment in 1994 allowed an organized and fully mobilized opposition to exploit Democratic weaknesses and push for change.

The new Republican majority was extraordinarily homogeneous. The seventy-three newly elected members were "true believers," deeply committed to balancing the budget and reducing the size and scope of government. John Shadegg, a newly elected member from Arizona, said, "The freshmen aren't interested in coming here to be reasonable and to settle for what they can get. They don't want to go along to get along." Matt Salmon, another freshman member from Arizona, said, "This is an ideological class . . . that really believes we were sent here to make a difference" (Aldrich and Rohde 1997–1998, 562). Most new members were aggressively anti-politics-as-usual; they were not interested in learning about House norms. Sophomore members were ideologically similar to the freshmen, and, together, they made up over half of the Republican Conference membership. Many of the party's senior conservatives were thrilled by the chance to finally move conservative policy. And most Republican moderates strongly supported acting on the Contract because they believed the party had to deliver on its campaign promises in order to maintain the majority (Aldrich and Rohde 1997–1998, 562; Sinclair 1999, 434).

On January 4, 1995, Newt Gingrich was chosen as Speaker of the House. Cheering Republicans filled the House gallery, and visitors packed the Capitol Building to witness the momentous event. Outgoing Democratic Speaker Richard Gephardt handed the gavel to Gingrich and said, "With resignation but with resolve, I hereby end 40 years of Democratic rule of the House. You are now my Speaker. Let the great debate begin" (Remini 2006, 483). Dick Armey (R-TX) was elected Majority Leader, and another Texan, Tom DeLay, was elected Majority Whip. DeLay was challenged by Bob Walker (R-PA) and Bill McCollum (R-FL), but he won the Majority Whip post with 119 votes to Walker's 80 and McCollum's 28, even though Walker and McCollum were more senior than DeLay. All three Majority Whip candidates had contributed money to Republican candidates and the NRCC during the 1994 campaign. DeLay, a Gingrich ally, had firmly established himself as an aggressive conservative with a large network of conservative contacts. He also proved himself to be a prolific fundraiser, who worked hard to connect his wealthy business contacts with the NRCC. While the top three leadership posts went to southern conservatives, the position of Republican Conference chair went to John Boehner, a conservative two-term member from Ohio. Susan Molinari (R-NY), a moderate and the wife of NRCC Chair Bill Paxon, won the position of conference vice chair. The Republican leadership team reflected Gingrich's preference for active, energetic members (Gimpel 1996, 33).

The New Republican Majority and Institutional Reform

Comprehensive institutional change is most likely to occur when a party gains majority status after having spent an extended period of time in the minority (Schickler 2001). Like the progressive wing of the Democratic Party in the 1970s, conservative Republicans believed they could improve their chances of moving their policy agenda forward by changing the rules and centralizing power in the leadership. Eager to take charge, the Republicans opened the 104th Congress with a marathon fourteen-and-a-half-hour session. Newt Gingrich was anxious to change the House rules and brought a broad set of institutional reforms to the House floor immediately. Republicans voted to adopt the changes, and on January 5, 1995, the House began to operate under a new set of rules. Just as the 1970s reforms had emboldened liberal House Democrats, the 1995 reforms encouraged conservative Republicans to actively pursue their agenda.

As fundraising has become more central to securing majority control, congressional reform has taken on a more partisan tone and has become more reflective of members' campaign finance concerns (Adler 2002). Following their success in the 1994 elections, Republican leaders believed that if the Republicans were to maintain majority control, the party and its members needed to keep up their vigorous fundraising efforts. Newt Gingrich lauded GOPAC and the NRCC for their fundraising and sought out ways to institutionalize party-based fundraising.

The 1995 institutional reforms were an essential part of this strategy because, as discussed later, they effectively advanced the collective fundraising goals that had propelled the party to victory in 1994.

Because some of the House reforms simultaneously promoted party goals and rewarded individual members, they provided Republican House leaders with a way to manage the tensions that surface when individually oriented members are expected to advance party goals. Of particular importance were the six-year term limit placed on committee and subcommittee chairs and the enhanced power the leadership was given in the chair selection and committee appointment process. Committee chair selection was at Gingrich's discretion, and his main goal was to select chairs who shared his basic philosophy. Because chairs were given the power to appoint their subcommittee chairs and hire committee staff, Gingrich was careful to appoint loyalists. Bill Archer (R-TX), who was named chair of Ways and Means, said that Gingrich understood and trusted that he was "going to be part of the leadership, and not a maverick" (Wolf 1995). For the most part, seniority ruled. However, Gingrich bypassed seniority in three crucial instances. In naming Robert Livingston (R-LA) chair of the Appropriations Committee, Gingrich passed over four more senior committee members. Representative John Myers (R-IN), the highest-ranking Republican on the committee, was "not considered the right person to initiate the huge budget cuts favored by Republicans" (Aldrich and Rohde 1997–1998, 549). Indeed, all Republicans who were appointed to the Appropriations Committee were required to sign a letter agreeing to cut the budget in accordance with Gingrich's wishes. Gingrich also ignored seniority in appointing Thomas Bliley (R-VA) chair of the Energy and Commerce Committee, and Henry Hyde (R-IL) chair of the Judiciary Committee (Foerstel 1994; Salant 1994). In both of these cases, the ranking member was Carlos Moorhead (R-CA), who didn't "project the right image," according to a committee staff person. "He's not an activist and we need an activist person" (Aldrich and Rohde 1997–1998, 550). Aside from John Kasich, who was named chair of the Budget Committee, and Bob Walker, who was named chair of the Technology and Competitiveness Committee, Representatives Livingston, Bliley, and Hyde were the only newly appointed chairs to have contributed money to other candidates during the 1994 election cycle. Of the five, Livingston was by far the biggest contributor, giving $140,900. All except four of the newly appointed chairs had contributed to the NRCC during the 1994 cycle. Gerald Solomon of New York, who was named chair of the powerful Rules Committee, had contributed $65,000—substantially more than the other chairs.

A staff person for Majority Leader Dick Armey explained that the decision to appoint party loyalists was strategic, and it "ended up sending a very clear signal that you don't just rely on seniority; you've got to prove yourself as someone willing to pursue . . . our agenda" (Owens 1997, 250). These appointments were the most significant departures from seniority since the Democrats had deposed three committee chairs in 1974. While freshman "insurgents" had been behind the 1974 ouster, Republican leaders were clearly responsible for the 1994 decisions (Aldrich and Rohde 1997–1998, 550).

When some members opposed the new rule that allowed committee chairs to appoint subcommittee chairs and hire committee staff, Gingrich argued that committee chairs needed to have full control over their panels. However, committee chairs were required to consult with Gingrich before they named their subcommittee chairs—an "understanding" that sometimes placed the chairs in an awkward position. Representative William Clinger (R-PA), chair of the Government Reform and Oversight Committee, appointed two freshman members to subcommittee chairs, at the behest of Gingrich. Following the Speaker's directives required Clinger to pass over two considerably more senior committee members (Aldrich and Rohde 1997–1998, 552). Committee hearing schedules were also expected to reflect the leadership's legislative priorities. Gingrich and Armey monitored the committees' activities, and their staff members met twice weekly with committee staff to ensure that the committees would comply with the leadership's orders. When one committee chair told Gingrich that he would not be able to meet a leadership-imposed hearing deadline, Gingrich warned him, "If you can't do it, I will find someone who will." The strict central control exercised by party leaders prompted Judiciary chair Henry Hyde to complain, "I'm really a sub-chairman. . . . I am a transmission belt for the leadership" (Owens 1997, 254).

The new rules prohibited members from serving as chair or ranking member on more than one committee or subcommittee and from serving on more than two full committees and four subcommittees. The Speaker's power to make multiple referrals was eliminated, but the power to make sequential and split referrals was retained. Sequential referrals send a bill to more than one committee sequentially, in an order determined by the Speaker. Split referrals send parts of a whole bill to the committees that have jurisdiction over the issues in the bill's separate parts. Gingrich was also granted the power to set committee reporting deadlines, a power that prevented committee chairs from sitting on bills they opposed. In addition, proxy voting in committee was eliminated; Representative Bob Walker (R-PA) claimed that removing the committee chair's ability to vote for absent same-party committee members would "cut down on the number of powerful little fiefdoms" because it would prevent chairs from controlling committee vote outcomes (Aldrich and Rohde 1997–1998, 551). Removing committee chairs' power to control vote outcomes was one way to prevent the fragmentation of authority.

Committee assignments were approved by a process that weighted the votes of Gingrich and Armey more heavily than the votes of other Steering Committee members. Gingrich cast five of the committee's thirty votes, and Armey cast two. Many freshmen who were known to support the leadership's agenda were placed on power committees (Salant 1994; Gimpel 1996): Three freshmen were placed on the Steering and Policy Committee, seven on Appropriations, eight on Commerce, and three on Ways and Means. Gingrich also appointed one freshman member and two sophomores to the Rules Committee. By placing loyal newcomers on these committees, Gingrich could ensure that he would have support in important places. Freshman members responded to this treatment by following Gingrich's lead on policy. A DCCC analysis of floor voting during the first hundred days of the 104th Congress found that average support for the party leadership's position among Republican freshmen was 97 percent. As freshman member Sam Brownback (R-KS) put it, "Basically [Gingrich] is using us to institute the revolution" (Aldrich and Rohde 1997–1998, 563–564). At the same time, Gingrich made certain that the freshmen he had handpicked would receive assistance in the form of campaign contributions from the well-funded groups that lobby these committees. By term-limiting the chairs, Gingrich also ensured that the freshmen he placed on key committees would have the opportunity to move up the committee ladder at a reasonably quick pace. And because serving on a power committee makes the task of raising money for the party and its candidates easier, Gingrich's loyalists enjoyed a further career boost.[2] Term limits also guaranteed that a constant stream of ambitious members would compete for chairs by demonstrating their party loyalty. Members who wanted to move up the House's power ladder understood that supporting the leadership's agenda and raising money for the party were key to this move.

Cutbacks in the committee system also made it easier for the Republican Party and its candidates to raise money. By eliminating three standing committees—District of Columbia, Merchant Marine and Fisheries, and Post Office and Civil Service—and thirty-one subcommittees, the Republicans cut a total of 484 committee and subcommittee seats. In doing so, they eliminated several forums that had served traditionally Democratic interests, and they narrowed the number of "contribution outlets" for outside donors.[3] According to Representative Bob Walker (R-PA), "The proliferation of committees and subcommittees has been a detriment to the legislative process" (Aldrich and Rohde 1997–1998, 551).

Republicans who favored reducing the number of committees and subcommittees wanted to prevent the committees from becoming independent power centers. By reducing committee staff by one-third and effectively eliminating many of the House caucuses by defunding them, the reforms also narrowed the number of information sources available to members. As a result, congressional committees relied more heavily on lobbyists when drafting legislation (Oppenheimer 1997, 381). The 1995 institutional reforms affected the redistribution of money in the House both directly and indirectly. Moreover, Republican leaders—particularly Newt Gingrich—pursued leadership strategies that emphasized collective party goals, including fundraising for the party and its candidates.

New Majority Leadership Strategies

Republicans pledged to bring all Contract items to a vote within the first hundred days of the 104th Congress. Gingrich, like Democratic leaders in the postreform era, believed that leading the House required a "strategy of inclusion." By involving Republican House members in the policy process, Gingrich hoped that they would support the leadership's goals (Sinclair 1999, 429). Gingrich established five task forces at the beginning of the 104th Congress to work on parts of the Contract, as well as several others to address hot-button issues like immigration. By March, the number of task forces had expanded to fifteen. Tony Blankley, Gingrich's spokesperson, said that Gingrich saw task forces "as a device for finessing some institutional obstacles to decision-making" (Aldrich and Rohde 1997–1998, 552). Task forces also provided Gingrich with a way to involve the party's junior members in developing legislation, working out compromises, and formulating strategy. That Gingrich sometimes used task forces to press committees to pass legislation conforming to the leadership's positions did not sit well with some committee staff members. One staff member said:

> The committees ought to be our task forces. The committee system in the House of Representatives was established . . . to develop expertise; to have members, based on their committee assignments, focus on specific issues; to utilize that area of expertise and for the people who are on other committees to rely on those committee members, because they've heard the testimony, they've been at the hearing, they've read the bills, they've participated in the mark up. And to sort of ignore all of that is to undermine the committee system, which is really the undermining of the legislative process. (Owens 1997, 262)

Gingrich worked hard to keep members in the policy and political loop. The Republican Conference met weekly, as did the extended party leadership. He met regularly with various party subgroups, including the freshman class, sophomore members, state delegations, and numerous single-issue and ideological groups. Part of Gingrich's strategy of inclusion was to make sure that all Republican members were frequently consulted and kept informed. He wanted all members to share in the action and feel that they were part of a team (Sinclair 1999, 430).

Gingrich built up the leadership's press operation and emphasized publicizing the party's message. He granted countless interviews, held daily press briefings, and insisted that each committee hire a press secretary. The leadership's communication team developed daily messages that members highlighted in one-minute floor speeches. Members were also advised about how to discuss various issues—which words and phrases to emphasize, and which messages to promote. Tremendous effort went into shaping the public's perception of the Republicans' policy agenda (Maraniss and Weisskopf 1996).

Another leadership strategy involved the Rules Committee. Because the majority party dominates the Rules Committee, it determines how legislation is brought to the floor. The majority can use the rules to structure floor debate and prevent certain amendments from being offered. Essentially, controlling the rules allows a cohesive majority party to pass the bills it wants to pass. When the Republicans were in the minority, they had complained bitterly about the Democrats' tendency to bring legislation to the floor under closed rules, which prevented the Republicans from offering amendments and restricted their ability to participate in the policy process. During the 1994 campaign, Republicans pledged that they would open up the rules process if they won control of the House. After the elections, they reiterated this pledge and promised to bring all Contract items to the floor under open rules. Gerald Solomon (R-NY), the chair designate of the Rules Committee, proclaimed, "The liberal Democrat leadership was so liberal and far to the left they couldn't afford to let bills come to the floor under open rules because their own conservative Democrats would have sided with the Republicans. . . . We don't have that situation. We are not factionalized in our party." Solomon declared that he would grant open rules (allowing all germane amendments) on 75 percent of the bills that the Rules Committee would consider in 1995 (Aldrich and Rohde 1997–1998, 555).

Before long, it became clear that promising to bring all Contract items up for a floor vote within the first hundred days of the session and promising to consider all Contract items under open rules were at odds. When the first Contract bill came to the floor under an open rule, 168 amendments were offered. The House considered the bill for five days, then set it aside. Majority Whip Tom DeLay accused the Democrats of deliberately holding the bill up, and Gerald Solomon threatened to impose restrictive rules if the Democrats did not cooperate. Claiming that they had promised a more open debate (as opposed to a totally open debate), the Republican leadership, working with the Rules Committee, eventually began to bring legislation to the floor under more restrictive rules. Despite their campaign promises, the Republicans proved willing to use the Rules Committee to control the floor debate and advance their legislative agenda (Aldrich and Rohde 1997–1998, 555).

Newt Gingrich and his leadership team were remarkably influential in shaping and managing legislation in the 104th Congress. The Republican members were willing to grant their leaders extraordinary power because they believed that doing so would ensure the passage of comprehensive policy change and help the party maintain its majority control. Party leaders controlled the agenda, determined legislative content, and kept committee chairs in line. If a chair could not get a bill out of committee, the leadership bypassed the committee. And if a committee reported out legislation that was unacceptable to the majority, the leadership revised the bill's language before sending it to the floor. Republican leaders also used the appropriations process to move members' policy objectives forward. The House Appropriations Committee provides funding for bills passed by the chamber's authorizing committees. For example, the House Armed Services Committee passes a bill that authorizes a certain level of funding for the Department of Defense, and the House Appropriations Committee's Subcommittee on Defense then considers the Armed Services Committee's authorizing bill and passes a bill to fund the Department of Defense. Sometimes the authorizers and the appropriators agree on funding levels, but often they disagree. Appropriations bills are not supposed to contain policy directives, but because the authorizing process tends to be much more cumbersome than the appropriating process, appropriators regularly insert

policy directives in their bills' report language. In 1995, if Republican
leaders did not get what they wanted in the authorizing bills, they asked
the appropriators to insert language in the must-pass appropriations
bills. Some senior Republican appropriators disapproved of this tactic
but succumbed to leadership pressure (Sinclair 1999, 435–436). They
had, after all, signed a "contract" at the beginning of the 104th Congress
agreeing to support the leadership's funding goals.

Republicans relied on their Whip system to mobilize votes on important party measures. Majority Whip Tom DeLay's team consisted of
a Chief Deputy Whip, thirteen Deputy Whips, and thirty-nine Assistant
Whips. Before a bill was scheduled for floor action, the Whips con-
tacted every Republican Conference member to determine if the party
had a majority. If a majority had not been secured, a vote was not
scheduled until the Whips could persuade enough members to vote
with the leadership to make a majority. During the 104th Congress, the
Whips' job was made easier by the presence of an ideologically homogeneous majority and by the pressure members felt to deliver on the
Contract. Republicans remained extremely unified on the Contract; on
average, fewer than five members defected from the party on each Contract item vote. During 1995, Republicans on average supported their
party 91 percent of the time on all party-line votes[4] (Sinclair 1997, 439).
A number of factors contributed to Republican unity, including pent-
up frustration at serving in the minority and growing support for Gingrich's hard-line partisan approach. Republicans developed a "strong
team spirit" and a willingness to trust in and defer to the leaders who
had gotten them into the majority.

In addition to encouraging a strong team spirit on policy matters,
Republican House leaders promoted electoral team spirit. Republican
House members were encouraged to establish leadership PACs so they
could raise money to help party candidates facing competitive races.
One Republican member's chief of staff said that his boss had established a leadership PAC after he was named a committee chair. "One of
the things the House leadership asked him to do was to establish a leadership PAC to help support other Republican candidates. The leadership suggested to a variety of members—many members—that they

establish leadership PACs as a way of raising additional funds to help Republicans." The director of another Republican member's leadership PAC said there was "pressure from the leadership" on all members to make contributions. He attributed this pressure to the rising cost of campaigning, and to the fact that "Republicans are much more organized than ever before." The chief of staff for a junior, up-and-coming Republican member said that his boss had not been pressured by the leadership to set up a PAC. Rather, he had gone to the Speaker and asked whether he should establish one: "The Speaker said, 'Yes, you really should,' and so he did. But he was never pushed to do it. Members are absolutely asked to give money to other members and that was another reason he decided to set up a PAC. It was really taking a toll on his personal campaign account to keep giving out of that" (interviews with author 2001).

After taking control of the House in 1995, the Republicans refined the conditional-party-government model that had characterized legislative organization and member behavior since the late 1980s. John Aldrich and David Rohde (1997–1998, 558) argue that conditional party government requires the majority party to have sufficient agreement on its goals and to empower party leaders with the resources they need to achieve those goals. To build a stronger, more cohesive majority party, House Republicans voluntarily adopted rules that removed some of their independence from the party and enhanced the leadership's power and control over the chamber.

The Republicans distinguished themselves ideologically from the Democrats and consistently referred to their policy agenda as a "profound transformation" and their takeover as a "revolution." In 1994, disproportionately more moderate Democrats lost elections or retired, and disproportionately more conservative Republicans won election. As a result, one of the major stipulations of conditional party government—intraparty homogeneity and interparty division—was strengthened (Aldrich and Rohde 1997–1998, 557–558; 2001). Republican opposition to President Bill Clinton's policy agenda further strengthened this condition. The intensity of this opposition became evident when House Republicans and President Clinton engaged in a bitter, protracted battle over the federal budget.

Trouble in the Ranks

Members will agree to empower their leaders only if they support their leaders' goals (Rohde 1991). After Republicans won majority control of the House in 1994, they almost universally embraced Newt Gingrich's vision for the new majority and they achieved an exceptionally high level of party unity in 1995, as they rallied around the Contract and other high-profile policy issues. Gingrich's strategy of inclusion brought House Republicans together and made them feel like part of a team. The political environment supported this approach to governance: Partisan margins were small, and most Republicans believed they had been mandated to pass the policies on which they had campaigned. In the budget battles of 1995 and 1996, this cohesiveness was put to the test. Newt Gingrich discovered that a unified majority's willingness to cede power to the leadership was not automatic, and that it depended on the issue and politics at hand.

In 1995, House Republicans and President Clinton clashed over the annual spending bills. Determined to make good on their promise to balance the budget, the House Republicans proposed a budget that slashed hundreds of federal programs. Clinton staunchly opposed the Republican budget. When no compromise was reached, he vetoed a stopgap spending bill, effectively shutting down most federal government offices on November 13, 1995. Almost eight thousand federal workers were ordered to stay home. Gingrich welcomed the shutdown. He argued that if the only way Republicans could demonstrate "that we were really going to balance the budget" was by closing the government, then so be it. Otherwise, "you never would have gotten Clinton and his staff to realize how deadly serious we were" (Remini 2006, 486).

A week later, Gingrich had decided that some compromise was necessary. President Clinton had managed to persuade an outraged public that the Republicans were responsible for the government shutdown, and a negotiated truce between Clinton and House Republicans sent government employees back to work on November 20. Congress passed a continuing resolution to keep the federal government running through December 15, and the president and House Republicans tried once again to negotiate. When they failed to reach a compromise, the government shutdown once again—this time for twenty-one days. In early January 1996, Gingrich realized that the public's opinion of the Republicans was plummeting and ordered the Republican Conference to end the shutdown. The House passed a series of funding bills soon after, government reopened, and Clinton emerged victorious (Smith and Gamm 2001).

What had made it possible for Gingrich to consolidate power— namely, an ideologically fervent followership—now made it difficult for him to lead. While Gingrich viewed the budget compromise as a necessary means to an imperfect end of restoring the Republicans' reputation, many House Republicans saw it as a betrayal of their principles. Junior members—particularly the freshmen—remained staunchly committed to the strategy of forcing Clinton to accept their demands. They were angered by Gingrich's willingness to negotiate. A top Clinton adviser said the freshmen had become "Newt's Frankenstein monster—and my new best friend. The more they dug in, the better off we were" (Zelizer 2006, 258). Divisions within the party, which had earlier been suppressed by a postelection sense of excitement and mandate, began to emerge, and the budget battle caused many House Republicans to reevaluate their policy goals in light of their constituencies rather than their party. Given the diversity of the constituencies these members represented, party unity began to splinter. Republican defections on party bills became more common in 1996, as did factional challenges to the leadership. To pass legislation, Republican leaders had to seek compromise within the party. They also reached out to vulnerable members and helped them secure pork for their districts.

This less aggressive leadership style, combined with enormous amounts of campaign money, helped the Republicans hold on to their House majority in 1996 (Sinclair 1999, 441–442), although the Republican majority fell to 227 (from 230) despite the party's active fundraising efforts. While the budget battle had damaged Gingrich's reputation within the conference, Republican leaders still managed to promote electoral party unity. House Republicans were determined to hold on to the majority they had claimed two years earlier. For the 1996 elections, Republican incumbents donated $4.9 million to House candidates and $4.1 million to the NRCC. House Republicans were also required to contribute to the Incumbent Support Fund, a separate NRCC account used to assist electorally vulnerable incumbents. The NRCC revived the 1994 Victory Accounts, which encouraged members to raise money for the committee in their home states. Speaker Gingrich appeared at events in most Republican candidates' districts and was credited with raising at least $65 million for the NRCC, the RNC, the state party committees, individual candidates, and himself (Kolodny and Dwyre 1998, 285–290; Bedlington and Malbin 2003).

Gingrich remained Speaker but faced growing criticism. House Democrats, led by Minority Whip David Bonior (D-MI), accused Gingrich of violating House ethics rules when he accepted a $4.5-million book advance from a publishing company. A House Ethics Committee's investigation forced Gingrich to return the money. The committee also investigated charges that Gingrich had violated campaign finance laws, and that his televised town hall meetings and a college course that he had taught between 1993 and 1995 had been financed by tax-deductible contributions diverted from his leadership PAC. Suddenly, Gingrich was subject to the same hostile tactics that he had pioneered to bring down former Democratic Speaker Jim Wright (Zelizer 2006).

While the Republicans were learning how to be a majority party, House Democrats adjusted to life in the minority. After the 1994 elections, the Democrats supported strengthening their leaders' powers, even though it meant relinquishing some member independence. They elected an aggressive Minority Leader, Richard Gephardt (D-MO), and strengthened his powers. The Democratic Caucus voted to strip Charlie Rose (D-NC) of his ranking-member seat on the Oversight Committee after he unsuccessfully challenged Gephardt for the party's top leadership post. Conservative Democrats angrily denounced the caucus's decision to vote in a slate of liberal leaders, and Gene Taylor, a conservative Democrat from Mississippi, described the decision as "the height of idiocy" (Cassata 1994). Gephardt responded to intraparty complaints about the need to diversify the party's upper ranks by expanding the leadership to include posts for conservatives, women, and minorities. Planning for their eventual return to majority status, House Democrats approved new rules abolishing committee chairs' power to appoint and fire committee staff and to hold subcommittee ranking positions while serving as chair. The caucus rejected a bid to follow the Republicans' lead and impose term limits on committee chairs and ranking members (Owens 1997, 271).

In 1996, House Democrats ran on a Families First agenda, a modest, twenty-one-point response to the Republicans' Contract with America. Democratic House leaders did not ask their members to endorse the agenda, claiming that the voters disapproved of party mandates. Instead, the leaders focused on promoting a positive view of the Democrats and their ideas. Unsurprisingly, the Families First agenda did not have much impact on the elections. Most Democratic House candidates chose to attack Gingrich and the House Republicans rather than promote their party's agenda.

President Clinton helped the DCCC raise millions of dollars in 1996 and also directed the DNC to give the DCCC an additional $2 million. House Democrats were newly motivated to raise money for the party and its candidates in 1996. Promoting the goal of regaining majority control, Minority Leader Richard Gephardt pressured Democratic House members to give for the good of the whole. Gephardt even announced member contributions at Democratic Caucus meetings to shame those who had not yet given. In 1996, Democratic incumbents contributed over $3 million to House candidates and $1.3 million to the DCCC. Some Democrats handed over as much as $50,000 to the DCCC (Kolodny and Dwyre 1998, 285–290; Bedlington and Malbin 2003).

Democratic leaders also encouraged their members to establish leadership PACs (or use their already established leadership PACs) to regain majority control. A spokesperson for one Democratic member said that her boss had established a leadership PAC "in order to raise money in hopes of taking back the majority." Explaining his decision to establish a leadership PAC, one Democratic House member said, "Some of us use them to contribute to competitive races and not just to solidify our positions with our colleagues." Another member's chief of staff said that his boss simply "wanted to be able to help other candidates." One House Democrat said that he had "established his PAC when we were still in the majority and now it's to help us get back in the majority" (interviews with author 2001).

Both parties greatly expanded their use of soft money during the 1996 elections. Soft money, also referred to as nonfederal money, was not subject to FECA rules on the size and source of contributions because it was raised and spent by the parties to support party-building activities. (Funds raised and spent in accordance with FECA regulations are known as hard money.) For example, the party committees used soft money to pay for building improvements and overhead. But in 1996, they began to use soft money to pay for issue advertising. While issue ads do not explicitly call for the election or defeat of a candidate, they typically carry a clear political message. Soft money also funded voter registration campaigns and get-out-the-vote drives.

On the heels of the protracted budget battle between President Clinton and House Republicans, and the 1996 election, the House grew increasingly partisan. Gingrich exercised caution in pushing policy because he knew he lacked support within his own party, where there was little consensus on policy goals and strategy, and members were much more likely to go their own way. By the summer of 1997, the Speaker was considered so ineffective that several top party leaders cooperated with a small group of neoconservatives and plotted to overthrow Gingrich. The plan was reported in the press, and Gingrich managed to avert the "coup" attempt. However, he never regained his aggressiveness. House Republicans were embarrassed by the reports of dissension in the ranks, and for the remainder of the 105th Congress, they struggled to regain their footing. Their policy accomplishments were meager, giving them little to run on in 1998 (Schickler 2001, 274; Smith and Gamm 2001, 261).

The End of the Gingrich Era

House Republicans lost 5 seats in the 1998 midterm elections, reducing their majority to a narrow 222 seats. No party in modern American history had ever before lost seats in the midterm election of an opposition president's second term in office (Smith and Gamm 2001, 261). "I was furious," said Bob Livingston, chair of the Appropriations Committee. "That's because I'd worked my butt off all year to campaign and raised a ton of money. And they were all turned into anti-Clinton ads and that's not what I'd raised them for. I said that I'd raised the money to spend it on pro-Republican ads. We didn't talk about what we had done right. We talked about what he [Clinton] had done wrong! And we blew it!" (Remini 2006, 488). House Republicans' focus on impeaching President Clinton contributed to the party's poor showing at the polls. The Republican Party campaign committees ran a series of last-minute attack ads during the 1998 campaign, designed to remind voters of the Monica Lewinsky scandal. By highlighting an episode voters wanted to forget, the ads backfired, and the public blamed the Republicans for the excessively partisan tone in Washington. The Republicans held Gingrich responsible for the party's poor showing at the polls, and support for his Speakership plummeted.

A number of Republicans claimed that they would not vote for Gingrich under any circumstances; they encouraged Bob Livingston to challenge Gingrich for the Speakership, and he agreed. Once Gingrich realized that he did not have the votes to hold back a challenge, he chose not to run for Speaker and resigned from the House. Livingston, who had contributed $1.4 million to Republican candidates and the party in 1998, ran unchallenged. One month after the Republican Conference had selected Livingston as Speaker, he resigned when reports of his extramarital affairs were made public. House Republicans were again without a leader. Dennis Hastert (R-IL), a virtual unknown, stepped in to fill the void. A close ally of Majority Whip Tom DeLay, Hastert was just as conservative as the other Republican House leaders. Perhaps most important, he had no enemies in the party and no skeletons in the closet (or mistresses in his bed!).

Conclusion

Newt Gingrich's rise to and fall from power were remarkable for a number of reasons. Most of his House career was dedicated to moving his party from a permanent minority to a sustainable majority. Throughout the 1980s and early 1990s, he led the charge against Democratic control. Gingrich attacked Democratic Party leaders, accusing them of ethics violations and unfair legislative gamesmanship. He coordinated and publicized Republican responses to the Democrats' policy agenda, and he promoted a much more aggressive style of politics. Gingrich was the Republican Party's lead electoral strategist as well. He was primarily responsible for the Contract with America, and for the NRCC's successful fundraising strategy in 1994. His ascension from Minority Whip to Speaker of the House went unchallenged, as his Republican colleagues credited him with leading the party into the promised land of majority control of the House.

House Republicans rewarded Gingrich by supporting his bid to centralize power in the Speakership. Gingrich was tremendously driven and sought to control almost all aspects of the party's policy and political strategy. He controlled committee chair and committee seat appointments, committee agendas, the floor schedule, and the House rules. He also coordinated the House Republican Party's message, took the lead on negotiating with congressional Democrats and the Clinton White House, and handled public outreach and press. He traveled the country, campaigning and raising money for the Republicans. And he established fundraising requirements for House Republicans. Gingrich's control over the chamber, combined with his penchant for highly visible and fiercely partisan politics, evoked Speaker Thomas Reed's dominating presence a century earlier (Schickler 2001, 273). Like Speaker Reed, Gingrich learned that fierce partisanship can have devastating electoral consequences.

Gingrich also discovered the consequences of excessive control. By stretching himself across a wide array of responsibilities, he opened himself up to broad criticism. His involvement in all levels of party politics meant that he was responsible for the party's failures as well as its successes. When the party faltered during the 1995–1996 budget showdown, and during the 1998 midterm elections, he was held responsible. The strict party discipline he encouraged had worked to his advantage when the political environment favored strong leadership. But when the political environment changed, Gingrich confronted a party that no longer supported his style of strong leadership.

Some of the collective electoral strategies that Gingrich supported— namely, fundraising—built up strong, independent actors in the party. While these members used their fundraising prowess to bring money to the party, they also positioned themselves to compete for power, should the leadership lineup shift. When Gingrich was forced to step down from the Speakership, Bob Livingston was primed to compete. In 1994, Gingrich had appointed Livingston to chair the Appropriations Committee. At Gingrich's direction, Livingston had used his chair to raise hundreds of thousands of dollars for the party and its candidates. While Livingston's fundraising had undoubtedly helped the party, it had also helped him take advantage of Gingrich's weaknesses following the 1998 elections. The fundraising strategies that Gingrich promoted clearly helped the party gain and maintain majority control. But they also created opportunities for political entrepreneurs to pursue their own agendas. This aspect of the party's collective fundraising efforts could create instability within the majority party and contribute to fragmentation. Perhaps in response to this new dynamic, Speaker Dennis Hastert and his leadership team developed new strategies for promoting the party's fundraising goals and enforcing party discipline.

Notes

1. In another estimate, using data from a personal interview with Maria Cino, former executive director of the NRCC, Kolodny and Dwyre (1998) claim that House Republicans contributed $1.2 million to the NRCC and $6.7 million to other candidates in 1994.

2. Heberlig and Larson (2003) found that House members who sat on "money committees" contributed the most campaign money to candidates and the CCCs during the 1990s, particularly in the second half of the decade.

3. See Scott Adler's discussion of how the committee-restructuring reforms, in particular, reflected the reelection goals of House Republicans. According to Adler, "Republican leaders had no problems in choosing to abolish committees that served traditionally Democratic constituencies like federal employees, maritime and environmental interests, and DC residents, but they were much more reluctant to eliminate panels oriented around policy matters important to Republican patrons, like the small business community or increasingly supportive military veterans" (2002, 210–212).

4. Party-line votes pit a majority of Democrats against a majority of Republicans. During 1995, 73 percent of all roll call votes were considered party-line votes.

6

Paying to Play

Redistributing Money in the Post-Gingrich Era

Newt Gingrich's strong Speakership proved no more durable than Jim Wright's experiment with assertive leadership in the late 1980s. Known for his "relaxed style and low profile" (Schickler 2001, 275), Dennis Hastert offered a dramatically different form of leadership from Gingrich's aggressiveness and yearning for the spotlight. Hastert allowed the committee chairs more independence and sought advice from a broader ideological range of Republicans than had Gingrich. But the House remained highly polarized, and Republicans continued to have difficulty agreeing on and adopting an agenda. Conservative Republicans emphasized ideological goals that the party's moderates resisted for reasons tied to their own electoral survival. As public support for the Republican policy agenda waned, the Republican-led impeachment proceedings against President Bill Clinton were criticized, and public views on issues like education, health care, and the environment shifted toward the Democrats. Hastert responded to the new political environment by pledging to work with both Republicans and Democrats to reduce partisanship. Heading into the 2000 elections, he produced a ten-point list of "items of agreement between Republicans and Clinton" that he hoped would result in policy action. The Republicans had entered a new era, in which their electoral concerns began to dominate their legislative strategy (Smith and Gamm 2001, 262).

In addition to promoting a politically feasible policy agenda, Republican House leaders pressured members to support the party's fundraising efforts. The 1998 elections had made clear that the party's majority was very fragile. Republican missteps and President Bill Clinton's popularity had helped the Democrats raise money. Hastert knew that House Republicans were going to need a lot of money to hold their majority in 2000, and he devised new ways to encourage member giving. Republican House leaders continued to enforce strict party discipline, emphasizing that cohesion was central to maintaining the majority. Most Republican House members were eager to move on from the Gingrich era and initially supported the leadership's legislative and electoral goals. House Democrats also adjusted to the new electorally driven political environment and stepped up their collective fundraising.

Newt Gingrich's departure in 1998 left open the question of whether his leadership team would retain their positions. All members of the leadership had increased their overall contributions to the party and its candidates between the 1994 and 1996 election cycles, and this pattern continued in 1998, when Republican House leaders increased their overall giving from the previous cycle. The only exceptions to this pattern were Newt Gingrich, who retired in 1998, and Susan Molinari, who retired in 1997. Majority Leader Dick Armey was challenged by Jennifer Dunn (R-WA) and Steve Largent (R-OK). Dunn had first been elected to the House in 1992, and Largent, in 1994. Armey faced a strong challenge from Largent in particular but managed to hold on to his position. Armey had outraised Largent and Dunn by far, contributing over $1 million to candidates and the NRCC in the 1996 and 1998 election cycles. Republican Conference chairman John Boehner was challenged and defeated by relative newcomer J. C. Watts (R-OK), who had first been elected to the House in 1994. Tillie Fowler (R-FL), first elected to the House in 1992, beat out three other candidates to win the position of conference vice chair. Fowler outraised two of her three challengers. Armey, Watts, and Fowler followed the same pattern as the other conference leaders and contributed more money to the party and its candidates after having secured a leadership post. That several members of the class of 1994 had challenged for leadership positions after only four years in office (and that one, J. C. Watts, had won) was remarkable. The institutional reforms of 1995 and changes in the political environment had altered the structure of opportunities in the House. Ambitious members could pursue their leadership ambitions early in their congressional careers, and their ability to raise and distribute money had become a major factor in this pursuit.

The majority of House committee chairs, who had contributed to the NRCC and Republican candidates during the 1994 election cycle, upped their overall contribution amounts in the 1996 cycle, and again in the 1998 cycle. Only those on their way out failed to contribute. Agriculture Chair Pat Roberts, whose contributions to the NRCC had dropped off substantially between the 1994 and 1996 cycles, began actively campaigning in 1996 for the Senate seat he was elected to in 1998. Bob Smith replaced Roberts as chair in 1996 but then retired in 1998. Of the four chairs who did not contribute any money to candidates or the NRCC during the 1994 and 1996 election cycles, two—Bob Goodling and Bill Archer—retired in 2000, once their committee chair terms expired. In the last cycle for which he had to raise money for his own reelection campaign (1998), Archer contributed $100,000 to the NRCC. Select Intelligence Chair Larry Combest was named chair of the more prestigious Agriculture Committee in 1998, perhaps because his fundraising had gone from nothing in the 1994 and 1996 cycles to $163,000 during the 1998 cycle. Committee chairs increased their contributions to the party and its candidates more than any other category of House member during the 1990s (Heberlig and Larson 2003).

The contribution patterns of Republican leaders and committee chairs following the 1994 elections suggest that most leaders and chairs abided by the party's fundraising expectations. In 1994, the committee chairs were handpicked by Newt Gingrich and understood the importance of party loyalty as expressed through fundraising. As the six-year term limit on these chairs inched closer, competition among Republican members who wished to replace them grew fierce. Many committee chair aspirants took a cue from the sitting chairs and began redistributing money to demonstrate their party loyalty.

Upon assuming the House Speakership, Dennis Hastert instituted a new system for selecting committee chairs. For the first time in the chamber's history, members who wanted to be considered for chairman-ships would be interviewed by the Steering Committee. The auditioning process, which required potential chairs to present their qualifications to the committee, encouraged party-building behavior. While chair aspi-rants were free to highlight whatever qualifications they chose, most fo-cused on their party-based fundraising. Expecting that seniority would be granted minimal consideration, most aspirants had begun laying the groundwork for their chair campaigns more than one year before the term limits were to take effect. In addition to lobbying the leadership and taking on high-profile issues, many of the potential chairs traveled the country and raised millions of dollars for the party and its candidates. The twenty-nine potential committee chairs appeared before the Steer-ing Committee in early December 2000 to tout their qualifications. Some prepared glossy brochures and PowerPoint presentations, and others brought snacks and beverages for the committee members. On January 4, 2001, Steering Committee members met to cast their secret ballots for each of the committee chairs. The results were then presented to the Republican Conference and endorsed on the House floor (Brewer and Deering 2005, 144).

Table 6.1 lists the twenty-nine members who were interviewed for committee chairmanships in the 107th Congress. The new chairs appear in bold and the most senior member in each chair race appears in italics. In six of the thirteen races, the member who was named chair was not the most senior member competing. In three of the seven cases where the most senior member was chosen as chair, no competition had emerged. Thus seniority was violated in six of the ten competitive races. Geography, party unity scores, and ideology did not seem to affect the chair races in any detectable way. The fundraising efforts of the members who competed for chairs, however, did seem to matter. In five of the six cases where seniority did not prevail, the member who had raised the most money won. And in seven of the ten competitive races, the chair went to the "highest bidder." James Leach (R-IA), the senior Republican on the International Relations Committee, lost the chair race to Henry Hyde (R-IL). Hyde had given the NRCC $105,000, and Leach had given the committee nothing. Tom Petri (R-WI), the senior Republican on the Education and Workforce Committee, had given $116,137 to his

Table 6.1 Contributions from Personal Campaign Funds and Leadership PACs Made to Congressional Candidates and the National Republican Congressional Committee by House Committee Chair Contenders, 2000 Election Cycle

Committee	Contenders[a]	Campaign to NRCC	Campaign to Candidates	Leadership PAC to Candidates	Total
Armed Services	*Bob Stump (AZ)*	40,000	11,000	0	51,000
	Duncan Hunter (CA)	5,000	20,827	0	25,827
	Curt Weldon (PA)	0	26,000	49,800	75,800
Banking	*Marge Roukema (NJ)*	40,000	0	0	40,000
	Richard H. Baker (LA)	150,000	42,000	0	192,000
Budget	**Jim Nussle (IA)**	100,000	3,505	7,500	111,005
	Saxby Chambliss (GA)	12,000	1,000	70,000	83,000
	Nick Smith (MI)	15,000	4,999	0	19,999
	John E. Sununu (NH)	15,000	1,000	0	16,000
Education and the Workforce	**John A. Boehner (OH)**	1,812	1,996	447,407	451,215
	Tom Petri (WI)	0	3,500	115,317	118,817
	Peter Hoekstra (MI)	15,000	12,150	0	27,150
Energy and Commerce	*"Billy" Tauzin (LA)*	270,000	27,060	293,204	590,264
	Michael Oxley (OH)[b]	170,000	59,100	193,000	422,100
International Relations	**Henry Hyde (IL)**	105,000	2,100	0	107,100
	James Leach (IA)	0	0	0	0
	Douglas K. Bereuter (NE)	57,500	3,500	0	61,000
Judiciary	**James Sensenbrenner (WI)**	84,000	0	0	84,000
	George W. Gekas (PA)	25,000	22,000	0	47,000
Resources	*James V. Hansen (UT)*	10,000	27,600	0	37,600
Science	*Sherwood Boehlert (NY)*	65,000	22,500	18,500	106,000
Small Business	**Donald Manzullo (IL)**	15,000	16,100	0	31,100
	Sue W. Kelly (NY)	65,000	5,000	0	70,000
Transportation	*Don Young (AK)*	25,000	0	45,390	70,390
Veterans' Affairs	*Christopher Smith (NJ)*[c]	50,000	3,000	0	53,000
	Michael Bilirakis (FL)	82,750	25,000	0	107,750
Ways and Means	**Bill Thomas (CA)**	252,000	43,000	133,000	428,000
	Philip M. Crane (IL)	80,000	56,000	132,000	268,000
	E. Clay Shaw (FL)	100,000	0	22,000	122,000

Source: Paul R. Brewer and Christopher J. Deering. 2005. Musical Chairs: Interest Groups, Campaign Fundraising, and Selection of House Committee Chairs. In *The Interest Group Connection,* Ed. Paul Herrnson, Ronald G. Shaiko, and Clyde Wilcox, 141–163. Washington, DC: CQ Press.

[a] New chairs appear in boldface; senior members appear in italics.

[b] Oxley interviewed for the Commerce chair but was named head of the Financial Services Committee, a somewhat expanded version of the former Banking Committee.

[c] Smith was interviewed for International Relations, but was the ranking member on Veterans' Affairs, where he was given the chairmanship.

colleagues. He lost to John Boehner, who had given almost $500,000 to the party and its candidates. Saxby Chambliss (R-GA), the senior Republican on the Budget Committee, lost the chair to Jim Nussle (R-IA). Chambliss had raised $70,000, while Nussle had raised $100,000 (Brewer and Deering 2005, 146–156).

One of the most contentious races was for the Ways and Means Committee chair. This committee is considered one of the most powerful in the House, as its jurisdiction encompasses taxation and entitlement spending. The race pitted three members against each other: Bill Thomas (R-CA), Phil Crane (R-IL), and Clay Shaw (R-FL). Crane, who had served fifteen terms in the House, was the most senior member of the committee. He was considered the early favorite because of his seniority and his close relationship with Speaker Hastert, a fellow Illinois Republican. However, some members complained about the seventy-year-old Crane's work ethic and his alcohol use. In 1999, Crane sought treatment for alcoholism and returned to the House after he had completed a rehabilitation program. He attracted broad industry support and was favored by the trade community, which backed his efforts to promote trade relations with China and Africa (Pershing 2000; Brewer and Deering 2005, 148).

Bill Thomas was considered a hard worker who was well versed in health policy. But he was known for having a bad temper and for having a questionable personal relationship with a health care lobbyist while serving as chair of the Ways and Means Committee's Subcommittee on Health. Health care lobbyists had contributed heavily to Bill Thomas's campaign committee and leadership PAC in 2000. As chair of the Ways and Means health subcommittee, Thomas was considered an expert on health care industry issues. He had formed close working relationships with many health and pharmaceutical representatives and had been the leading recipient of campaign money from these industries (Pershing 2000; Brewer and Deering 2005, 148).

Clay Shaw was considered a long shot. He had decided to enter the race after it was clear that party leaders were considering factors other than seniority. Several Ways and Means Committee members said they expected Shaw to pull votes away from Thomas rather than Crane (Pershing 2000).

Both Thomas and Crane had raised and redistributed large sums of money (see Table 6.1). In addition to contributing money to the NRCC and party candidates, both candidates had held fundraisers for the party and helped raise money for various NRCC programs. Thomas and Crane had raised over $1 million apiece on behalf of the party and its candidates in 2000. Clay Shaw had not raised nearly as much money as Thomas and Crane—another indicator that his candidacy was not in play (Brewer and Deering 2005, 148).

In January 2001, the Steering Committee chose Bill Thomas as the new chair of the Ways and Means Committee. In casting his allotted five votes for Thomas, Speaker Hastert put same-state loyalties aside and risked angering the party's conservative wing, which had heavily supported Crane. Press reports claimed that the leadership had favored Thomas because they believed he was more capable of enacting President George W. Bush's $1.6-trillion tax cut, as well as Bush's health care and entitlement reform proposals. The leadership also considered Thomas the better legislative tactician and policy expert, believing that his gruff personality might work to his advantage in pushing President Bush's agenda through the committee (Eilperin 2001). In addition to factors cited by the leadership, many members believed that Thomas's superior fundraising had won him the job. The chief of staff for the chair of one of the House's power committees said, "If you do some research on the race for chairmanship of the Ways and Means Committee, I would say that's a case where money was a factor. That was a case where a less senior member took over the chairmanship of the committee and that didn't used to happen. In all of these cases, the evidence is anecdotal, but in Crane's case, I'm sure money was a factor." Another House member's chief of staff observed, "Leaders are expected to lead, and raising money is part of that. Within the Republican Conference, there are definite expectations. Look at the race between Thomas and Crane for chairmanship of Ways and Means. Crane was told by the leadership that he had to raise more money" (interviews with author 2001).

A spokesperson for Crane said that the leadership now emphasized fundraising over other party-building activities because fundraising can be "measured on paper." The spokesperson pointed out that Crane had been in the House for thirty-two years and had always actively worked on behalf of other members. Crane had been instrumental in establishing Republican-affiliated organizations like the Heritage Foundation and the American Conservative Union—organizations that many newer members took for granted "as always having been there, but that's not the case." The difference between these kinds of activities and fundraising, according to Crane's spokesperson, was that the old-style activities were not measurable and were therefore not kept track of. More prominent members of the party just did them to help other members and the party. This spokesperson said:

> Congressman Crane has a long history of always helping out people in the party but he did not start a leadership PAC until 1998. And he was not very active with his leadership PAC until 1999 and 2000. A little of that was a slow recognition on his part that there had been a change in the way that you actually helped other members get elected. Members used to go out and help other members in key districts and things like that, but now they raise money. Once he saw that the leadership and folks within the party were more attentive to the fundraising than to the basic party-building activities he always did, he recognized that he had to participate in that also and did so. (interview with author 2001)

The race for the chair of the Ways and Means Committee in 2000 demonstrates how institutional reform and the political environment shape the structure of opportunities in the House. In 1974, House Democrats stopped using the seniority rule to choose their committee chairs; in 1995, House Republicans not only got rid of the seniority rule but term-limited their committee chairs and leaders to six years. By institutionalizing turnover within the party's upper ranks and rewarding loyalty, Republican leaders could expect that a constant stream of ambitious members would promote themselves by promoting the party. House members can demonstrate party loyalty in a number of ways, but fundraising ranks high on the list. As partisan margins have narrowed, both parties have emphasized electoral rather than legislative strategies in their quest for majority control. And in today's highly competitive environment, the party's electoral strategies center on fundraising.

While term limits on committee chairs proved extremely profitable for the Republicans, some senior House Republicans complained that the aggressive fundraising behavior of the potential chairs was fracturing the party. Another contentious chair race pitted Billy Tauzin (R-LA) against Michael Oxley (R-OH) for the gavel of the powerful Energy and Commerce Committee. Tauzin, who had recently switched from the Democratic Party to the Republican Party, was a ten-term veteran of the committee. Oxley, who chaired the committee's Subcommittee on Finance, had served on the committee for nine terms. While he was competing with Tauzin for the Energy and Commerce chair, Oxley's backup plan was to lobby for the chair of the newly formed Financial Services Committee. Marge Roukema (R-NJ), the most senior Republican on the Banking Committee, was competing against Richard Baker (R-LA) for the Banking chair. However, Republican leaders decided to dissolve the Banking Committee and create the Financial Services Committee. The new committee was given jurisdiction over the former Banking Committee's policy portfolio. The Steering Committee awarded the chair of the Energy and Commerce Committee to Billy Tauzin and the chair of the newly formed Financial Services Committee to Michael Oxley. Roukema and Baker came up empty-handed. Roukema, who had faced a costly primary battle in 2000, had contributed $40,000 to the NRCC and nothing to party candidates. Baker had given $150,000 to the NRCC and $42,000 to party candidates. Oxley's contributions to the NRCC and party candidates had totaled $422,100. While a number of factors may have influenced the outcome of the Financial Services chair race, many members considered money a primary one. Roukema, who claimed that someone in the party leadership had told her she had not raised enough money, said, "I don't think our Republican Party wants to be known as a party where you can buy a chairmanship." The *Bergen Record*, Roukema's hometown paper, ran an editorial with the headline "Sold to the Highest Bidder," and Roukema's Democratic opponent in the 2000 election wrote an op-ed for the same paper in which she complained about the Republican leadership's emphasis on fundraising: "Raise money, your party notices. Raise the most money, you get elected. Raise even more money, give it back to your party, you chair a committee" (Brewer and Deering 2005, 155).

While some members decried the emphasis on money, others complained that ideology was a deciding factor. Tom Petri (R-WI), a moderate who had challenged John Boehner (R-OH) for the Education and Workforce Committee chair, sent out a press release labeling the chair-selection process a "purge of moderate Republicans" (Foerstel and Ota 2001). Because more money is raised at the ideological extremes, moderates tend to attract less money than their more conservative or liberal colleagues (Heberlig, Hetherington, and Larson 2006). Thus, appealing to the party's conservative leaders may be more difficult for moderate Republicans both financially and ideologically.

Republican members voiced similar complaints about committee chair races in the 108th Congress. At the beginning of the 108th Congress, five House members were tapped to fill vacant chairs on the Armed Services, Resources, Government Reform, Agriculture, and Homeland Security Committees. Together, the five new chairs had contributed more than $1 million to the NRCC and nearly $500,000 to Republican candidates during the 2002 election cycle. Of the five new chairs, two held seniority. Joel Hefley (R-CO), who had been passed over in 2003 for chair of the House Resources Committee, said, "Fundraising evidently was an enormous part of it. It's unseemly. It's like buying seats and we shouldn't do that" (Kratz 2003). Richard Pombo (R-CA), a conservative ally of Tom DeLay, was elevated over five more senior members to the House Resources Committee chair. Voicing the concerns of some of the conference's more senior members, Wayne Gilchrest (R-MD) said that deviating from seniority could result in a loss of stature for the House and that "arbitrary politics is not consistent with good government" (Willis 2003, 91).

Democrats Rev Up the Money Machine

The intensification of money-oriented politics was not limited to the Republicans. In their effort to regain majority status, Democratic leaders promoted party-building strategies. House Democrats were urged to unify in opposition to the Republicans' agenda, and to raise money for the party and its candidates. Democratic leadership aspirants heeded this call and competed for power by redistributing money at record-breaking levels.

While House Republicans were deciding who would take the committee chair gavels in 2001, House Democrats were deciding who would take over as Minority Whip when David Bonior (D-MI) stepped down later that year to run for governor of Michigan. Though Bonior did not announce his plans to launch a gubernatorial bid until May 2001, the race to replace him had begun in 1998. Several months before the 1998 elections, Nancy Pelosi (D-CA), Steny Hoyer (D-MD), and John Lewis (D-GA) privately began to solicit the backing of their House colleagues. If the Democrats had reclaimed majority status in 1998, Minority Leader Richard Gephardt (D-MO) would presumably have been elevated to House Speaker, David Bonior would have become Majority Leader, and the Whip position would have opened. Pelosi was the first of the three contenders to publicly signal her intentions; in August 1998, she distributed to her Democratic colleagues a letter stating her desire to become the next Majority Whip and asked for their support. Lewis, a Chief Deputy Whip, had sought support through informal phone calls to his colleagues all year, and Hoyer began phoning colleagues after Pelosi distributed her letter. By fall 1998, the prospect of a Democratic takeover of the House looked dim. However, there was speculation that Gephardt might launch a bid for the presidency in 2000, a move that would open up the Whip position, assuming Bonior would replace him as Minority Leader. Because of the uncertainty over Gephardt's plans, the campaign for Minority Whip continued through the fall of 1998.

The Democrats' failure to gain majority status in 1998 and Gephardt's announcement that he would not seek the Democratic nomination for president in 2000 put the Whip's race into temporary remission. However, the race was revived the following year, and by July 1999, Pelosi had given $120,000 to Democratic candidates—much more than any of her Democratic colleagues, including Gephardt, who was second in giving with just $38,000. Hoyer had raised over $100,000 for his leadership PAC, and Lewis had been relatively less active (Wallison and VandeHei 1999). While Pelosi actively lobbied her colleagues for their support and continued to fundraise, Hoyer and Lewis expressed dismay over the race's early start. "This shouldn't be going on right now. It should really wait until we've taken the House back—that is where our focus should be," said Hoyer. "Quite honestly, since it has started, I don't intend to sit on the sidelines." Lewis expressed "real reservations" about campaigning so early but said that "if there are other people out there lining up members and gathering support, I feel that I must get out there" (Wallison 1999). Just as real competition between the parties spurred intensive fundraising, real competition within parties for leadership posts stimulated the redistribution of money.

By August 1999, Pelosi and Hoyer had established Whip teams and were arranging dinners and other events for groups of potential supporters. Some members, particularly freshmen, expressed discomfort with the amount of pressure they were getting from the Whip candidates for pledges of support. Each candidate claimed to stand for an important faction of the party that was underrepresented: Pelosi emphasized her gender and her liberal stance; Hoyer played up his moderate leanings; and Lewis suggested a need for African-American representation in the leadership. Fearing that aligning themselves with one faction would isolate them from the others, some members sought to avoid making early commitments. Gephardt said that there was little he could—or would—do to discourage political ambition, and that if the early race meant more campaign money for other members, then so much the better (Rich 1999, 8). The Republican committee chair races had demonstrated to Gephardt the financial value of internal party competition.

By February 2000, Pelosi had donated $550,000 to her House colleagues, while Hoyer had given $115,000. Although Lewis had raised about $700,000 for his personal campaign committee, he was comparatively less active in spreading the wealth (Ghent 2000). While Pelosi relied heavily on her national appeal as a woman and as one of the party's most prolific fundraisers, Hoyer stressed his institutional footing and his willingness to give other members a voice (Wallison 2000a). A Hoyer spokesperson described the essential differences between the two front-runners: "Pelosi has a lot of money, she's a woman, and she's from California. All of those things and her ability to raise a lot of money are what she wants the race to be about. Hoyer is a leader and a consensus builder and people see that, too" (interview with author 2001).

In July 2000, Lewis announced he was dropping out of the race and supporting Hoyer's candidacy. His endorsement of Hoyer came as a surprise to many who had expected him to support Pelosi, a fellow liberal. Hoyer was ecstatic and expected to pick up a substantial number of endorsements from Lewis's supporters. Approximately one week after Lewis's announcement, Pelosi declared that she had enough votes to claim victory—a claim Hoyer chalked up to strategy and strongly disputed (Wallison 2000b). By the end of August 2000, Pelosi had raised more than $1 million and contributed $678,144 to House candidates. Among House and Senate Democrats, Pelosi's fundraising was second only to that of Senate Minority Leader Tom Daschle. Hoyer, by contrast, had raised $588,651 and given out $457,500 to candidates and to the DCCC. Pelosi insisted her fundraising efforts were not about breaking records but about winning back the House. Hoyer claimed he would rely on the personal relationships he had established with other members, rather than campaign contributions, to win support for his Whip bid (Crabtree and Kane 2000).

More than two-and-a-half years after it had begun, the campaign for the Whip post again came to a halt when Democrats failed to win back the House in November 2000. Hoyer and Pelosi announced they would keep their organizations in place, should another opportunity surface. Table 6.2 depicts the contributions Hoyer and Pelosi made to the DCCC and to party candidates during the 2000 elections cycle. These figures do not include the money Hoyer and Pelosi raised on behalf of party candidates and the DCCC by hosting fundraisers, speaking at fundraising events, and traveling with candidates in their districts. Both Hoyer and Pelosi hosted events and provided services such as transportation at the Democratic National Convention in the summer of 2000.

When Bonior announced in May 2001 that he would step down from the minority Whip post to run for governor of Michigan, Hoyer and Pelosi hit the ground running. Several House members and chiefs of staff pointed to the Whip's race as an example of how members used money to pursue their political ambitions. A Hoyer spokesperson said, "I don't think ever in the history of the Democratic Caucus has it reached where it is now, as far as the level of contributions." The main reason fundraising had become so central to the race was that "it plays

Table 6.2 **Personal Campaign Committee and Leadership PAC Contributions, Steny Hoyer (MD) and Nancy Pelosi (CA), 1999–2000**

Committee Name	Total Disbursements ($)	Total Disbursements to House Candidates ($)	Total Disbursements to the DCCC ($)
Hoyer for Congress	1,268,702	127,000	125,500
AmeriPAC (Hoyer's leadership PAC)	658,473	572,000	0
Pelosi for Congress	608,318	135,709	120,000
PAC to the Future (Pelosi's leadership PAC)	1,162,284	792,800	30,000

Sources: Center for Responsive Politics, www.crp.org; Federal Elections Commission, www.fec.gov.

to Pelosi's strengths. . . . She's made the race about that. She's been double-maxing to members who don't need the money, just because she can. But we've been just as competitive with Pelosi when it comes to the members who the contributions matter to most. Pelosi has a safe seat and California as her fundraising base. Hoyer has a competitive seat in Maryland, so compared to her, the amount he's raised isn't too shabby and I think everyone knows that." Hoyer's spokesperson responded to member complaints about the protracted and increasingly bitter nature of the race by stating, "It's not going to let up. If we let up just to make members who are complaining feel better, then that gives her an opportunity to raise even more" (interview with author 2001). When the Democratic Caucus convened in the fall of 2001 to choose their next Whip, Nancy Pelosi won 118 votes to Hoyer's 95.

During the 1970s and 1980s, money factored into several of the Democratic leadership races. Pelosi was a protégé of former Representative Phil Burton (D-CA), who had introduced the concept of redistributing money in leadership races when he competed for the Majority Whip post in 1976. Like Burton, Pelosi had built up a strong network of wealthy California Democrats whom she could count on for contributions. Her framework for competing centered on fundraising—this was how she had learned to win political battles, and the Minority Whip race was another such battle. Hoyer also understood the value of redistributing money but found it difficult to match Pelosi's generosity. The protracted race benefited the House Democrats, who received multiple contributions from the Minority Whip candidates. The race also made the members consider the longer-term value of having a proven fundraiser in the leadership. If the party benefited from having Pelosi compete, it would certainly benefit from having her serve in the leadership. As both parties began increasingly to emphasize their electoral strategies, leaders who could raise tremendous amounts of money became more appealing.

Broader Trends in the Redistribution of Campaign Money

The redistribution of campaign money clearly played a role in a number of committee chair and leadership races in the 107th and 108th Congresses. But this strategy for expressing party loyalty was not limited to committee chair and leadership aspirants. Throughout the 1990s and into the twenty-first century, both parties emphasized electoral strategies that centered on fundraising. Close partisan margins meant that majority status was at stake every two years, and competition for that prize was intense. Party-based fundraising efforts compelled all members of the party, not just those who were competing for higher positions within the chamber, to give for the good of the whole. Figure 6.1 depicts the amount of money Democratic and Republican House members gave to other candidates between 1990 and 2006, and Figure 6.2 depicts the amount of money these members gave to the CCCs during this same period.

The amount of money that Democratic and Republican House members gave to candidates and the CCCs increased steadily over the sixteen years from 1990 to 2006. After 1996, members began giving a higher proportion of their campaign funds to the CCCs rather than to candidates. This change suggests that the parties began to play a more active role in coordinating electoral strategies as the margins between the parties narrowed. By giving money to the CCCs, House members allow the committees to decide which party candidates need the most

Figure 6.1 Contributions from Democratic and Republican House Members' Leadership PACs and Personal Campaign Committees to Candidates, 1990–2006

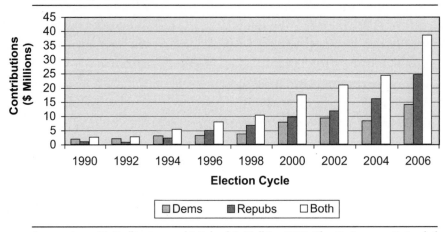

Source: Anne H. Bedlington and Michael J. Malbin. 2003. The Party as an Extended Network: Members Giving to Each Other and to Their Parties. In *Life after Reform,* Ed. Michael J. Malbin, 121–140. Lanham, MD: Rowman & Littlefield. Campaign Finance Institute, http://www.cfinst.org/data/VitalStats.aspx.

Figure 6.2 Contributions from House Members' Leadership PACs and Personal Campaign Committees to CCCs, 1990–2006

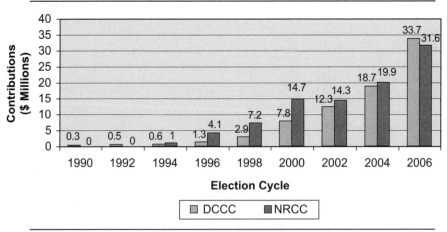

Source: Anne H. Bedlington and Michael J. Malbin. 2003. The Party as an Extended Network: Members Giving to Each Other and to Their Parties. In *Life after Reform,* Ed. Michael J. Malbin, 121–140. Lanham, MD: Rowman & Littlefield. Campaign Finance Institute, http://www.cfinst.org/data/VitalStats.aspx.

help, decisions that help mitigate the vast fundraising disparities that tend to arise between incumbents and outside challengers (Larson 2004, 160). By contributing money to the CCCs, members also accrue credit for their party-building efforts. And this credit can help members who seek higher positions within the chamber. Figure 6.3 shows House member contributions as a percentage of the CCCs' hard money receipts between 1990 and 2006. While the DCCC and the NRCC stepped up their efforts to attract outside donors, they increasingly relied on House members as a source of campaign funds (Bedlington and Malbin 2003). As a result, members today must spend more time raising money for their parties than members have in the past.

The success of these party-building efforts depends in large part on how much pressure the parties are willing to exert on their members. In 2000, the Democrats urged incumbent members to support certain candidates but provided no selective benefits for doing so. Minority party leaders typically have a more difficult time providing their members with benefits because their party does not control the chamber's most

Figure 6.3 Contributions from House Members' Leadership PACs and Personal Campaign Committees as a Percentage of the CCCs' Total Receipts, 1990–2006

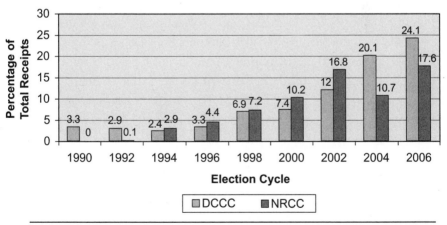

Source: Anne H. Bedlington and Michael J. Malbin. 2003. The Party as an Extended Network: Members Giving to Each Other and to Their Parties. In *Life after Reform*, Ed. Michael J. Malbin, 121–140. Lanham, MD: Rowman & Littlefield. Campaign Finance Institute, http://www.cfinst.org/data/VitalStats.aspx.

prestigious positions. As a result, House Democrats were less willing
to give for the good of the whole in 2000. The Republican strategy
rewarded member contributions. The NRCC's Battleground 2000 program strongly encouraged incumbent members to contribute by publicizing the names of members who had donated, and by rewarding the
top donors with crystal elephants (Kanthak 2007). Republican House
leaders also made clear that members' fundraising efforts would be considered when committee chairs and assignments were determined at the
beginning of the 107th Congress. Party leaders in previous congresses
had granted committee transfers (especially transfers to power committees) in return for party loyalty (Cox and McCubbins 1993). Republican
leaders in the 107th Congress did the same, but they measured party
loyalty in terms of dollars raised for the party and its candidates. Indeed,
members who gave generously to the party and to other candidates were
more likely to receive prestige committee assignments than those who
had not. By rewarding generous members with these benefits, Republican leaders were able to circumvent the member-versus-party collective
action problem (Heberlig 2003; Kanthak 2007, 395). Majority Whip
Tom DeLay (R-TX) launched an additional fundraising effort for the
2000 elections. The Retain Our Majority Program was designed to help
ten vulnerable Republican incumbents. DeLay required each of his
sixty-five Deputy Whips to contribute $3,000 to the ten endangered Re-
publicans (Eilperin 1999). In this case, cooperative Deputy Whips were
rewarded with the selective benefit of keeping their Deputy Whip posts!

Majority status translates into more money for a party. Outside contributors tend to favor the party that controls the chamber, and majority
party members tend to raise and therefore redistribute more money than
their minority party counterparts. Until 1994, House Democrats had redistributed more money to candidates than had House Republicans.
That equation changed when House Republicans launched an aggressive
effort to raise money and redistribute it to strong challengers and open-
seat candidates during the 1994 elections. While Republicans pursued a
seat-expansion strategy, House Democrats focused on protecting incumbents. Figure 6.4 shows how House Democrats distributed their contributions among incumbents, challengers, and open-seat candidates
from 1990 to 2006. Figure 6.5 shows the distribution patterns for House

169

Figure 6.4 Contributions from Democratic House Members' Leadership PACs and Personal Campaign Committees to Incumbents, Challengers, and Open-Seat Candidates, 1990–2006

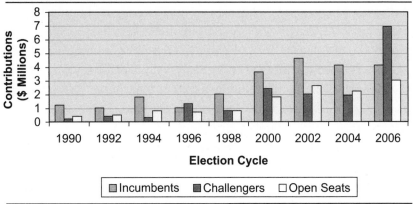

Source: Anne H. Bedlington and Michael J. Malbin. 2003. The Party as an Extended Network: Members Giving to Each Other and to Their Parties. In *Life after Reform,* Ed. Michael J. Malbin, 121–140. Lanham, MD: Rowman & Littlefield. Campaign Finance Institute, http://www.cfinst.org/data/VitalStats.aspx.

Figure 6.5 Contributions from Republican House Members' Leadership PACs and Personal Campaign Committees to Incumbents, Challengers, and Open-Seat Candidates, 1990–2006

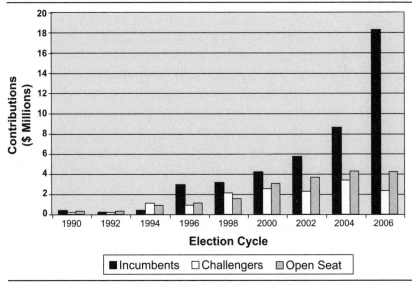

Source: Anne H. Bedlington and Michael J. Malbin. 2003. The Party as an Extended Network: Members Giving to Each Other and to Their Parties. In *Life after Reform,* Ed. Michael J. Malbin, 121–140. Lanham, MD: Rowman & Littlefield. Campaign Finance Institute, http://www.cfinst.org/data/VitalStats.aspx.

Republicans over the same period. In 1996, in the first election cycle following the 1994 Republican takeover, Democrats had considerably less money than Republicans to give. In an effort to expand their numbers, Democrats contributed twice as much money to challengers and open-seat candidates than to incumbents. Republicans chose to focus their efforts on protecting their newly elected incumbents. During the 1998 election cycle, the House was in the throes of the Clinton impeachment scandal. Republicans wrongly assumed that the scandal would help them pick up additional seats, and so they increased their contributions to outside challengers. Democrats assumed the scandal would hurt their members, and so they reacted by pursuing an incumbent protection strategy. Over the next few election cycles, both parties continued to increase their overall giving totals. The Republicans increased their giving to incumbents and open-seat candidates, but their contributions to challengers did not consistently rise or fall. Democrats did not exhibit consistent giving patterns across candidate types between 1998 and 2006 (Bedlington and Malbin 2003; Campaign Finance Institute).

Pursuing Intrainstitutional
Power within a Party Framework

Within these party-based strategies, individual members still have the ability to pursue contribution strategies consistent with their own intrainstitutional ambitions. An exploration of leadership PAC giving during the 1990s found that committee and subcommittee chairs consistently gave a much higher percentage of their leadership PAC funds to incumbent candidates. These members also consistently contributed money to their committee colleagues (1998 was an exception to this pattern). This redistribution strategy allows committee and subcommittee chairs to simultaneously pursue the party's incumbent protection goals and their own intrainstitutional goals.

Democratic and Republican core leaders in the 1990s tended to adhere to party-oriented contribution strategies, whereas extended leaders tended to emphasize their individual goals over party goals. Core leaders are the senior leaders elected by House party members and include the

Speaker, the Majority Leader, the Minority Leader, the Majority Whip, the Minority Whip, the Chief Deputy Whips, and the Democratic Caucus and Republican Conference chairs. The extended leadership includes secondary elected leadership posts, including the junior party Whips, the caucus and conference vice chairs, the House Steering and Policy Committee chairs, and the CCC chairs. In the 1990s, extended leaders gave a higher proportion of their contributions to incumbent candidates, regardless of their majority or minority party status, than did core leaders. They also tended to contribute on a more ideologically select basis than the core leaders. Members of the extended leadership who aspired to core leadership positions wanted to build support inside the chamber and contributed in ways that supported this goal. Core leaders tended to give in ways that reflected their party's majority or minority status; when in the majority, they supported at-risk incumbents, and when in the minority, they supported strong challengers. Core leaders did not want to isolate different ideological factions within their parties and tended to contribute to a broad range of party members (Currinder 2003).

Rank-and-file members with leadership PACs consistently gave a higher proportion of their contributions to incumbents, regardless of their own majority or minority party status. This pattern suggests that nonleaders who establish leadership PACs are driven by progressive ambition and are primarily concerned with gaining the colleague support they need to advance up the chamber's power ladder (Currinder 2003).

Members who aspire to higher positions in the chamber uniformly agree that fundraising is necessary to achieving their goals. Because members can give more money to their colleagues through leadership PACs, many leader aspirants view them as necessary. The chief of staff for a Democratic party leader said, "It's like peer pressure to set one up. They can give out money to people on the Steering Committee and say, 'Look, I'm a team player, put me on the Appropriations Committee or whatever.' When my boss was running for leadership, what we were doing in some cases was giving in $1,000 chunks so every time certain members saw my boss, they'd think to themselves, 'Gee, he has more money he can give me.' Obviously, that's a benefit." One member said that leadership PACs are a necessity for members with leadership

ambitions. "It's a common denominator. . . . Obviously, the more involved you get financially, the more clout you have." A Democratic
member claimed that "it is very important to be seen as a team player.
Democrats have one goal and that is to become the majority party and
whatever you can do to demonstrate your commitment to that effort is
going to be viewed favorably by the overall caucus." Another member
remarked that "it's difficult to get further in the leadership without
having one [a leadership PAC]. It probably is becoming more preva-
lent in terms of showing yourself to be a team player and participant
in the process." A Democratic leader said that for those who aspire to
leadership, the ability to raise money matters: "The names of members
are published in our caucus report and we can all see who has risen to
the occasion and who hasn't, and that's obviously important for
people seeking committee assignments and for people running for
leadership positions. People aspire to move on to exclusive committees, or to leadership, or to improve their committee assignments and
to do that, it's important to have made a major contribution to the
party." Another member acknowledged that "having a leadership PAC
helps me tremendously with my colleagues, whether it's getting legislation through, getting their support for it, . . . or, if I ever get in trouble,
they will be more willing to help me. If I ever run for a leadership post,
hopefully these people will feel like they know me and want to help
me" (interviews with author 2001).

Members—whether they aspire to higher positions or not—also
contribute in ways that support their broader ideological or personal
goals. In 1996, Democrat Charles Rangel, a black representative from
Harlem, contributed $739,082 mostly to black candidates. He also gave
money to help neighborhood groups in his district and to mobilize
black voters in his district and others. David McIntosh, a conservative
Indiana Republican, gave $61,500 from his Faith, Family, and Freedom
PAC to fifty-two conservative candidates for Congress. McIntosh's
PAC sought contributions from wealthy conservative donors, then directed the funds to candidates these donors supported (Wayne 1996;
Pritchard 1997). Ideological giving is one way members can attempt to
shape the House's political environment.

All of these contribution strategies demonstrate how members can redistribute money in ways that satisfy the party's collective fundraising goals and, at the same time, emphasize their own personal ambitions. While the overall focus on fundraising has been good for the party's campaign coffers, it has also induced competition among members who seek higher positions in the chamber. By encouraging competition between members, the parties may inadvertently stoke members' entrepreneurial tendencies, and this dynamic, as we have seen, can lead to fragmentation.

Beyond 2000: The Republican Majority Hangs On, but for How Long?

During the 1990s, electoral strategies began to dominate legislative strategies as Democrats and Republicans fought for control of the House. The presence of real competition dictated both parties' strategy in Congress, and both Democrats and Republicans used their resources to pursue electoral rather than legislative goals. For a party to successfully pursue its policy goals, it must exercise majority control. But when the partisan margins are narrow, majority parties have difficulty focusing on their policy goals because they are constantly at risk of losing their majority. Put simply, practical politics outweighed broader consideration of the policymaking role of parties in our political system during the 1990s (Damore and Hansford 1999, 383). As electoral politics took center stage, the pressure to raise campaign money increased.

These dynamics continued to drive congressional party politics in the first years of the twenty-first century, and both parties continued to focus on fundraising. House Democrats hoped that Nancy Pelosi's election as Democratic Whip would help fill the fundraising void left by Bill Clinton's departure from the White House in 2000. Pelosi excelled at large events featuring big names that attracted wealthy donors. Her San Francisco district was home to some of the party's most reliable big donors, and California has long been a fundraising haven for Democratic candidates. Even moderate and conservative House Democrats who did not support Pelosi in the Whip's race praised her ability to raise money. "She's very political, and she has raised lots of money," said Chris John (D-LA), co-chair of the conservative Blue Dog Coalition. "She delivered four of the seats in California" that Democrats won in the 2000 elections. Patrick Kennedy (D-RI), who chaired the DCCC during the 2000 election cycle, concurred. "She's the best fundraiser outside Gephardt. Nancy is better than I am." Nita Lowey (D-NY), who replaced Kennedy as DCCC chair in 2001, said Pelosi called her "five minutes after" Pelosi was elected Democratic Whip to arrange a strategy meeting (Willis 2001). Pelosi used her new leadership status to raise even more money and also directed her Democratic colleagues to follow her example and give for the good of the whole.

Republican Whip Tom DeLay was also a prolific fundraiser. After the 1994 Republican takeover, DeLay aggressively courted the lobbying community for campaign money. He kept a book in his office that tracked which PACs had given to the Democrats and which had given to the Republicans. PACs that had supported Democrats were labeled "unfriendly," and DeLay refused their lobbyists access to the party's leadership. News of DeLay's book spread quickly throughout the lobbying community. To be a friend of the Republican leadership, groups had to give the party a lot of money—and they did (Maraniss and Weisskopf 1995). They also gave a lot of money to DeLay. In the 2000 election, his leadership PAC donated $1 million, more than any other House leadership PAC, to 120 Republican candidates. DeLay's fundraising skills, along with his lobbying and organizational skills, propelled him to the position of Majority Leader when Dick Armey retired in 2002 (Foerstel 2001).

Roy Blunt (R-MO), who described himself as an aggressive fundraiser and an aggressive giver, replaced DeLay as Majority Whip in 2002 (Ferrechio and Willis 2002). After ascending to this post, Blunt developed a sophisticated fundraising operation and raised hundreds of thousands of dollars for his Republican colleagues. Blunt described fundraising as "critically important" to maintaining the Republicans' narrow majority and said he had "an obligation and an opportunity to help other members" (Ferrechio and Willis 2002).

Both parties established member-based fundraising programs in 2002. House Republicans' Battleground 2002 effort, directed by Roy Blunt and Tom Reynolds (R-NY), set a minimum hard-money goal of $16 million. Republican core leaders were asked to contribute $750,000 each, and power committee chairs were asked to contribute $300,000 each. Other members of the Republican Conference were assessed fundraising goals based on their positions in the chamber. House Democrats launched their TEAM (Together Everyone Achieving the Majority) Builders program and appointed eight captains to direct fundraising efforts and mentor challengers and open-seat candidates. The program involved fifty House Democrats, who concentrated on raising money for candidates in competitive races. A number of Republican and Democratic leaders and would-be leaders participated in these programs to help both their colleagues and themselves. Tom Reynolds (R-NY), who was interested in chairing the NRCC, held a number of fundraisers for his colleagues, as did Jerry Weller (R-IL), who also wanted to chair the NRCC. Bob Menendez (D-NJ) and Rosa DeLauro (D-CT), who were competing for the Democratic Caucus chair position, hosted a number of fundraising events and traveled to raise money for their colleagues facing close races (Cillizza 2002).

The 2002 election cycle marked the last election during which the national party committees and federal candidates could raise and spend soft money. The Bipartisan Campaign Reform Act (BCRA), which became effective on November 6, 2002, banned unlimited soft-money contributions to the national political parties and regulated preelection issue advertising by independent groups. The new law also doubled the hard-money contribution limits for individuals from $1,000 per candidate, per election, to $2,000 per candidate, per election. BCRA indexes individual contributions for inflation; as of this writing, individuals can give $2,300 per candidate, per election. The new law kept PAC contribution limits at $5,000 per candidate, per election. BCRA also contained new provisions regarding party expenditures on behalf of federal candidates. National, congressional, and state party committees may contribute $5,000 apiece to a House candidate, per election. The party committees were also limited to spending $33,780 in coordinated expenditures per

House candidate, per race. Coordinated expenditures are funds a party spends for services such as polling or buying media time on behalf of a candidate who has requested it. The law allows the parties to make unlimited independent expenditures on behalf of House candidates. Independent expenditures are funds spent on behalf of a candidate, but not coordinated with the candidate's campaign (Currinder 2005). House members responded to BCRA by helping the CCCs offset the loss of soft money. Eric Heberlig and Bruce Larson (2005, 14) found that in 2002, House incumbents gave $45.4 million to local, state, and federal party organizations, with $24.5 million (54 percent) going to the CCCs. Two years later, House incumbents gave $41.6 million to the party organizations, with $37.4 million (90 percent) going to the CCCs. BCRA did not significantly affect member-to-member redistribution activity in the House; members continued to increase their giving from one cycle to the next.

Republicans scored major victories in the 2002 elections and maintained majority control of the House (229–205). The party kicked off the 108th Congress by reelecting Speaker Dennis Hastert and swearing in new members. But the pageantry quickly devolved into partisanship when the Republicans passed a major rules package that left Democrats crying foul. Some of the rules, such as the elimination of the term limit on the Speaker and the creation of a new Select Homeland Security Committee, were expected. While most Republicans supported eliminating the Speaker's term limit, others denounced the term limit removal as a "betrayal of principle." One senior member was quoted in the *Wall Street Journal* as saying that if the "Republicans water down term limits, they will show that they are falling prey to the same careerist impulses that they said had distanced Democrats from average Americans back in 1994" (Anderson 2003).

Democrats were particularly angry about rules making it more difficult for them to move bills and propose alternatives. They were also angry about a provision to keep the previous year's budget in place until Congress passed a conference report on the 2003 budget blueprint. Republicans reinstated the "Gephardt rule," which allowed Congress to increase the debt limit in the budget resolution without requiring a separate vote. For decades, Republicans had used votes on the debt limit to make larger political points about out-of-control government spending. When Gephardt imposed a rule bypassing votes on debt limits, Republicans angrily protested. But now that they were in the majority and a Republican was in the White House, the Republicans found the Gephardt rule appealing. The party adopted another rule that allowed committee chairs to postpone votes indefinitely to avoid losses. This rule meant that bills could be brought up for vote at a time entirely separate from the committee debate over the bill. Republicans also weakened limits on the types of gifts that members could receive from lobbyists and allowed for unlimited food and beverages to be delivered to members' offices. Democrats accused the Republicans of going back on their 1995 pledge of fairness and openness in the legislative process. Republicans countered that they had been treated far worse when the Democrats controlled the chamber, and they claimed that the new rules reflected their ideas of how best to run the House (Billings and Crabtree 2003; Ornstein 2003).

Democratic and Republican House leaders also predicted that the House would become even more partisan because of the elevation of conservative hard-liner Tom DeLay to Majority Leader and stalwart liberal Nancy Pelosi to Minority Leader. Republicans accused Pelosi of starting off the new Congress on a partisan note when she broke with the tradition of deference and voted for herself for Speaker. Hastert, who was elected to another term as Speaker with 228 votes, had voted merely "present."

As their parties' top fundraisers, Tom DeLay and Nancy Pelosi made clear their intentions to fight a financial battle in the 108th Congress. DeLay deemed member-to-member giving a top priority and gave out $131,000 to his Republican colleagues in the first three months of 2003. Speaker Hastert doled out $110,000, and Majority Leader Roy Blunt gave out $71,000. Tom Reynolds (R-NY), who had been named chair of the NRCC, raised $1.5 million for his personal campaign committee, even though he had a safe seat. Reynolds also formed a leadership PAC. The NRCC raised an incredible $44 million in the first six months of 2003, though only $500,000 of that amount came from Republican House members. On the Democratic side, Pelosi contributed $85,000 in the first three months of 2003, and Minority Whip Steny Hoyer gave out $104,000. Pelosi worked with the DCCC to establish the Frontline program, which raised money for the party's most vulnerable incumbents. She also pressured Democratic members to give a lot and to give early. In the first six months of 2003, the DCCC raised about $14 million, $3.8 million of which came from House Democrats. "All members have gotten the message that they are part of the Democratic team by being unified on the floor with their votes and giving to the DCCC and other members in competitive races," said Pelosi spokesperson Brendan Daly. Bob Menendez (D-NJ), the newly installed DCCC chair, expressed the sentiments of both parties when he observed that "early money breeds success" (Billings 2003; Stevens 2003).

Despite predictions that BCRA's ban on soft money would significantly impact the parties' ability to raise money, the CCCs managed to bring in about as much money in 2004 as they had in 2002. The NRCC and the DCCC were particularly aggressive in seeking out new sources of hard money. Although the DCCC met its goal of raising $75 million, that total did not come close to the $169 million that the NRCC raised. During the 2004 election, the NRCC spent $85 million to build up its hard-money donor list—an investment that paid off. The Democrats also undertook a major effort to reach out to new contributors in 2004 but did not enjoy the same level of success as the Republicans. The NRCC raised more than $16 million from House Republicans, and the DCCC collected $20 million from Democratic incumbents. House Republicans topped the list of highest member-to-member contributors: Majority Leader Tom DeLay gave $846,278; Speaker Dennis Hastert gave $643,000; John Boehner gave $552,077; and Ralph Regula gave $535,500. Minority Whip Steny Hoyer was the top Democratic contributor, giving $709,000 to his colleagues. The CCCs invested heavily in competitive races, and most of their money went to television advertising. Because of the partisan battle over redistricting in Texas, the House races in that state were very important to both parties. The NRCC spent more than $8 million on five Texas House races and established Team Texas, a separate fundraising program to help the Republican candidates in these districts. The DCCC poured a lot of money into the Texas races and also established a separate Texas Fund (Currinder 2005, 127–128).

Republicans won control of the House (232–202) for the sixth consecutive election and, in January 2005, entered their tenth year in the majority. Following the 2004 elections, Democratic leaders made good on their promise to reward team players with the party's few available power committee assignments. A senior leadership aide said that the leaders would most heavily consider how much money a member had raised and contributed, as well as the strength of his or her loyalty to the leadership: "Those members that haven't taken advantage of building relationships in the right places usually find themselves on the short end of the stick" (Billings 2004a). One member who almost found himself on the short end of the stick was Collin Peterson (D-MN). Peterson was in line for the ranking slot on the Agriculture Committee but almost lost the position because he had failed to contribute to the DCCC and to other members. Shortly after the 2004 elections, Pelosi met with Peterson and pressed him on his allegiance to the party. After the meeting, Peterson wrote a check for $45,000 to the DCCC. He also began to show up at caucus meetings and to send letters to his colleagues seeking their support. Democratic leaders' concern over the lack of member giving in 2004 was not limited to Peterson. Minority Whip Steny Hoyer reminded members that committee assignments do not come without an obligation; he threatened to revoke the power committee assignments of members who did not meet their dues obligations. "I think this issue is bubbling," said one Democratic member. "It started in the last cycle and it's now percolating. People are saying, 'Why should you serve on an exclusive committee if you aren't willing to participate?'" (Billings 2004b).

Conclusion

Under the leadership of Minority Leader Nancy Pelosi and Minority Whip Steny Hoyer, House Democrats began to coalesce around an electoral strategy that focused on fundraising. Party loyalty, as expressed through fundraising and support for the leadership, was emphasized as never before. Patrick Kennedy (D-RI), who chaired the DCCC during the 2000 election cycle, remembered how hard it had been for him to convince members to give, and he applauded the new tough standards. Past experiences, according to Kennedy, "helped make the DCCC into the tougher collector that it is today. . . . It isn't something that could have happened overnight but it's good that it's taken hold" (Bolton 2004).

As the Democratic leadership pushed party unity, House Republicans showed signs of fissure. Speaker Dennis Hastert avoided many of the problems that had helped undo Newt Gingrich, but in the process he became more of a broker than a strong leader. Hastert delegated much of the responsibility for passing the party's policy agenda to Tom DeLay, a conservative hard-liner known as "The Hammer." Under DeLay's guidance, the Republican leadership regularly attached revisions to bills already approved in committee and then declared the bills "emergency measures" so that they could be brought to the floor for a vote with as little as thirty minutes' notice. Leadership intervention in the appropriations process also became routine. Republican leaders retained control over the content of all appropriations bills, and subcommittee chairs were expected to adhere to the leadership's directives. The appropriations process regularly broke down, and the breakdowns strengthened the leadership's leverage. Multiple continuing resolutions, omnibus bills, negotiations with the White House, and severe time constraints maximized the leadership's ability to control appropriations outcomes (Price 2004, 8).

The election (and reelection) of President George W. Bush led to further consolidation of power within the Republican House leadership. In order to put together winning majorities for Bush's right-of-center agenda, Republican House leaders pushed legislation from the "right in." The strategy was to bring conservative bills to the House floor, then—if necessary—go "one-on-one" with Republican moderates, pressuring them on the spot to vote with the conservative faction (Eilperin 2003). While the idea was to pass conservative legislation so that the Republican leaders would have an advantage when it came time to compromise with the more moderate Senate, the use of such strong-arm tactics demonstrated that Republican leaders were willing to ratchet up their own influence in order to control Republican Conference members who did not automatically toe the conservative party line. While such tactics may have worked in the short run, Republican leaders alienated some Republican moderates as well as Republican members who put constituency interests ahead of party interests.

Republican House leaders also used increasingly restrictive rules to control the content of legislation brought to the House floor. By pressuring members who favored a more deliberative process to consistently vote the party line, the leaders may have jeopardized their long-term ability to rely on these members for support.

In the conditional party government model, House members support giving their leaders the powers they need to advance the party's agenda. But when dissension within the party grows, the party members are less willing to grant their leaders excessive powers. The Republican Conference continued to be dominated by ideological conservatives, but its willingness to support an overly assertive leadership faltered. In dictating how and when members are permitted to express their entrepreneurial tendencies—whether they are writing legislation, offering amendments, crossing party lines, or fundraising—leaders risk offending members who wish to play an active role in their party's policy and political process. And if party members begin to feel alienated from the process, the party becomes susceptible to fragmentation. Heading into the 2006 elections, House Republicans faced the collective challenge of responding to an electorate that was unhappy with the status quo.

7

Campaign Funds and the New Democratic Majority

The 2006 elections returned House Democrats to the majority for the first time in twelve years. While the switch in majority control was a major change for the House, other aspects of congressional party politics remained relatively static. Small partisan margins, and hence a competitive political environment, remained the norm. As both parties looked toward the 2008 elections, electoral politics continued to overshadow legislative politics in the House. The Democrats focused on politics and policies that would help them hold (and build) their majority. They also concentrated on protecting their freshman members, many of whom represented conservative districts. Democratic House leaders faced the difficult task of trying to keep their ideologically diverse caucus unified. House Republicans focused on undermining the majority party's efforts to pass its legislative agenda. They believed that the less the Democrats accomplished, the easier it would be for the Republicans to expand their numbers and win back majority control of the House. Campaign money remained central to these competitive strategies. The fundraising expectations placed on individual House members increased, as did overall party fundraising goals. Events in the two years leading up to the 2006 elections help explain how Democrats recaptured majority control of the House.

Following the 2004 elections, Republican leaders continued to emphasize member fundraising and loyalty to the party's conservative agenda. Speaker Dennis Hastert and Majority Leader Tom DeLay worked closely with the Bush White House to ensure that the president's conservative policy initiatives would clear the House. Hastert continued to operate more or less behind the scenes, while DeLay enforced strict party discipline and punishment. Moderate Republicans complained that they were being increasingly marginalized. Tight leadership control over the committees—particularly the Appropriations Committee—meant that moderates had little input in terms of bill content. And tight leadership control over the House floor meant that moderates and other party "dissidents" had little opportunity to offer policy alternatives or express disagreement. Party loyalty was the criterion for exercising any sort of power in the chamber. Whether they wanted to advance up the leadership ladder or bring their bills to the House floor for a vote, Republican members were expected to support the party's fundraising and policy goals.

When the 109th Congress convened in January 2005, the Republican Steering Committee faced the important task of deciding who would chair the powerful House Appropriations Committee. Bill Young (R-FL) was term-limited out of the chairmanship, which he had held since 1999. Ralph Regula (R-OH), the most senior candidate for the chairmanship, faced Jerry Lewis (R-CA) and Harold Rogers (R-KY). The three candidates competed by aggressively raising money for the party, promising to support the leadership's spending goals, and pledging to make the traditionally bipartisan committee more partisan. The race was very competitive and difficult to predict; Speaker Hastert claimed that the differences between the candidates were marginal. Regula's seniority and popularity within the Republican Conference made him the early favorite. However, some of Regula's conservative colleagues viewed him as too moderate. He did not consistently toe the party line and sometimes complained that the Republican leadership was too tight-fisted. His bipartisan approach to passing spending measures was also out of step with the party's leaders and conservatives, who wanted the Appropriations Committee more in line with their partisan goals. Heading into the chair race, Regula stepped up his party loyalty efforts, although his refusal to accept PAC contributions made it difficult for him to raise and redistribute money. After he had been named chairman of the Subcommittee on Labor, Health, and Human Services in 2000—and

the full committee chair was within reach—Regula established a leadership PAC and begun to raise money for the party and its candidates. In
addition to pushing the leadership's spending priorities, he contributed
$595,000 to Republican candidates, including $27,000 to his Appropriations Committee colleagues, during the 2004 election cycle. Though
he significantly increased his redistribution efforts in 2003 and 2004,
Regula could not match Jerry Lewis's long-established fundraising
record.

Jerry Lewis was second in seniority on the Appropriations Committee and chaired the Defense Subcommittee. He gave $1.37 million from
his personal campaign committee and $400,000 from his leadership
PAC during the 2004 election cycle. Of that amount, $21,000 went to
his committee colleagues. Lewis had consistently supported the party
and its candidates since 1989.

Harold Rogers, chairman of the Subcommittee on Homeland Security, was viewed as the wild card in the race. A pragmatic conservative,
Rogers sought to impress Tom DeLay with his proposal to overhaul the
structure of the Appropriations Committee by changing the committee's subcommittee structure and bipartisan culture. Rogers even hosted
a fundraiser for Tom DeLay's legal fund, netting $100,000 for the Major-
ity Leader. In addition to raising money for DeLay, Rogers contributed
$431,500 to Republican candidates during the 2004 election cycle. Like
Lewis, Rogers was a long-term contributor to the party's fundraising
efforts, although his fundraising totals came nowhere near Lewis's.

After the Republican Steering Committee completed its interviews,
members who had not already pledged to support one of the candidates
waited for guidance from Speaker Hastert and Majority Leader DeLay.
Hastert, who had five votes on the committee, and DeLay, who had two
votes, exerted vast influence over the committee's decisions. After the
Speaker and the Majority Leader signaled their support for Lewis, the
committee held a secret vote and named Lewis as chair. A few hours
later, Lewis issued a press release pledging to reform the culture of the
committee and to support the Republican leadership's spending goals.
Hastert publicly praised the three candidates and said the decision had
been a difficult one. Lewis, however, was viewed as the candidate who

had done the most to support the party over the long haul. His "prolific record over the past quarter-century of collecting funds to expand the number of GOP seats in the House, and his pledges to stick with increasingly tight GOP budgets" (Schatz 2005) won him the chair (Mabeus 2004; Schatz 2004).

After naming a strong party loyalist as chair of the Appropriations Committee, the Republican Steering Committee issued a stern warning to Charles Taylor (R-NC), chair of the Appropriation Committee's Subcommittee on the Interior. Taylor was in danger of losing his chair because he had failed to contribute enough money to the party and its candidates. Every other Appropriations subcommittee chair had given at least $150,000 during the 2004 election cycle, while Taylor had given only $23,000 to the North Carolina Republican Executive Committee (and nothing to the NRCC or Republican House candidates). Ernest Istook, another Appropriations subcommittee chair, had already lost his chair after he failed to demonstrate sufficient loyalty to the leadership. And Chris Smith (R-NJ) had been stripped of his Veterans' Committee chair after he clashed with Hastert and DeLay over funding for veterans. Many congressional observers interpreted these actions as part of an ongoing effort by Hastert and DeLay to enforce the loyalty of committee and subcommittee chairs (Bolton 2005).

The efforts appeared to pay off, as committee chair aspirants looked toward January 2007, when the chairs of several key committees would turn over. Jim McCrery (R-LA), who was competing with Nancy Johnson (R-CT) and Clay Shaw (R-FL) for future chair of the Ways and Means Committee, argued that "fundraising is one of the things that should be considered" (Pershing 2005). McCrery's leadership PAC raised $808,000 during the first six months of 2005, while Johnson's raised $171,000, and Clay's raised $36,000. Buck McKeon (R-CA), who planned to compete for the Education and Workforce Committee chair, agreed that "fundraising is part of it." McKeon's leadership PAC raised $208,000 during the first six months of 2005. His potential competitor, Tom Petri (R-WI), raised $56,000 for his leadership PAC. Ileana Ros-Lehtinen (R-FL) and Dan Burton (R-IN) had begun competing for the International Relations Committee chair in 2004. Ros-Lehtinen's PAC raked in $289,000 between

January and June of 2005. Burton did not have a leadership PAC, but he did have $953,000 in his personal campaign account that he could use to help his colleagues. Burton said that fundraising would be one of several factors taken into consideration and claimed he would "be as helpful to other candidates as I can be" (Pershing 2005). Potential chair candidates for the Financial Services Committee and the Judiciary Committee also began raising early money for their leadership PACs. Spencer Bachus (R-AL), a contender for the Financial Services gavel, raised $139,000 in the first six months of 2005. And Lamar Smith (R-TX), a Judiciary chair candidate, raised $163,000. In 2001, when the six-year term limit on committee chairs was implemented for the first time, fundraising had played a significant role in the chair races. Republican members who planned to compete for chairs in 2007 had clearly learned from the example set by their predecessors (Pershing 2005).

While Republican committee chair aspirants were busy raising and redistributing money, Minority Leader Nancy Pelosi and DCCC Chair Rahm Emanuel were issuing threats to House Democrats who failed to pay their party dues. As of June 2005, only half of the House Democratic Caucus had contributed to the DCCC. "From now on you have to pay your dues to avail yourselves of member services," Pelosi told members at a caucus lunch. "Fair is fair." Members who failed to pony up were told they could no longer expect a free ride and would miss out on such DCCC benefits as telephones for fundraising. Federal law prohibits members of Congress from making fundraising calls from their congressional offices. The DCCC and NRCC are located next to the Capitol so that members have a convenient place to go to make their fundraising calls. A staff person for one Democratic member said, "I don't know where members would go to make fundraising calls if they couldn't go to the DCCC. And every member needs to raise money" (Billings 2005b). Pelosi and Emanuel followed up their verbal threats with a letter demanding timely dues as a condition for receiving DCCC services. While some members complained that the threats lowered morale and created divisions, others viewed them as reasonable. Chris Van Hollen (D-MD) said that early contributions were a "signal of commitment by members to the cause" and a test of the party's strength (Billings 2005b).

Republican Turmoil

In addition to imposing strict fundraising requirements on party members, Democratic House leaders were looking for campaign themes that would help the party win majority control in 2006. Majority Leader Tom DeLay inadvertently provided them with one important theme: ethics reform. Before the 2004 elections, DeLay had raised substantial amounts of money and used his considerable political influence to orchestrate a redistricting plan in Texas. District lines had been redrawn to favor Republican candidates; as a result, several prominent Texas Democrats had lost their House seats. DeLay's involvement in the redistricting scheme was questioned, and an investigation was launched. In the fall of 2005, two Texas grand juries indicted DeLay for alleged money laundering and conspiracy in connection with his fundraising activities for Texas state legislature candidates. Because House rules prohibit a member who is under indictment from serving in the leadership, DeLay was forced to step down temporarily from his leadership post. DeLay maintained that he had never done anything illegal and attributed the charges to blatant partisanship. He was also under scrutiny for his involvement with Jack Abramoff and Michael Scanlon (a former aide to DeLay), lobbyists who were under federal investigation for allegedly bilking Native American tribes out of millions of dollars. DeLay had taken at least three overseas trips with Jack Abramoff that were paid for by lobbyists or foreign interests—a violation of House ethics rules (Drinkard 2005b).

The House Ethics Committee, which had already admonished DeLay five times since 1997, stalled on launching an investigation into DeLay's foreign travels because all five Republican members of the committee had financial links to him. Four of the five committee members had received campaign contributions from DeLay and two of the five had contributed money to DeLay's legal defense fund. The five Democratic members of the committee refused to adopt rules put forth by their Republican counterparts, claiming they were designed to protect DeLay (Drinkard 2005a). Meanwhile, DeLay's supporters in the Republican Conference were pushing for a vote to waive House rules requiring an indicted member to step down from his leadership post until his case is resolved. House Democrats (along with some Republicans) angrily protested. As the DeLay "scandal" intensified and attracted more media attention, Republican House leaders decided against waiving the rules for one of their own. DeLay announced he would resign from the House in June 2006. With DeLay's departure, House Republicans lost their most prolific fundraiser and their most partisan advocate. John Boehner (R-OH), who had built up goodwill over the years by raising money for his colleagues, was chosen as the party's new Majority Leader. During 2005, Boehner had contributed $445,000 from his campaign committee and leadership PAC to Republican candidates (Ferrechio 2006).

Several other House Republicans were investigated for their ties to Jack Abramoff, their connections to other lobbyists, and their campaign fundraising practices. One member, Mark Foley (R-FL), was forced to resign after his improper relationships with several House pages were made public. Congress's public approval ratings plummeted, and Republicans found themselves on the defensive. House Democrats sought to capitalize on these scandals by promoting ethics reform. Public support for the Iraq war was also faltering. President Bush's approval ratings dropped off as his administration continued to promote an increasingly unpopular war. Democrats tried to link their Republican colleagues to the beleaguered president and pushed for an end to the war. The Bush administration's incompetent response to Hurricane Katrina also hurt congressional Republicans. Democrats promoted their party as an alternative to the unpopular status quo.

As electoral tensions escalated, both parties stepped up their fundraising efforts. Democratic House leaders sent a letter to caucus members stating, "National polling continues to show that the American public overwhelmingly prefers Democratic candidates of change and new ideas over the old and tired status quo Republican candidates" (Billings 2005a). Members were directed to pay their party dues to help the party "continue its fight." Dues ranged from $100,000 for rank-and-file members to $600,000 for top party leaders, and only the most threatened incumbents were exempt from contributing. Democratic leaders publicized the names of those who had given and those who had not, arguing that fundraising was a team goal. The DCCC also established the

Red to Blue program, which urged House Democrats to contribute to candidates in competitive races. Chris Van Hollen (D-MD), who co-chaired the program with Debbie Wasserman Schultz (D-FL), claimed that member enthusiasm was high and getting stronger every day. Another DCCC program, dubbed Calling for a New Majority, solicited contributions from a targeted list of donors. The committee asked all members of the Democratic Caucus to participate in the effort and provided them with a portfolio of names, talking points, and campaign information. By December 2006, the DCCC had collected a record $33.7 million from Democratic House members. These contributions accounted for almost one-quarter of the DCCC's total intake of $140 million during the 2006 election cycle (Billings 2005a; Carney 2006; Davis 2006). Nancy Pelosi's staff estimated that her fundraising activities on behalf of the party and its candidates in 2006 had generated about $50 million. She also had contributed $659,000 to Democratic candidates out of her personal campaign committee funds and leadership PAC. Pelosi became a main target in Republican campaign ads, which warned that a "San Francisco liberal" would become the Speaker of the House if the Democrats prevailed in November, but her colleagues were willing to risk being associated with her as long as she helped them raise money. Through her fundraising efforts, Pelosi was able to build a strong network of loyal supporters in the Democratic Caucus (Epstein 2006).

For many Democrats, the desire to win back control of the House replaced ideological purity. Rahm Emanuel, whom Nancy Pelosi had picked to chair the DCCC in late 2004, took the lead in recruiting Democratic candidates to compete for open seats or against vulnerable Republican incumbents in 2006. Emanuel focused on candidates' ability to win tough races rather than their ideological leanings. "He did not care where a candidate stood on abortion or the Iraq war, or whether that candidate was displacing a 'better' Democrat, if such purity cost a House seat" (Naftali Bendavid, quoted in Glass 2007). Emanuel did not try to nationalize the elections the way Republicans had in 1994. He studied the demographics of competitive districts and recruited candidates who could win in those districts. Because many of the competitive districts leaned Republican, he recruited a number of conservative Democrats whose ideologies were out of line with the party's more liberal leaders.

Emanuel then directed substantial campaign assistance to these candidates and made sure they had the money they needed to run competitive races. The candidates were not expected to promote a broad party manifesto; rather, they were encouraged to localize their campaigns and run on issues that mattered to the people in their districts.

Emanuel also was responsible for enforcing member dues requirements. His aggressiveness, combined with his junior status (he had first been elected in 2002), rubbed some members of his party the wrong way. When some members of the conservative Blue Dog Coalition and the Congressional Black Caucus failed to pay their DCCC dues, Emanuel threatened to deny them access to party-based services. Senior members of the Blue Dog Coalition and the Black Caucus were outraged by Emanuel's demands, but he had the backing of Minority Leader Pelosi. And he was not one to shy away from confrontation. Part of the problem that Emanuel faced was that, historically, Democratic members had not paid any penalty for ignoring their dues requirements. Because the rewards handed out were based mostly on seniority, there was little incentive for senior members to be financially generous. Emanuel borrowed a page from the Republicans' 1994 playbook and argued that the team goal of majority status required all members to contribute for the good of the whole. Once winning control of the House seemed possible, Emanuel's high-pressure tactics began to pay off (Mercurio 2006). House members contributed a total of $33.7 million to the DCCC during the 2006 election cycle, $15 million more than they had given during the 2004 cycle.

While Democratic members were raising unprecedented amounts of money for the DCCC, House Republicans were on the defensive. "There is no question that we are in a very difficult political environment," said Majority Leader John Boehner (Lawrence and Locker 2006, A2). The party revived its Battleground program for the 2006 elections and set an initial fundraising goal of $22 million. NRCC Chair Tom Reynolds (R-NY) and Eric Cantor (R-VA), chair of the Battleground 2006 program, steadily pressured Republican Conference members to give as much as they could. Leading by example, Republican leaders used almost all of the money they had raised to fund incumbent candidates in tight races. Speaker Dennis Hastert, Majority Leader John

Boehner, and NRCC Chair Tom Reynolds gave $1.9 million to approximately seventy Republican incumbents facing strong challengers. This amount represented 85 percent of their combined total contributions. In 2004, Hastert's leadership PAC had given 32 percent of its contributions to Republicans challenging Democratic incumbents. Two years later, his PAC gave less than 16 percent of its contributions to Republican challengers. In contrast, Minority Leader Nancy Pelosi, Minority Whip Steny Hoyer, and DCCC Chair Rahm Emanuel gave $963,000 to approximately fifty Democratic candidates who were challenging vulnerable Republican incumbents. This amount came to 64 percent of their combined total contributions. Very few Democratic incumbents were considered vulnerable, so the party could invest the majority of its campaign funds in strong challengers (Davis 2006; Lawrence and Locker 2006).

As competition between the parties tightened, Republican incumbents upped their contributions to the party. The NRCC collected $31.6 million from House members during the 2006 election cycle— approximately $2 million less than the Democrats. The committee raised more overall, however: $180 million, compared to the DCCC's $140 million. Despite collecting more in total contributions, Republican House members failed to raise as much money for the NRCC as Democratic members did for the DCCC. For the first time in twelve years, minority party members contributed more for the good of the whole than did their majority party counterparts.

Democrats Take the Reins

The House Republicans could not stem the anti-status-quo tide that swept Congress in 2006. The Democrats regained control of the House for the first time in twelve years. Forty-two new Democrats were elected to the chamber, giving the party a 233–202 margin over the Republicans. Democrats also captured the Senate, 51–49. Nancy Pelosi was elected to the House Speakership, Steny Hoyer was named Majority Leader, and James Clyburn (South Carolina) was selected Majority Whip. Rahm Emanuel, who was credited with formulating the Democrats' takeover of the House, was named Democratic Caucus chairman. Chris Van Hollen was chosen as chair of the DCCC. Republicans chose John Boehner as their Minority Leader, Roy Blunt of Missouri was named Minority Whip, and Floridian Adam Putnam was named Republican Conference chair. Tom Cole of Oklahoma was chosen as chair of the NRCC. While all of the newly elected leaders operated leadership PACs, Steny Hoyer, John Boehner, and Roy Blunt controlled the wealthiest PACs and had given over $1 million apiece during the 2006 election cycle. Clearly, raising money for the party and its candidates remained a leadership prerequisite.

Democrats kicked off the 110th Congress in January 2007 by adopting a new set of rules. The rules package proposed earmark, ethics, and travel reforms. These proposals were meant to demonstrate the party's commitment to reducing corruption and increasing transparency. The new earmark rules required that a list of sponsors, justifications, and beneficiaries accompany all earmark requests. Members were also required to attach their names to their earmarks, along with a statement verifying that neither they nor their spouses would benefit from their earmarks. However, the new rules did not lower the number or the size of the earmarks that members could request. New ethics rules banned members from traveling on corporate jets and from trying to influence lobbyists. In addition, members were prevented from accepting gifts, meals, or travel paid for by lobbyists. The new ethics rules did not address campaign contributions.

The package also contained new budget rules, requiring new mandatory spending to be offset (known as pay-as-you-go budgeting). Additional rules focused on reforming House operations. One provision prohibited holding floor votes open for the purpose of changing the outcome—a tactic Republican leaders had used on several important votes. Another rule required conference committees to give adequate notice and allow all conferees to attend committee meetings. When Democrats were in the minority, they had complained that Republicans regularly shut them out of conference committee meetings. These new rules were portrayed as making the system more fair than it had been under Republican control. However, the Democrats included a few bill-specific provisions in their rules package, designed to prevent the Republicans from interfering with the passage of several top Democratic priorities. Majority Leader Hoyer claimed that the Democrats were not reneging on their campaign promise of more openness; they were simply making sure their top priorities would be passed because they were a "unique part of the 2006 campaign and our promise to the American people" (Ferrechio 2007; see also Dennis 2007).

One of the most significant changes the Democrats adopted was not a provision they added to the House rules but one they left in. While Speaker Pelosi had adhered to seniority in naming the new committee chairs, House Democrats rejected their party's historical deference to seniority and decided to impose six-year term limits on committee chairs. The rule was buried on page 498 of the 1,200-page House rules document. When the term limits rule was first adopted by Republicans in the 104th Congress, Democrats had rejected a proposal to impose similar limits on their leaders and ranking members (Ferrechio 2007). But twelve years later, Democratic leaders saw the value in term-limiting committee chairs. Speaker Pelosi did not publicize the inclusion of term limits in the rules package. In fact, some senior Democrats who strongly opposed term limits had voted to adopt the rules package, not knowing that term limits were a part of it. Afterward they angrily protested the leadership's decision and pushed to have the rule removed. Most junior Democrats—including the forty-two freshman majority makers— favored term limits and urged the Speaker to leave the rule intact. "Old bulls" like John Dingell (D-MI), who chaired the Energy and Commerce Committee, and Henry Waxman (D-CA), who chaired the Government Oversight and Reform Committee, did not support any effort that would impinge on their long-accrued power. Speaker Pelosi sought to defuse the tension by promising the party's senior members that the rule would be revisited in a couple of years, before the term limits took effect. She urged them to avoid setting off an intraparty battle over the issue, arguing that the new majority needed to present a unified front at the beginning of the 110th Congress.

Democratic House leaders' electoral concerns were likely reflected in their decision to endorse the rule that had indirectly helped House Republicans raise millions of dollars. By imposing term limits on committee chairs, Democratic leaders could expect that ambitious members would compete by raising money for the party and its candidates. They also could expect that ambitious members would toe the party line to demonstrate their loyalty to the party's leaders. Democratic leaders may have had their electoral concerns in mind when they promised full five-day workweeks, as well. When the new schedule was announced, lobbyists immediately saw more opportunities to hold fundraisers for members in Washington. "Honestly, we've already begun to schedule them," said Monica Notzon, a political fundraiser. "I think we're going to see events every day of the week" (Ackley 2007). Indeed, thousands of lobbyists began preparing for a full calendar of fundraisers as soon as the Democrats proposed a longer workweek. "If they're [House members] here more, that's what they'll do," said Dan Danner, the top lobbyist at the National Federation of Independent Business. "There'll be more fundraisers" (Ackley 2007). By passing new ethics rules that prevent lobbyists from buying meals for members and congressional staff, Democrats had automatically increased the importance of fundraisers. "You're going to have 100 percent attendance at fundraisers" because face-to-face interaction with members would be at a premium, according to one corporate lobbyist (Ackley 2007). H. Stewart Van Scoyoc, another lobbyist, predicted that the demand for campaign money would go up: "Particularly with the ethics package, it'll put more pressure on fundraising because it will limit the interaction between lobbyists and staff and push more of it into the fundraising context" (Ackley 2007). For example, the DCCC hosted a December 2007 fundraiser attended by top congressional aides; the admission price was $1,000 per person. "Members tap us all year, so why not the staff?" said one lobbyist, referring to the increasingly common fundraising practice (Hearn 2007c). Congressional history shows that institutional reforms often have unintended consequences. But when electoral competition dominates congressional politics, it becomes more difficult to label these money-generating consequences unintended.

Having won the House, Democrats began the 110th Congress by pursuing an incumbent protection strategy. After passing their "100-hour agenda"—a set of campaign promises that Democrats had promised to implement if they won majority control—the Democrats turned their attention to a slate of popular issues that appealed to voters across the ideological spectrum. The initiatives included measures dealing with election reform, children's health, energy independence, and climate change. Democratic House leaders wanted to ensure that their party members had a strong record of accomplishment to run on in 2008, and they chose issues that had broad appeal. Sixty House Democrats represented districts that George W. Bush had carried in the 2004 presidential election. Holding those seats was a priority for the party, and their policy agenda reflected this goal. The DCCC also focused on providing support to the party's at-risk candidates. The committee's Frontline program, which provides support to vulnerable Democrats, adopted a memorandum of understanding requiring incumbents to play a more active role in grassroots and get-out-the-vote efforts in their districts. DCCC Chair Chris Van Hollen established new fundraising goals for members. While his personal style was less aggressive than his predecessor Rahm Emanuel's, he pledged to enforce discipline in just the same way (Hearn and O'Connor 2007).

Despite their attempts to unify on policy, the House Democrats faced divisions, particularly on Iraq. The party's liberal faction favored cutting off spending for the war and withdrawing troops immediately. Conservative Democrats pushed for continued spending and phased withdrawals. During the first few months of the 110th Congress, Democratic leaders avoided bringing potentially divisive issues to the House floor. However, they eventually had to address supplemental war funding and other contentious issues, and Speaker Pelosi struggled to bring her party's various factions together on a series of war-spending votes. Some senior Democrats were angered by her willingness to bring unpopular bills to the floor and began calling for a majority-of-the-majority rule. Speaker Dennis Hastert had adhered to this rule and had not brought any bill to the floor that a majority of the majority party members did not support. Pelosi refused to adopt the rule and said she would continue to try to negotiate compromises between her party's factions. On many issues, getting a majority of the majority to agree was difficult, if not impossible.

While Democrats adjusted to life in the majority, Republicans struggled to maintain a unified minority. The party fractured over the Iraq war, with some members deserting the White House. Other members defied the leadership and voted with the Democrats on popular domestic issues. Eighty-two Republicans voted with the Democrats to approve an increase in the minimum wage, sixty-eight backed a Democratic measure to put into force the remaining recommendations of the September 11 Commission, forty-eight supported the Democrats' pay-as-you-go budget rules, and thirty-seven voted in favor of expanding embryonic stem cell research. Leaders of both parties attributed Republican splintering to the president's low public approval ratings, the unpopularity of the war, and public demand for some of the policies pushed by the Democrats. Conference Chair Adam Putnam predicted that Republicans would return to the fold once the Democrats moved on to tougher issues. Republican House leaders had in the past been able to control dissension within the ranks and were determined to continue enforcing discipline (Hulse 2007).

House Republicans, well aware of the divisions within the majority party, used various procedural motions to make life difficult for the Democratic leadership. They frequently targeted the conservative freshman Democrats by offering amendments or motions that were difficult for these members to reject. For example, Republicans offered a motion to send the Washington, DC, voting-rights bill back to committee with instructions to amend the bill to repeal DC's ban on handguns and assault weapons. The motion to recommit (or send back) is a minority right that has been in place since 1822, allowing the minority party a last chance to send a majority party bill back to committee for further consideration before a vote is taken. The full chamber votes on the motion to recommit, and it typically fails because it is a vehicle of the minority party. In the case of the DC voting-rights bill, Republicans knew that there were enough conservative Democrats who could not afford to vote against a gun rights measure. Democratic leaders pulled the bill from the floor rather than force their members to take a vote on gun control. Had they not pulled the bill, the motion to recommit would have passed because enough conservative Democrats would have voted with the Republicans on the gun control motion. As Republicans continued to target conservative Democrats with these types of procedural votes, the Democratic leaders moved to limit the minority party's ability to participate in the process. Despite their pledges to allow open debate and participation, Democrats brought more bills to the floor under totally closed rules than Republicans had when they were in the majority. Closed rules prevent members from offering any amendments to bills. After the DC voting-rights bill debacle, the Democrats threatened to change the rule governing motions to recommit. Republicans responded by bringing the floor to a standstill. Lynn Westmoreland (R-GA) called for a procedural vote every thirty minutes (a dilatory tactic) until the Democrats agreed to withdraw the proposed rule (O'Connor 2007).

Procedural heavy-handedness is the prerogative of the majority party. When the Republicans took control of the House in 1995, they had pledged a more open process. But they reneged on those promises once they realized how difficult it was to manage the process. The Democrats in 2007 followed the same pattern. When the margins between parties are small, as they have been since 1994, the majority party has a much more difficult time controlling legislative outcomes. Allowing the House to work its will through debate and compromise is less an option when the goal is to win. As partisan margins have narrowed, closed rules have become a standard tool in the majority party's arsenal. As a result, members devote less time to debating the merits of policy measures. But less time on the floor means more time to raise money. A former House member who had served in the Republican leadership during the 1990s and the early years of the twenty-first century argued in favor of open rules because he believed that the Republicans would benefit from engaging in public debates with the Democrats. If members were forced to explain and defend their policy positions, the "Republicans would win every time." His colleagues in the leadership agreed with his premise but still refused to open the rules. "I was told that if we opened the rules, members would have to spend more time on the floor debating policy and less time over at the party headquarters making their fundraising calls. And we needed to raise money to stay in power" (interview with author 2007). The legislative process is thus held hostage by the desire for power and the need for money.

Consequences and Challenges

In a 2006 survey, former House members were asked about the biggest challenges facing Congress. Three-quarters of the nearly one hundred respondents offered the same three responses: the undue influence of moneyed interests, the inability to control federal spending, and—the biggest response by far—the pervasiveness of partisan polarization (Adler and Wilkerson 2006). That money and partisanship top the lists of those who have served in the House speaks volumes about contemporary congressional party politics. Narrow margins have divided the parties since 1994. Electoral politics has replaced legislative politics, as real competition makes the fight for majority control relevant every two years. And in order to compete, the parties need to raise money. These dynamics have increased the role that money plays both between and within the parties in Congress. The CCCs engage in fundraising battles every election cycle, as they race to fund their most promising and most vulnerable candidates. Ambitious members who seek to move up the chamber's power ladder engage in almost constant fundraising battles with each other in an effort to impress their party leaders. The presence of competition between parties and among members of the same party has intensified the role of money in congressional politics.

Before the 1970s, House members did not compete for power in the chamber; they earned it through long-term service. The demise of the seniority rule, together with party-imposed term limits on committee chairs and leaders, means that all members have the opportunity to move up in the chamber. Because narrow margins and fierce partisanship increase the value of party loyalty, ambitious members compete by toeing the party line and supporting the party's fundraising goals. Following the 2006 elections, several newly elected Democrats established leadership PACs to raise money early in hopes that it would pay off later (Mayer 2007). Establishing a leadership PAC can also help members meet their party dues requirements—something they are made aware of as soon as they arrive in Washington. As competition for leadership posts and committee chairs has opened up, leadership PACs are no longer limited to party leaders. Members who raise money for the good of the whole demonstrate that they are loyal team players.

As money has become central to the way parties compete for majority control, partisan polarization and the influence of wealthy interests have intensified. Party leaders have taken on increased fundraising responsibilities. Speaker Nancy Pelosi's pledge to raise over $25 million for her party during the 2008 election cycle illustrates just how high the stakes are. Contemporary party leaders have to be well connected to individuals and organized interests that can provide campaign funds. Thus some members—because of their district constituencies, their professional backgrounds, and their personal connections—are better positioned than others to become party leaders. Moreover, contributors tend to favor members who are at the far ends of the ideological spectrum—the Republicans' conservative faction or the Democrats' liberal faction—so these members are better able to compete for power in the chamber. Members are attracted to leaders who can help them raise money—so much so that they may be willing to overlook a leader's more extreme ideological views. This dynamic has driven the congressional parties to choose leaders who do not represent the median party voter (Heberlig et al. 2006). Leaders such as Nancy Pelosi, a liberal San Francisco Democrat, and Tom DeLay, a conservative Texas Republican, epitomize this phenomenon. Leaders may also feel compelled to advance the agendas of those who have funded their leadership campaigns.

The constant pressure to raise money has created a number of questionable fundraising practices, including thickening ties between House members and lobbyists. Just before the November 2006 elections, Republican-oriented tax lobbyists, as well as corporate lobbyists, received late-campaign solicitations from Charlie Rangel's (D-NY) leadership PAC. Rangel, who was running unopposed in his Harlem district, was positioned to become chair of the Ways and Means Committee if the Democrats won majority control. The lobbyists were told that their contributions would be "a nice gesture for Charlie." The solicitations were widely interpreted as a requirement for a ticket to enter Rangel's office, should he become chair of the Ways and Means Committee. While Rangel denied these claims, the implications of not contributing were clear to the lobbyists who wheel and deal in the world of campaign politics (Novak 2006).

As lobbyists have become closer and closer to campaigns, members have begun hiring them as the treasurers of their campaign committees and leadership PACs. Since 1998, seventy-nine members of Congress have tapped lobbyists to serve as the treasurers of their fundraising committees. A treasurer's job is to raise money for the member, and many lobbyists have well-heeled connections. Lobbyists also organize fundraisers for members, and sometimes bundle campaign contributions for members' reelection efforts. In return, they get access and influence—invaluable commodities on the Hill (Shesgreen 2006).

Some House members have also put family members on the payroll of their leadership PACs. Tom DeLay's wife was paid more than $170,000 over four years by his leadership PAC, for fundraising and consulting services. The wife of John Doolittle, a Republican from California, worked as a fundraiser for his PAC and kept 15 percent of the contributions she brought in as payment. In recent years, leadership PACs have spent an increasing proportion of their funds on items other than contributions to candidates. These expenses range from travel, hotels, and meals to flowers, jewelry, and spa packages for campaign supporters. "My impression is that a lot of people use leadership PACs as a slush fund," said Joel Hefley, a Colorado Republican and former chair of the House Ethics Committee. Lawmakers use their accounts, he said, to pay for "all kinds of things that can be justified, but certainly are questionable" (Mullins 2006). All of these practices contribute to the appearance if not the reality of corruption, and they diminish popular faith in government.

Between raising money for their own campaigns and raising money for the party and its candidates, members devote tremendous amounts of time to fundraising. As a result, less time is spent on the business of legislating. Floor debate is limited and committee hearings are poorly attended. As party loyalty has become the criterion by which ambitious members are judged, incentives for specializing in policy have decreased.

And when the legislative agenda is tightly controlled by the leadership, members have even less incentive to hone their policy skills. In an environment that emphasizes electoral politics over legislative politics, members' political skills are more important than their legislative expertise. This reality makes life in the House difficult for those members who lack wealthy connections, represent poor constituencies, face competitive races, or simply find fundraising distasteful.

Epilogue

The 1970s reforms sought to democratize the House by dispersing power more evenly throughout the chamber. While removing the seniority rule leveled the playing field between junior and senior lawmakers, it also increased competition among members hoping to advance in the chamber. The redistribution of campaign funds was an outgrowth of this new, more competitive environment. The reforms also strengthened party leaders, who began to take full advantage of their new powers during the 1980s. Since 1994, narrow partisan margins have dominated congressional party politics, and the presence of real competition in the House has prompted leaders to enforce strict party discipline. The majority party has to remain unified to pass its agenda and the minority party has to stick together (and attract a dozen or so majority party members) to block the majority's bills. In a highly competitive political environment, party loyalty is at a premium. A party cannot produce results unless its members are willing to put the team's interests ahead of their own personal ambitions.

The challenge for majority party leaders in the House is to find ways to prevent members from putting their own goals ahead of the party's goals. Having placed their own ambitions on the back burner to help their party win majority control, members are typically anxious to pursue their own political and policy goals once they achieve power in the chamber. With majority status comes the opportunity to consolidate power. Ambitious members can pursue leadership posts, committee and subcommittee chairmanships, and seats on desirable committees. By virtue of their majority status, they are also better able to pursue their own policy goals.

Members can also consolidate power in the chamber by raising and redistributing money. Beginning in the 1970s, ambitious members used their own campaign committees and their leadership PACs to direct money to their colleagues. Spreading the wealth allowed members to build support for their own intrainstitutional ambitions. In the process, they weakened the influence of the party leaders in determining chairmanships, leadership posts, and committee appointments. By contributing to colleagues who could help them achieve their own personal ambitions, members did not always give to those who needed the most help. From the party's standpoint, then, campaign funds were sometimes distributed inefficiently. If the goal is to maximize the party's ability to maintain or gain majority status, money should go to the most vulnerable candidates. But if the goal is to build personal support networks in the chamber, money is directed to members who can help a donor achieve this goal. Throughout the 1970s and 1980s, party leaders had little control over how members chose to redistribute their campaign money. The Democrats had a comfortable majority over the Republicans, so it was difficult for leaders to dictate campaign finance redistribution strategies.

Beginning in the early 1990s, the Republicans began to centralize their campaign finance strategies. The minority party typically has an easier job convincing its members to support the group goal of majority status. Minority party members are more willing to unify and to push the party's agenda because they cannot reasonably pursue their own personal goals if they are not in the majority. Heading into the 1994 elections, the Republican House leaders convinced incumbent members to contribute their excess campaign funds for the good of the whole. By supporting Republican candidates, these members increased their own chances of moving into the majority and consolidating power. The strategy worked: Large sums of campaign money, combined with the right political circumstances, propelled the Republicans into the majority. The Republican majority, unlike the previous forty years of Democratic majorities, was quite narrow. Party leaders knew that enforcing strict party discipline was key to holding the majority. Power was centralized in the leadership, and ambitious members understood that if they wanted to advance in the chamber, they had to be loyal to the party. In a system where loyalty (as it is defined by the party leaders) is the key to advancement, the party as a whole benefits from its members' ambitious pursuits. By structuring a system in which the individual goal of intrainstitutional power is inextricably linked to the group goal of majority status, Republican House leaders could promote competition between members while avoiding internal fragmentation. And because members competed by raising money for the party rather than for colleagues of their choosing, campaign finances could be distributed more proficiently. The Democrats soon followed suit and began promoting and rewarding party loyalty.

Today, both parties emphasize member contributions to the CCCs. With the exception of those who are facing tough reelection campaigns, all members are required to give for the good of the whole. Members who wish to climb the chamber's power ladder are expected to give beyond the minimum requirements in order to demonstrate their strong commitment to the team. By refusing to participate in this game of "give and go," members may deny themselves the chance to realize their personal ambitions.

Just as individual members tried to adapt the system for redistributing campaign money to serve their own personal ambitions, the congressional parties have adapted the system to serve collective party goals. This new system still encourages members to develop relations with outside interests and individuals who can provide support in the form of campaign funds. But rather than use these resources to build individual fiefdoms within the chamber, members are encouraged to hand these resources over to the party. Those who provide the party and its candidates the greatest amount of money are then rewarded for their efforts. By rewarding loyalty to the party, leaders offset the tendency toward fragmentation.

By containing internal fragmentation, the parties have addressed one problem but opened themselves up to others. If power goes to those who raise the most money, power goes to those who are well connected to the organized interests and the individuals who can provide campaign funds. This system can build policy biases and obligations into the party's agenda that are at odds with the party's historic positions and ideological orientation. The effort to create a unified campaign system that raises a lot of money could ironically result in the fragmentation of the party's political and policy agenda. As a result, divisions within the party may form, and core partisan support may drop.

The increased emphasis on campaign money may also lead to ethical lapses. A system that relies so heavily on money gives political and policy leverage to those who can contribute. To compete for power in the chamber, ambitious members need to raise money, so by directing money to their favored candidates' campaign committees and leadership PACs, outside interests and individuals can indirectly help determine who among the elected will lead. If those members are then elected to chairs or other leadership posts, the outside interests who funded their campaigns are well positioned to get a foot in the policy door. This dynamic favors private interests over the public good and can erode public confidence in government.

Finally, a system so focused on fundraising leaves little time for legislating. During the 1960s and 1970s, the average two-year session of the House met for 323 days. During the 1980s and 1990s, the average dropped to 278 days. Today, the average House session hovers around 250 days. In addition, the average number of committee and subcommittee hearings during a two-year session of Congress has significantly declined (Ornstein 2006). Raising money requires members—particularly House leaders—to spend tremendous amounts of time meeting with contributors and "dialing for dollars." As well as raising money for their own campaigns, all members have to raise money for their parties. The constant need to fundraise creates cross pressures for the House leaders, who are charged with developing their party's policy agenda and shepherding it through the legislative process. Whose goals are prioritized in a system so focused on raising money? The persistence of narrow majorities suggests that these conditions will not change in the foreseeable future. In the absence of reform, money will continue to dominate party politics in the House.

Bibliography

Ackley, Kate. 2007. Maxing Out. *Roll Call,* January 8.

Adamany, David. 1984. Political Parties in the 1980s. In *Money and Politics in the United States: Financing Elections in the 1980s,* Ed. Michael J. Malbin, 70–121. Chatham, NJ: Chatham House.

Adler, E. Scott. 2002. *Why Congressional Reforms Fail: Reelection and the House Committee System.* Chicago: University of Chicago Press.

Adler, E. Scott, and John Wilkerson. 2006. The Biggest Problem Facing Congress? Ex-Members Say: Itself. *Roll Call,* October 26.

Aldrich, John H. 1995. *Why Parties?* Chicago: University of Chicago Press.

Aldrich, John H., and David W. Rohde. 1997. The Transition to Republican Rule in the House: Implications for Theories of Congressional Politics. *Political Science Quarterly* 112, no. 4:541–567.

_____. 2001. The Logic of Conditional Party Government: Revisiting the Electoral Connection. In *Congress Reconsidered,* Ed. Lawrence C. Dodd and Bruce I. Oppenheimer, 264–292. Washington, DC: CQ Press.

Alexander, Herbert E. 1984. Financing Politics. Washington, DC: CQ Press.

Allen, Mike. 2000. House GOP Goes within for Money. *Washington Post,* June 14.

Alston, C. 1991. Members with Cash on Hand Reach Out to Help Others. *CQ Weekly,* September 28.

Anderson, Nick. 2003. GOP Seeks End to Term Limit of House Speaker. *Los Angeles Times,* January 5.

Babcock, Charles R., and Ruth Marcus. 1998. PAC Gave Speaker-to-Be Some Reach; New in Spring, It Grew to $1 Million, Most of Which Went to Aid House Candidates. *New York Times,* November 11.

Babson, Jennifer. 1994. Coelho's 1981 Overhaul. *CQ Weekly,* April 2.

Bailey, Holly. 2001. Buying Leadership: House Republicans and the Scramble for Committee Chairmanship. *Money in Politics Alert,* January 4.

Baker, Ross K. 1989. *The New Fat Cats.* New York: Priority Press.

Barry, John M. 1989. *The Ambition and the Power.* New York: Viking.

Bedlington, Anne H., and Michael J. Malbin. 2003. The Party as Extended Network: Members Giving to Each Other and to Their Parties. In *Life after Reform,* Ed. Michael J. Malbin, 121–140. Lanham, MD: Rowman & Littlefield.

Bendavid, Naftali. 2007. *The Thumpin': How Rahm Emanuel and the Democrats Learned to Be Ruthless and Ended the Republican Revolution.* New York: Doubleday.

Benenson, Bob. 1986. Even Some Critics Use Them: In the Struggle for Influence, Members' PACs Gain Ground. *CQ Weekly,* August 2.

Bibby, John F. 1981. Party Renewal in the National Republican Party. In *Party Renewal in America: Theory and Practice,* Ed. Gerald M. Pomper, 102–115. New York: Praeger.

Billings, Erin P. 2003. DCCC's Member Infusion. *Roll Call,* July 17.

––––––. 2004a. Peterson, in Ag Bid, Pays Up. *Roll Call,* November 22.

––––––. 2004b. Steering to Repay Donors. *Roll Call,* November 29.

––––––. 2005a. Democratic Leaders Issue Call for Outstanding Dues. *Roll Call,* December 12.

––––––. 2005b. Pelosi Gets Tough on Member Dues. *Roll Call,* June 29.

Billings, Erin P., and Susan Crabtree. 2003. House Rules Spark Fight. *Roll Call,* January 8.

Black, Gordon. 1972. A Theory of Political Ambition: Career Choices and the Role of Structural Incentives. *American Political Science Review* 66:144–159.

Bolton, Alexander. 2004. Democrats Feel Pressure to Give More to House Caucus. *The Hill,* July 15.

––––––. 2005. House GOP Puts Taylor on Warning. *The Hill,* February 15.

Brewer, Paul R., and Christopher J. Deering. 2005. Musical Chairs: Interest Groups, Campaign Fundraising, and Selection of House Committee Chairs. In *The Interest Group Connection,* Ed. Paul S. Herrnson, Ronald G. Shaiko, and Clyde Wilcox, 141–163. Washington, DC: CQ Press.

Broder, David. 1971. *The Party's Over: The Failure of Politics in America.* New York: Harper & Row.

Brown, Lynne P., and Robert L. Peabody. 1984. Dilemmas of Party Leadership: Majority Whips in the U.S. House of Representatives, 1962–1982. *Congress and the Presidency* 11, no. 2:179–196.

––––––. 1992. Patterns of Succession in House Democratic Leadership: Foley, Gephardt, and Gray in 1989. In *New Perspectives on the House of Representatives,* Ed. Robert L. Peabody and Nelson W. Polsby. Baltimore: Johns Hopkins University Press.

Campaign Finance Institute, http://www.cfinst.org/data/VitalStats.aspx.

Canon, David T. 1989. The Institutionalization of Leadership in the U.S. Congress. *Legislative Studies Quarterly* 14, no. 3:415–443.

Carney, Eliza Newlin. 2006. The New Rainmakers. *National Journal,* October 27.

Caro, Robert A. 1990. *The Years of Lyndon Johnson.* New York: Vintage Books.

Cassata, Donna. 1994. Conservatives' Pleas Go Unheeded as Democrats Keep Old Guard. *CQ Weekly,* December 3.

Cigler, Allan J. 1993. Political Parties and Interest Groups: Competitors, Collaborators, and Uneasy Allies. In *American Political Parties,* Ed. Eric Uslaner, 407–435. Itasca, IL: F. E. Peacock.

Cillizza, Chris. 2002. Money Chase: Parties Push for Late Cash; Campaign Committees Set Fundraising Goals for Members. *Roll Call,* June 27.

Conway, M. Margaret. 1983. Republican Political Party Nationalization, Campaign Activities, and Their Implications for the Party System. *Publius* 13, no. 1:1–17.

Cooper, Joseph, and William West. 1981. The Congressional Career in the 1970s. In *Congress Reconsidered,* Ed. Lawrence C. Dodd and Bruce I. Oppenheimer, 83–106. Boulder, CO: Westview Press.

Corrado, Anthony. 1992. *Creative Campaigning: PACs and the Presidential Selection Process.* Boulder, CO: Westview Press.

Corrado, Anthony, Thomas E. Mann, Daniel R. Ortiz, Trevor Potter, and Frank J. Sorauf, Eds. 1997. *Campaign Finance Reform: A Sourcebook.* Washington, DC: Brookings Institution.

Cox, Gary W., and Mathew D. McCubbins. 1993. *Legislative Leviathan.* Berkeley: University of California Press.

Crabtree, Susan, and Paul Kane. 2000. GOP Keeps PAC Edge: Leaders' Funds Help Majority in Final Days. *Roll Call,* October 26.

Crotty, William J. 1984. *American Parties in Decline.* Boston: Allyn & Bacon.

Currinder, Marian. 2003. Leadership PAC Contribution Strategies and House Member Ambitions. *Legislative Studies Quarterly* 28:551–577.

———. 2005. Campaign Finance: Funding the Presidential and Congressional Elections. In *The Elections of 2004,* Ed. Michael Nelson, 108–132. Washington, DC: CQ Press.

Damore, David F., and Thomas G. Hansford. 1999. The Allocation of Party Controlled Campaign Resources in the House of Representatives, 1989–1996. *Political Research Quarterly* 52, no. 2:371–385.

Davidson, Roger H. 1981. Subcommittee Government: New Channels for Policymaking. In *The New Congress,* Ed. Thomas E. Mann and Norman Ornstein, 99–133. Washington, DC: American Enterprise Institute.

Davis, Susan. 2006. "Battleground" Gets Late Push. *Roll Call,* September 25.

Davis, Susan, and Tory Newmyer. 2007. Boehner Takes Up Money Challenge. *Roll Call,* July 24.

Deering, Chris, and Steve Smith. 1997. *Committees in Congress.* Washington, DC: CQ Press.

Dennis, Steve T. 2007. Budget Rules Will Alter Lawmaking Landscape. *CQ Today,* January 3.

Dodd, Lawrence C. 1977. Congress and the Quest for Power. In *Congress Reconsidered,* Ed. Lawrence C. Dodd and Bruce I. Oppenheimer, 269–307. Boulder, CO: Westview Press.

_____. 1986. The Cycles of Legislative Change: Building a Dynamic Theory. In *Political Science: The Science of Politics,* Ed. Herbert F. Weisberg, 82–104. New York: Agathon Press.

_____. 2001. Re-envisioning Congress: Theoretical Perspectives on Congressional Change. In *Congress Reconsidered,* Ed. Lawrence C. Dodd and Bruce I. Oppenheimer, 389–414. Washington, DC: CQ Press.

Dodd, Lawrence C., and Richard L. Schoff. 1979. *Congress and the Administrative State.* New York: Wiley.

Downs, Anthony. 1957. *An Economic Theory of Democracy.* New York: Harper & Row.

Drew, Elizabeth. 1983. *Politics and Money: The New Period of Corruption.* New York: Macmillan.

Drinkard, Jim. 2005a. DeLay Politics May Carry Heavy Price. *USA Today,* October 18.

_____. 2005b. Donations Link DeLay, Ethics Panel. *USA Today,* April 27.

Edsall, Thomas B. 1984. Money, Technology Revive GOP Force. *Washington Post,* June 17.

Ehrenhalt, Alan. 1991. *The United States of Ambition.* New York: Times Books.

Eilperin, Juliet. 1999. DeLay Enlists His Deputies as Fund-Raisers: Plan Aims to Protect 10 Vulnerable House GOP Colleagues, Retain Majority in 2000. *Washington Post,* March 25.

_____. 2001. GOP Leaders Make Choice of Necessity: Many Confident Thomas Can Best Shepherd Bush's Agenda through Ways and Means Panel. *Washington Post,* January 6.

_____. 2003. House GOP Practices Art of One-Vote Victories. *Washington Post,* October 14.

Epstein, Edward. 2006. Pelosi Is Dealing Dollars to Win: For the House, the Party, Herself. *San Francisco Chronicle,* October 25.

Evans, C. Lawrence, and Walter J. Oleszek. 1997. *Congress under Fire: Reform Politics and the Republican Majority.* Boston: Houghton Mifflin.

Fenno, Richard. 1973. *Congressmen in Committees.* Boston: Little, Brown.

———. 1978. *Home Style: House Members in Their Districts.* Boston: Little, Brown.

Ferrechio, Susan. 2006. Part Rabble-Rouse, Part Back-Slapper, Boehner Becomes Party's Top Insider. *CQ Today,* February 2.

———. 2007. House Democrats Keep Term Limits. *CQ Today,* January 3.

Ferrechio, Susan, and Derek Willis. 2002. As Republican Whip, Blunt Will Be Forceful in His Own Way. *CQ Monitor News,* April 8.

Fiorina, Morris P. 1977. *Congress, Keystone of the Washington Establishment.* New Haven, CT: Yale University Press.

———. 1989. *Congress: Keystone of the Washington Establishment.* New Haven, CT: Yale University Press.

Foerstel, Karen. 1994. House Chairmen: Gingrich Flexes His Power in Picking Panel Chiefs. *CQ Weekly,* November 19.

———. 2001. "The Hammer" Becomes the Heir Apparent. *CQ Weekly,* December 15.

Foerstel, Karen, and Alan K. Ota. 2001. Early Grief for GOP Leaders in New Committee Rules. *CQ Weekly,* January 6.

Fowler, Linda L., and Robert D. McClure. 1989. *Political Ambition.* New Haven, CT: Yale University Press.

Francis, Wayne L., and Lawrence W. Kenny. 2000. *Up the Political Ladder.* Thousand Oaks, CA: Sage.

Friedrich, Carl J. 1963. *Man and His Government: An Empirical Theory of Politics.* New York: McGraw-Hill.

Ghent, Bill. 2000. The Return of Steny Hoyer. *National Journal,* February 19.

Gimpel, James G. 1996. *Fulfilling the Contract: The First 100 Days.* Boston: Allyn & Bacon.

Glass, Andrew. 2007. Talking a Blue Streak. *The Politico,* May 9.

Glasser, Susan B., and Juliet Eilperin. 1999. A New Conduit for "Soft Money"; Critics Decry Big, Largely Untraceable Donations to Lawmakers' "Leadership PACs." *Washington Post,* May 16.

Green, Donald P., and Ian Shapiro. 1994. *Pathologies of Rational Choice Theory.* New Haven, CT: Yale University Press.

Hall, Richard L. 1996. *Participation in Congress.* New Haven, CT: Yale University Press.

Hall, Richard L., and Robert VanHouweling. 1995. Avarice and Ambition in Congress: Representatives' Decisions to Run or Retire from the U.S. House. *American Political Science Review* 89, no. 1:121–136.

Hearn, Josephine. 2007a. DCCC Raises $24 M, Asks Members for More. *The Politico,* June 20.

_____. 2007b. Dems Demand More Cash. *The Politico,* March 14.

_____. 2007c. Lobbyists Point to Dem Surge. *The Politico,* December 11.

Hearn, Josephine, and Patrick O'Connor. 2007. Democrats Plan Agenda to Help Incumbents in Red States. *The Politico,* January 29.

Heberlig, Eric S. 2003. Congressional Parties, Fundraising, and Committee Ambition. *Political Research Quarterly* 56, no. 2:151–161.

Heberlig, Eric S., Marc Hetherington, and Bruce Larson. 2006. The Price of Leadership: Campaign Money and the Polarization of Congressional Parties. *Journal of Politics* 68, no. 4:992–1005.

Heberlig, Eric S., and Bruce Larson. 2003. Committee Leaders and the Redistribution of Campaign Funds. Paper presented at the Symposium on Empiricism and Theory in the Study of Legislative Institutions, Annual Meeting of the Northeastern Political Science Association.

_____. 2005. Redistributing Campaign Funds by U.S. House Members: The Spiraling Costs of the Permanent Campaign. *Legislative Studies Quarterly* 30, no. 4:597.

Herrick, Rebekah, and Michael K. Moore. 1993. Political Ambition's Effect on Legislative Behavior: Schlesinger's Typology Reconsidered and Revisited. *Journal of Politics* 55:765–776.

Herrnson, Paul S. 1986. Do Parties Make a Difference? The Role of Party Organizations in Congressional Elections. *Journal of Politics* 48, no. 3:589–615.

_____. 1988. *Party Campaigning in the 1980s.* Cambridge, MA: Harvard University Press.

_____. 1989. National Party Decision Making, Strategies, and Resource Distribution in Congressional Elections. *Western Political Quarterly* 42, no. 3:301–323.

_____. 1996. Party Strategy and Campaign Activities in the 1992 Congressional Elections. In *The State of the Parties,* Ed. John C. Green and Daniel M. Shea, 84–107. Lanham, MD: Rowman & Littlefield.

_____. 1997. Money and Motives: Spending in House Elections. In *Congress Reconsidered,* Ed. Lawrence C. Dodd and Bruce I. Oppenheimer. Washington, DC: CQ Press.

_____. 1998. *Congressional Elections: Campaigning at Home and in Washington.* Washington, DC: CQ Press.

Hibbing, John R. 1986. Ambition in the House: Behavioral Consequences of Higher Office Goals among U.S. Representatives. *American Journal of Political Science* 30:651–665.

_____. 1993. Careerism in Congress: For Better or for Worse? In *Congress Reconsidered,* Ed. Lawrence C. Dodd and Bruce I. Oppenheimer. Boulder, CO: Westview Press.

Hirschfield, Julie R. 2000. Committees: Power Plays and Term Limits. *CQ Weekly,* November 11.

Hook, J. 1990. New House Fundraisers in the Wings? *CQ Weekly,* November 3.

_____. 1991. Gray's Exit Roils Leadership as Party Seeks Stability. *CQ Weekly,* June 22.

Hulse, Carl. 2007. Newly in the Minority, G.O.P. Shows Signs of Division on Iraq and Domestic Policies. *New York Times,* January 14.

Huntington, Samuel P. 1965. Congressional Responses to the Twentieth Century. In *The Congress and America's Future,* Ed. David Truman, 5–31. Englewood Cliffs, NJ: Prentice Hall.

Jackson, Brooks. 1990. *Honest Graft.* Washington, DC: Farragut.

Jacobson, Gary C. 1984. Money in the 1980 and 1982 Congressional Election. In *Money and Politics in the United States: Financing Elections in the 1980s,* Ed. Michael J. Malbin, 38–69. Chatham, NJ: Chatham House.

_____. 1985–1986. Party Organization and Distribution of Campaign Resources: Republicans and Democrats in 1982. *Political Science Quarterly* 100, no. 4:603–625.

Kane, Paul. 2007. Freshmen Padding Their Independence: Procedural Votes Become Safe Nays. *Washington Post,* December 26.

Kanthak, Kristin. 2007. Crystal Elephants and Committee Chairs. *American Politics Research* 35, no. 3:389–406.

Kayden, Xandra, and Eddie Mahe, Jr. 1993. Back from the Depths: Party Resurgence. In *American Political Parties,* Ed. Eric Uslaner, 175–205. Itasca, IL: F. E. Peacock.

Kazee, Thomas A. 1994. The Emergence of Congressional Candidates. In *Who Runs for Congress?,* Ed. Thomas A. Kazee. Washington, DC: CQ Press.

Kenworthy, Tom. 1988. Democratic Caucus Race Heats Up: Rep. Gray Is Front-Runner for Increasingly Important House Post. *Washington Post,* July 5.

_____. 1989. House Democratic Campaign Unit Running into Turbulence. *Washington Post,* August 2.

_____. 1991. Collaring Colleagues for Cash: Fazio's Method Eases Campaign Panel Debt. *Washington Post,* May 14.

Kingdon, John W. 1973. *Congressmen's Voting Decisions.* New York: Harper & Row.

Kolodny, Robin. 1996. The Contract with America in the 104th Congress. In *The State of the Parties,* Ed. John C. Green and Daniel M. Shea, 314–327. Lanham, MD: Rowman & Littlefield.

_____. 1998. *Pursuing Majorities: Congressional Campaign Committees in American Politics.* Norman: University of Oklahoma Press.

Kolodny, Robin, and Diana Dwyre. 1998. Party-Orchestrated Activities for Legislative Party Goals. *Party Politics* 4, no. 3:275–295.

Koopman, Douglas L. 1996. *Hostile Takeover: The House Republican Party, 1980–1995.* Lanham, MD: Rowman & Littlefield.

Kratz, Vikki. 2003. The House Money Built. *Capital Eye,* January 16.

Kraushaar, Josh. 2007. Frontline Freshman Democrats Show Strong Numbers. *The Politico,* April 17.

Kucinich, Jackie. 2007. Pay Your Dues or Lose in Nov., Tom Cole Says. *The Hill,* November 7.

Larson, Bruce. 2004. Incumbent Contributions to the Congressional Campaign Committees, 1989–90 through 1999–2000. *Political Research Quarterly* 57:155–161.

Lawrence, Jill, and Ray Locker. 2006. House GOP Going for Broke to Hold Seats: Tables Turn as Democrats Go on Offensive, Fund Challenges. *USA Today,* September 12.

Loomis, Burdett A. 1984. Congressional Careers and Party Leadership in the Contemporary House of Representatives. *American Journal of Political Science* 28, no. 1:180–202.

_____. 1988. *The New American Politician.* New York: Basic Books.

Mabeus, Courtney. 2004. Buying Leadership. *Capital Eye,* December 8.

Maisel, L. Sandy. 1994. Political Parties in a Non-party Era: Adapting to a New Role. In *Parties and Politics in American History,* Ed. L. Sandy Maisel and William G. Shade, 259–278. New York: Garland.

Maisel, L. Sandy, Kara E. Falkenstein, and Alexander M. Quigley. 1997. Senate Retirements and Progressive Ambition among House Members in 1996. *Congress and the Presidency* 24, no. 2:131–149.

Malbin, Michael J. 1974. New Democratic Procedures Affect Distribution of Power. *National Journal,* December 14.

_____. 1981. Delegation, Deliberation, and the New Role of Congressional Staff. In *The New Congress,* Ed. Thomas E. Mann and Norman Ornstein, 134–177. Washington, DC: American Enterprise Institute.

_____. 1984. Looking Back at the Future of Campaign Finance Reform: Interest Groups and American Elections. In *Money and Politics in the United States: Financing Elections in the 1980s,* Ed. Michael J. Malbin, 232–276. Chatham, NJ: Chatham House.

Maraniss, David, and Michael Weisskopf. 1995. Speaker and His Directors Make the Cash Flow Right. *Washington Post,* November 27.

_____. 1996. *Tell Newt to Shut Up.* New York: Simon & Schuster.

Mayer, Lindsay Renick. 2007. Barely Unpacked, New Members of Congress Start PACs. *Capital Eye,* January 31.

Mayhew, David R. 1974. *Congress: The Electoral Connection.* New Haven, CT: Yale University Press.

Mercurio, John. 2006. The Shame Game. *NationalJournal*.com, October 26.

Mitchell, Alison. 1989. A New Form of Lobbying Puts a Public Face on Private Interests. *New York Times,* September 30.

Mullins, Brody. 2006. Loose Change: Lawmakers Tap PAC Money to Pay Wide Array of Bills; Funds for Candidates at Risk Also Cover Hotels, Meals and Gifts for Big Donors; $5,000 for a Texas Funeral. *Wall Street Journal,* November 2.

Novak, Robert. 2006. Democratic Committee Chair Selling Access for Late Campaign Donations. *Chicago Sun Times,* October 15.

O'Connor, Patrick. 2007. Dems Bend Rules, Break Pledge. *The Politico,* May 17.

Oppenheimer, Bruce I. 1997. Abdicating Congressional Power: The Paradox of Republican Control. In *Congress Reconsidered,* Ed. Lawrence C. Dodd and Bruce I. Oppenheimer, 371–389. Washington, DC: CQ Press.

Ornstein, Norman. 1981. The House and the Senate in a New Congress. In *The New Congress,* Ed. Norman Ornstein and Thomas E. Mann, 363–383. Washington, DC: American Enterprise Institute.

_____. 2003. Congress Inside Out: Narrow Majorities, New Rules Will Pose Challenges for the White House and Both Parties in Congress. *Roll Call,* January 27.

_____. 2006. Part-Time Congress. *Washington Post,* March 7.

Ornstein, Norman, Thomas E. Mann, and Michael J. Malbin. 1999. *Vital Statistics on Congress.* Washington, DC: American Enterprise Institute.

Owens, John E. 1997. The Return of Party Government in the US House of Representatives: Central Leadership—Committee Relations in the 104th Congress. *British Journal of Political Science* 27, no. 2:247–272.

Pershing, Ben. 2000. Members Play Show and Tell for a Day: Chairmanship Interviews Begin with Lots of Intrigue over House Committees. *Roll Call,* December 7.

_____. 2005. House Gavel Hopefuls Stock PACs. *Roll Call,* July 25.

Pitney, John J. 1996. Understanding Newt Gingrich. Paper presented at the Annual Meeting of the American Political Science Association, San Francisco.

Polsby, Nelson W. 1968. The Institutionalization of the U.S. House of Representatives. *American Political Science Review* 62, no. 1:144–168.

Polsby, Nelson W., Miriam Gallagher, and Barry Spencer Rundquist. 1969. The Growth of the Seniority System in the U.S. House of Representatives. *American Political Science Review* 63, no. 3:787–807.

Price, David. 1992. *The Congressional Experience: A View from the Hill.* Boulder, CO: Westview Press.

Price, David E. 2004. House Democrats under Republican Rule: Reflections on the Limits of Partisanship. Paper presented at the Miller Center for Public Affairs, University of Virginia. January 16.

216 Bibliography

Pritchard, Justin. 1997. Rep. McIntosh Helps "Right" Donors Spread Campaign Cash. *Legi-Slate News Service,* July 3.

Reichley, James A. 1985. The Rise of National Parties. In *The New Direction in American Politics,* Ed. John Chubb and Paul Peterson, 175–200. Washington, DC: Brookings Institution.

Remini, Robert V. 2006. *The House.* Washington, DC: Smithsonian Books.

Rich, Andrew. 1999. Whipped. *New Republic,* October 13.

Rieselbach, Leroy N. 1977. *Congressional Politics.* Morristown, NJ: General Learning Press.

———. 1995. *Congressional Politics.* Boulder, CO: Westview Press.

Rohde, David W. 1979. Risk-Bearing and Progressive Ambition: The Case of Members of the United States House of Representatives. *American Journal of Political Science* 23:1–26.

———. 1991. *Parties and Leaders in the Postreform House.* Chicago: University of Chicago Press.

Sabato, Larry, J. 1984. *PAC Power.* New York: W. W. Norton.

———. 1990. PACs and Parties. In *Money, Elections, and Democracy,* Ed. Margaret Latus Nugent and John R. Johannes, 187–204. Boulder, CO: Westview Press.

———. 2007. Congressional Combat. *Larry J. Sabato's Crystal Ball '08,* December 20. http://www.centerforpolitics.org/crystalball/article.php?id=LJS2007122001.

Salant, Jonathan D. 1994. Committees: New Chairmen Swing to Right; Freshmen Get Choice Posts. *CQ Weekly,* December 10.

Schatz, Joseph J. 2004. Claiming Appropriations Chair a Bit Trickier on House Side. *CQ Weekly,* May 15.

———. 2005. Lewis Wins Favor of GOP Leaders—and Coveted Appropriations Chair. *CQ Weekly,* January 10.

Schickler, Eric. 2001. *Disjointed Pluralism: Institutional Innovation and the Development of the U.S. Congress.* Princeton, NJ: Princeton University Press.

Schickler, Eric, and Kathryn Pearson. 2005. The House Leadership in an Era of Partisan Warfare. In *Congress Reconsidered,* Ed. Lawrence C. Dodd and Bruce I. Oppenheimer, 207–226. Washington, DC: CQ Press.

Schickler, Eric, and Andrew Rich. 1997. Controlling the Floor: Parties as Procedural Coalitions in the House. *American Journal of Political Science* 41, no. 4:1340–1375.

Schlesinger, Joseph A. 1966. *Ambition and Politics.* Chicago: Rand McNally.

———. 1991. *Political Parties and the Winning of Office.* Ann Arbor: University of Michigan Press.

Shade, William G. 1994. Introduction: Elections, Parties, and the Stages of American Political Development. In *Parties and Politics in American History*, Ed. L. Sandy Maisel and William G. Shade, 1–26. New York: Garland.

Shepsle, Kenneth A. 1978. *The Giant Jigsaw Puzzle: Democratic Committee Assignments in the Modern House.* Chicago: University of Chicago Press.

Shesgreen, Deirdre. 2006. Shimkus Campaign Losing Lobbyist amid D.C. Scandal: The Treasurer of a Congressman's Political Action Committee Is Quitting. *St. Louis Post-Dispatch*, February 16.

Sinclair, Barbara. 1981. Majority Party Leadership Strategies for Coping with the New U.S. House. *Legislative Studies Quarterly* 6, no. 3:391–414.

———. 1983. *Majority Leadership in the U.S. House.* Baltimore: Johns Hopkins University Press.

———. 1992. The Emergence of Strong Leadership in the 1980s House of Representatives. *Journal of Politics* 54, no. 3:657–684.

———. 1995. *Legislators, Leaders, and Lawmaking.* Baltimore: Johns Hopkins University Press.

———. 1997. Party Leaders and the New Legislative Process. In *Congress Reconsidered*, Ed. Lawrence C. Dodd and Bruce I. Oppenheimer, 229–245. Washington, DC: CQ Press.

———. 1999. Transformational Leader or Faithful Agent? Principal-Agent Theory and House Majority Party Leadership. *Legislative Studies Quarterly* 24, no. 3:421–449.

Smith, Steven S. 1989. *Call to Order.* Washington, DC: Brookings Institution.

Smith, Steven S., and Gerald Gamm. 2001. The Dynamics of Party Government in Congress. In *Congress Reconsidered*, Ed. Lawrence C. Dodd and Bruce I. Oppenheimer, 245–268. Washington, DC: CQ Press.

Sorauf, Frank. 1984. *What Price PACs?* New York: The Twentieth Century Fund.

———. 1992. *Inside Campaign Finance: Myth and Realities.* New Haven, CT: Yale University Press.

Stevens, Allison. 2003. Leaders Take the Lead in Member-to-Member Donations. *CQ Today*, April 30.

Thayer, George. 1973. *Who Shakes the Money Tree? Campaign Practices from 1789 to the Present.* New York: Simon & Schuster.

Van Dongen, Rachel. 2000. NRCC Expands Targets. *Roll Call*, October 26.

Wallison, Ethan. 1999. House Democrats Get Head Start on Whip Race: Pelosi's Activity Forces Hoyer, Lewis to Campaign. *Roll Call*, August 2.

———. 2000a. Pelosi, Hoyer Battling: Californian Claims "Aura of Inevitability." *Roll Call*, February 24.

———. 2000b. Pelosi Claiming Victory in Whip Race. *Roll Call*, July 27.

Wallison, Ethan, and Jim VandeHei. 1999. House Leaders Make Sure Members Have Campaign Cash. *Roll Call,* July 1.

Wayne, Leslie. 1996. Political Twist: Spread the Wealth. *New York Times,* October 27.

Wilcox, Clyde. 1989. Share the Wealth. *American Politics Quarterly* 17, no. 4:386–408.

_____. 1990. Member to Member Giving. In *Money, Elections, and Democracy,* Ed. Margaret Latus Nugent and John R. Johannes, 165–186. Boulder, CO: Westview Press.

Willis, Derek. 2001. Democrats See Fundraising Gains from Pelosi's Win. *CQ Monitor News,* October 10.

_____. 2003. Republicans Mix It Up When Assigning House Chairmen for the 108th. *CQ Weekly,* January 11.

Willis, Derek, and Susan Ferrechio. 2002a. As Republican Whip, Blunt Will Be Forceful in His Own Way. *CQ Monitor News,* April 8.

_____. 2002b. Blunt's Fundraising Prowess Improves with Position. *CQ Monitor News,* April 8.

Wolf, Richard. 1995. Speaker's Team Concept Has Put His House in Order. *USA Today,* March 8.

Wright, John R. 2000. Interest Groups, Congressional Reform, and Party Government in the United States. *Legislative Studies Quarterly* 25, no. 2:217–235.

Zelizer, Julian E. 2006. *On Capitol Hill: The Struggle to Reform Congress and Its Consequences, 1948–2000.* Cambridge: Cambridge University Press.

Zeller, Shawn, and Michael Teitelbaum. 2007. Money Hungry. *CQ Weekly,* January 15.

Acknowledgments

After completing my first year of graduate school, I applied for a summer internship at the Center for Responsive Politics, a nonpartisan, nonprofit research group that tracks money in politics. I was interested in campaign finance issues and figured that spending a few months at the Center would be a good way to learn more. As an intern, I wrote for *Capital Eye*, the Center's newsletter. I enjoyed the experience so much, I continued to freelance for the Center once I returned to graduate school. One day, the Center's communications director called me and asked if I would write a story about congressional leadership PACs. I had never heard of leadership PACs but agreed to write the story. Thus began my decade-long fascination with members of Congress giving money to each other. I would like to thank the Center for Responsive Politics for introducing me to the captivating world of campaign finance, and for providing me with continuous support over the years.

I thank my dissertation advisers, Lawrence C. Dodd and M. Margaret Conway, for helping me think like a political scientist. I am grateful for their mentoring and friendship over the years. I would also like to thank Ken Wald, Wayne Francis, and Ron Formisano, all of whom served on my dissertation committee. Thanks also to Michael Malbin and the Campaign Finance Institute for generously providing me with data over the years, and for data used in this book. I'd also like to thank the many House members and chiefs of staff who agreed to talk to me about this project. Thank you to Jeff Biggs and the American Political

219

Science Association Congressional Fellowship Program for providing me with the opportunity to see Congress from the inside. And thanks to Representative David Price for allowing me to spend a wonderful year as a fellow in his office. I am also grateful to Representative Price's staff for their guidance and support.

My colleagues at the Government Affairs Institute at Georgetown University deserve a big thank-you for supporting me as I worked on this book. Special thanks to Ken Gold for generously granting me a writing leave. I am grateful for all of the help I received from Steve Catalano, Kate Hendrickson, Erica Lawrence, and Annie Lenth at Westview. My copyeditor, Margaret Ritchie, also deserves a special thanks for wading through my manuscript. I would like to thank numerous friends and colleagues, including Kevin Blythe, John Creed, Claire Curtis, Lynne Ford, Christy Grier, Angela Halfacre, Amy Leonard, Liz Oldmixon, Craig Plaketta, Melford P. Thomas, and Grace Wong for their encouragement and friendship.

This book would not have been possible without my family's support. Thanks to my mom and dad for always believing in me, and thanks to Chris, Mike, Michelle, and Teresa for shaping the way I see the world. Finally, I'd like to thank my husband, Adam. His unconditional love and support made writing this book possible.

Index